Navigating Precarity in Educational Contexts

This volume offers a timely collection of research-based studies that engage with contemporary conditions of precarity across an array of locations, exploring how it is understood, experienced, and acted upon by educators in schools, universities, and nonformal educational spaces. Precarity presents as layered, unpredictable, destabilizing, and rapidly shifting sociopolitical and economic dynamics, shown here in various forms, including the global pandemic, divisive populist politics, displacement of refugees and the landless, race and gender injustices, and neoliberal policies that constrain educational and social possibilities. Grouped around reflection, educational practice, and social activism, the authors show how educators engage these precarious conditions as they work toward a more interconnected, humane, and just society.

This text will benefit researchers, academics, and educators with an interest in social foundations of education, multicultural and social justice education, educational policy, and international and comparative education, sociology and anthropology of education, and cultural studies within education, among other fields.

Karen Monkman is Professor Emerita of Education at DePaul University, USA.

Ann Frkovich is Associate Professor in the Department of Research at Concordia University, USA.

Amira Proweller is Associate Professor and Program Director in the Department of Teacher Education at DePaul University, USA.

Routledge Research in Education

This series aims to present the latest research from right across the field of education. It is not confined to any particular area or school of thought and seeks to provide coverage of a broad range of topics, theories and issues from around the world.

Multimodal Signs of Learning
Tracking semiosis in the classroom
Shirley Palframan

A Retrospective Study of a Dialogic Elementary Classroom
Understanding Long-Term Impacts of Discursive Pedagogies
Lynn Astarita Gatto

Thinking with Stephen J. Ball
Lines of Flight in Education
Maria Tamboukou

A History of Inspiration through Metaphors of Learning
The Height of Teaching
Robert Nelson

Relational Aspects of Parental Involvement to Support Educational Outcomes
Parental Communication, Expectations, and Participation
for Student Success
Edited by William Jeynes

Navigating Precarity in Educational Contexts
Reflection, Pedagogy, and Activism for Change
Edited by Karen Monkman, Ann Frkovich, and Amira Proweller

Navigating Precarity in Educational Contexts

Reflection, Pedagogy, and Activism for Change

Edited by Karen Monkman, Ann Frkovich, and Amira Proweller

Routledge
Taylor & Francis Group

NEW YORK AND LONDON

First published 2023
by Routledge
605 Third Avenue, New York, NY 10158

and by Routledge
4 Park Square, Milton Park, Abingdon, Oxon, OX14 4RN

Routledge is an imprint of the Taylor & Francis Group, an informa business

© 2023 selection and editorial matter, Karen Monkman, Ann Frkovich, and
Amira Proweller; individual chapters, the contributors

Library of Congress Cataloging-in-Publication Data
A catalog record for this book has been requested

ISBN: 978-1-032-19223-9 (hbk)
ISBN: 978-1-032-19224-6 (pbk)
ISBN: 978-1-003-25822-3 (ebk)

DOI: 10.4324/9781003258223

Typeset in Bembo
by Apex CoVantage, LLC

Contents

PART II
Educational Practice in Precarious Spaces

PART III
Pushing Back Against Precarity

Contributors

Yacoub Aljaffery holds a PhD degree in education (curriculum studies) from DePaul University, and a master's degree in teaching English as a second language (ESL). He has been teaching in the field of ESL for 17 years. He has taught regionally (within the United States) and internationally (Kuwait, South Korea, Costa Rica, and Saudi Arabia). He has also trained teachers in different countries as a volunteer. His research interests include ESL teaching methodologies and refugee and immigrant students. Aljaffery is trilingual in Arabic, English, and Spanish. Traveling and learning about people's cultures and traditions are two of his favorite hobbies.

Kevin Ballou is a Lecturer in the Faculty of Architecture at Kindai University in Japan. He holds an MA in English as a Second Language from the University of Hawaii and has been teaching English in the Asia-Pacific region for over 20 years. His research interests include curriculum and materials design, project-based language learning, study abroad, and computer-assisted language learning.

Tameka Carter-Richardson is a high school Spanish teacher and Assistant Dean of Pluralism and Multicultural Affairs at Lake Forest Academy in Lake Forest, Illinois. She earned her bachelor's degrees in Spanish and Political Science from Stetson University, where she was also a member of the NCAA women's basketball team. In 2009, she received her MA in Teaching from National-Louis University and is currently completing her doctorate in Education at DePaul University. Her research interests and studies include intellectual emancipation, experiential learning, diversity in study abroad programming, teaching intercultural competencies in high school, and the construction of predominantly black education in the United States.

Beth S. Catlett is an Associate Professor in the Department of Women's and Gender Studies at DePaul University, and the Director of the Faculty Scholarship Collaborative in DePaul's College of Liberal Arts and Social Sciences. Beth also co-founded and directs the Beck Research Initiative for Women, Gender, and Community that specializes in community-based research involving gendered violence and social movements to create community change. Her areas of scholarly interest include development of youth critical consciousness, community-based participatory action research, violence in intimate relationships, feminist research methodologies, and the uses of contemplative practices to inspire social justice.

Phillip M. Clark is an adjunct instructor at the School of International Studies, Kwansei Gakuin University, Japan. His research interests include returnees in Japan and elsewhere in the world, bilinguals and biculturalism, and second language acquisition. He received his doctorate from Temple University, Japan, where he wrote his dissertation on Japanese returnee students studying at a foreign language university. Prior to attending Temple, he received his master's degree in TESOL and bachelor's degree in English from the University of Alabama.

Richard H. Derrah is an Associate Professor in the Faculty of Applied Sociology at Kindai University in Japan. He holds a PhD degree in Education from Temple University, a master's in East Asian Studies from Harvard University Graduate School of Arts and Sciences, and an MEd from Boston College. He has held secondary teaching licenses in the United States and Japan and has worked as a high school teacher in both countries. His research focuses on secondary education and teacher licensing in Japan as well as the wider area of East Asia.

Ann Frkovich is Associate Professor of Research and Doctoral Studies at Concordia University Chicago. She teaches courses related to research epistemologies and qualitative methods. Her scholarship explores the globalized educational experiences of teachers and students, with work to date related to China and the United States. Recent publications include the edited book from Routledge: *Belonging in Changing Educational Spaces: Negotiating Global, Transnational, and Neoliberal Dynamics* (2022, with Karen Monkman). A high school English teacher and administrator for 18 years, she consults widely in the United States, China, and West Africa around English and international education.

Beth L. Goldstein is Professor Emeritus in the Department of Educational Policy Studies & Evaluation at the University of Kentucky (UK). With expertise in comparative and international education and in anthropology, her research, teaching, and program development activities have focused on East and Southeast Asia regions and on Kentucky. Her research revolves around empirical study, participatory action research, and formative evaluation of educational border crossing, adult and family literacy, and internationalization of education in Asia and the United States. Projects have included implementation of a Malaysian twinning program with US universities, a nationwide higher education development project with Indonesian colleagues, expansion of Asian Studies at UK, and currently research as an adult ally with the Prichard Committee's Student Voice Team.

Sabrina González is a PhD candidate in the Department of History at University of Maryland. She graduated from Universidad Nacional de La Matanza, Buenos Aires, Argentina, with a BA in social communication. Her dissertation, entitled "Schools as Laboratories: Science, Children's Bodies, and School Reformers in the Making of Modern Argentina (1880–1930)," examines the historical processes by which schoolteachers in South America used education as a tool for emancipation and built a transnational school reform movement that both challenged and contributed to children's disciplining. In Argentina, she has taught classes at public universities, high schools, and alternative schools for adults.

Sawsan Jaber holds a PhD in Curriculum and Instruction from Concordia University Chicago, and is currently a high school English teacher at East Leyden High School in Illinois. She is the founder of Education Unfiltered Consulting and one of the founders of the Arab American Education Network. Sawsan is a Board Director of Our Voice Alliance charged with amplifying the voices of teachers of color to create more equity for students of color. Additionally, Sawsan is a member of ISTE's Education Leaders PLN. She is an educational leader with over 20 years of experience in the United States and abroad.

Rebecca John is Assistant Professor of Education at Virginia Wesleyan University. She holds a PhD degree in Curriculum and Instruction from Old Dominion University with an emphasis in Early Childhood Education. Her dissertation work focused on resettled refugee women and their experiences with early childhood education in the United States. Her research agenda focuses on giving voice to refugee and immigrant families and their experiences with the education system and exploring how trauma-informed and culturally sustaining pedagogies can impact students and families from diverse backgrounds. She has presented at national and international conferences for education such as American Education Research Association and Reconceptualizing Early Childhood Education and has published in journals such as *Contemporary Issues in Early Childhood*.

Karen Monkman is Professor Emerita at DePaul University and a visiting scholar at University of Pittsburgh's Institute for International Studies in Education (IISE). She specializes in comparative and international, and US-based, issues related to equity in education. Her research focuses on gender, migration, transnationalism, and globalization, as they relate to educational processes. Pertinent publications include *Belonging in Changing Educational Spaces: Negotiating Global, Transnational, and Neoliberal Dynamics* (2022, with co-editor Ann Frkovich; Routledge), Educating Girls: Complexities of Informing Meaningful Social Change (in *Studies in Social Justice*, 2018), Emerging Youth Leaders in a Civic Leadership Program (with Amira Proweller, in *Schools: Studies in Education*, 2016), and *Globalization* *and Education: Integration and Contestation across Cultures* (with co-editor Nelly P. Stromquist, 2000 and 2014). She is President of the Comparative and International Education Society (CIES), 2021–2022.

Jennifer Lee O'Donnell is Assistant Professor of Education at Texas State University, San Marcos. She holds a PhD degree in Teacher Education and Curriculum Studies from the University of Massachusetts, Amherst. Her research agenda is focused on curriculum and instructional practices in Latin American social movements. Specifically, she uses ethnography and affect theory to explore the ways in which race, class, and gender intersect in the mobilization practices and career trajectories of women activists in popular education projects. Her publications can be found in peer-reviewed journals like *Gender & Education, Anthropology & Education Quarterly, Adult Education Quarterly, The International Journal of Bilingual Education & Bilingualism, Social Identities,* and *The International Journal of Applied Linguistics.*

Amira Proweller is Associate Professor of Educational Policy Studies and Research at DePaul University, Chicago. She is the author of *Constructing Female Identities: Meaning Making in an Upper-Middle Class Youth Culture.* Her publications have focused on the cultural politics of schooling, youth culture and identity, educational policy in urban contexts, community-based service-learning, and critical youth participatory action research. She teaches courses in the sociology of education, social and historical issues in education, social justice education, and qualitative research methodology.

Cara K. Snyder is Assistant Professor of Women's, Gender, and Sexuality Studies at the University of Louisville. She has also taught courses at Federal and State Universities in Bahía and Pernambuco, Brazil. Snyder earned her PhD degree from the Harriet Tubman Department of Women's, Gender, and Sexuality Studies, with certificates in Teaching and Learning and Digital Studies, at the University of Maryland, College Park. Her research interests include transnational feminism, Latin American/Brazilian Studies, physical cultural/sport studies, and digital studies.

Bianca Ayanna Suárez is an independent researcher and graduate of the Detroit Public Schools. She earned her doctorate in Social and Cultural Studies in Education at the University of California Berkeley. Her research employs anticolonial critique and oral history/archival methods to uplift the rise of educational consciousness and social movements in Detroit. She is an affiliate of the We the People of Detroit Research Collective and her published work can be found in the *Encyclopedia of African American Education* and *Teachers College Record.*

Nisha Thapliyal is an activist-scholar and Senior Lecturer in Comparative Education at the University of Newcastle, Australia. Her teaching and scholarship are shaped by critical, feminist and postcolonial theories of education and social justice. Her research occurs in solidarity with education social movements in Brazil, the United States, South Africa, and India. Nisha teaches courses in Comparative Education, International Education Policy, Global Citizenship Education, Social Movements for Education and Peace Education. Her research profile can be found at www.newcastle.edu.au/profile/nisha-thapliyal

Guadalupe Valdivia is an advocate, counselor, and researcher. She has a doctorate in Educational Leadership from California State University, San Bernardino. Guadalupe has two decades of working experience in student affairs, student support, and student services. She volunteers at several non-profits, has obtained training and conducted research on topics related to adverse childhood experiences, educational disparities, ethnic identity, meaningful activities, significant relationships, future orientations, and resiliency. As a Youth Service Specialist at Torres Martinez Tribal-TANF, she created the "Agents of Change for Social Justice" program with the goal of empowering Native youths to work toward improving the Tribal Nation by taking action in community issues. Her goal was to prepare the next generation of tribal leaders by creating culturally sensitive programs that embrace education, character development, and leadership skills.

Salma Waly holds a PhD degree in Instruction and Learning from the School of Education at the University of Pittsburgh, PA. She is the founder and CEO of *Universal Narratives*, an educational consultancy company. She also hosts the *Universal Narratives Podcast* in which she interviews global educators on a wide range of issues. She is an expert pedagogical coach, teacher-trainer, curriculum developer, and educational leader. Her research focuses on teacher identity, education at times of sociopolitical change as well as creating equitable learning and teaching spaces. She recently published her first children's book series titled *Maryam the New Yorker*, featuring immigrant and multiracial characters. She teaches and supervises public and private school teachers in New York City.

Yan Wang received her PhD degree from the Department of Educational Policy Studies & Evaluation at the University of Kentucky. Her research focuses on college students' identity development and racism with a focus on students of Asian descent. She is a qualitative researcher. Her project includes Asian-identifying college students' lived experience during the pandemic. She is a strong advocate for racial justice advocating diversity, equity, and inclusion for racially minoritized populations, including international students.

Erica Zuniga Fuentes was born and raised in San Antonio, Texas. A Gates Millennium Scholar, she received her Bachelor of Arts at Texas A&M University (BA English, BA Theatre Arts, 2012), and completed the writing program at The Second City's Training Center in Chicago. She holds a master's degree in Social and Cultural Foundations in Education from DePaul University. Her research aims to recognize the importance of Mexican-American and Latinx people in the history, culture, and society of the United States. Some interests include the history of the United States-Mexico border; race and ethnic identity; Latinx mental health; colonialism and language politics; the Latinx experience; and Latin American folklore.

Acknowledgements

The editors would like to acknowledge the vision and determination of the chapter authors, who wrote and researched (as an act of love, brute force, or both) through times of unimaginable hardship, sadness, hopelessness, indignity, and isolation about those experiencing the same.

Thank you also to Connie McCabe for her editorial contributions in fine-tuning language and achieving clarity while honoring the rhetorical conventions of diverse voices.

1 Navigating Education in Precarious Times

Ann Frkovich, Amira Proweller & Karen Monkman

Introduction

One morning early in 2021, we abruptly stopped a meeting in which we were conceptualizing this book because, as Americans, we were shocked by the news flash that right-wing insurrectionists had suddenly stormed the US Capitol. The truth is, by then we had become used to living with much of the unpredictability of our times, we were used to disruption and the onslaught of media messages, to living in an increased state of instability and fragility, and to the never-ending feeling of despair. Working on a book related to precarity in education was something we took up while simultaneously experiencing precariousness ourselves. Together, as white women, we processed how we were dealing with a global pandemic and the rise of political extremism (Rogers et al. 2017), our country's racial reckoning (Jones & Hagopian 2020) overlapping with the #MeToo movement (Williams, Singh, & Mezey 2019), along with the irreversible environmental change related to global warming, all while institutions around us downsized and restructured to avoid or delay further demise.

Those of us working in universities with students who are also teachers and school leaders not only kept track of our own unpredictable circumstances but also watched an uptick in the stress of our students. We engaged with those who were sick or caring for the sick, who lost loved ones, or were grieving the dead. Many expressed a resigned sadness and confusion, as they found themselves in a state of perpetual destabilization as the schools in which they taught, and the schools of their children, shut down for in-person teaching and learning and shifted suddenly to online platforms (Pressley & Ha 2021). Similarly, students who worked in grocery stores, restaurants, and other spaces providing essential services that required public contact worried about their own well-being and that of their families as they found themselves on the front line (USDOE 2021). Furthermore, the conditions that existed prior to COVID-19 – the tensions related to school leadership in a neoliberal world (Scott & Holme 2016), challenges of balancing work and home life (Hochschild 2012; Gerstel 2000), the instability of many jobs and the inadequacy of earnings, the inequity of access to resources for quality

DOI: 10.4324/9781003258223-1

schools and healthcare (Lipman 2011) – were only brought into sharper focus because of the pandemic. While some of these realities were not brought on by the global pandemic, they were accelerated and magnified by it, adding to the layers of precarity.

Our collective experiences with the global pandemic, wide-ranging and diverse, offer us a lens for seeing more clearly the various layered and entangled dimensions of precariousness (Butler 2009; Fine, Greene, & Sanchez 2016; Ahmed 2020; Perry, Aronson, & Pescosolido 2021). Precariousness, in a generic sense, connotes a state of being characterized by uncertainty, unpredictability, and anxiety, along with instability and disruption. Our shared precariousness becomes a gateway for a new understanding of and commitment to equity, a vision for human care and responsibility toward others. In this book, the chapter authors examine how those engaged in education experience precarity in a wide variety of settings and times. They take up the pandemic; exclusionary politics; involuntary mobility; neoliberal policies; social injustices related to race, gender, ethnicity, religion, and language; and contested dynamics of identity construction. Examining these kinds of manifestations of precarity situates educators to also identify spaces for possibility.

Precarity Beyond Education

Historically, the concept of precarity had its inception in the field of labor studies examining the implications of economic change stemming from neoliberal economic and social policies which emerged over the past three to four decades (Sassen 2013). Labor studies scholarship has mined how such economic shifts, globally and locally, have directly impacted work and people's livelihoods, rendering both unstable, unpredictable, and temporary (Kasmir 2018; Means 2019; Standing 2016). Other studies prioritize a broader engagement of focus on neoliberalism as a force that creates experiences of precarity – both economically and also politically, socially, and culturally (Harvey 2003; Means 2018). Political science examines the relationship of democracy and precarity (Schapp et al. 2020; Goodson & Schostak 2021). Another realm of scholarship examines forms of violence such as war, torture, and kidnapping, with a focus on the affective experience of precarity (Butler 2008; Kasmir 2018). And yet another area of research focuses on precarity's relationship to social movements (Casas-Cortés 2021; Kasmir 2018). In this sense, precarity can give rise to the emergence of a new politicized awareness, along with changes in one's sense of self, using the term "precarity pride" to emphasize how precarity evokes conditions for action that are positive (Casas-Cortés 2021, p. 511). What is important in these instances is developing an understanding of precarity that is grounded in a deep knowledge of the underlying conditions.

In turning to what precarity is, Lorey (2015) argues: "precarization means living with the unforeseeable, with contingency. . . . The conceptual composition of 'precarious' can be described in the broadest sense of insecurity and vulnerability, destabilization and endangerment" (p. 10). It is about how people experience displacement, vulnerability, and hopelessness (Kasmir 2018; Mason & Megoran 2021), which is where the fragility of life becomes evident.

While the conditions of precarity can affect all lives, they take shape and unfold in varied ways and to different degrees. Ultimately, the underlying conditions of precarity are differentially distributed and experienced (Butler 2004, 2009; Standing 2016). Butler (2009) argues that precarity is a politically induced condition, in which:

> certain populations suffer from failing social and economic networks of support and become differentially exposed to injury, violence, and death. Such populations are at a heightened risk of disease, poverty, starvation, displacement, and of exposure to violence without protection.
>
> (p. 25)

Those on the social margins are impacted the most (Perry, Aronson, & Pescosolido 2021). When intersections of multiple types of disorientation, insecurity, vulnerability, and destabilization are present, the experience of precariousness is layered and amplified.

Although we are not using Judith Butler's (2009, 2004) notion of precarity in its full sense, her contributions are important to recognize. Precariousness, in her work, refers to a generalized human condition, grounded in the interdependence among all humans, making all vulnerable. Butler (2009) emphasizes that "If we take the precarious life as a point of departure, then there is no life without the need for shelter and food, no life without dependency on wider networks of sociality and labor, no life that transcends injurability and mortality" (p. 25). She distinguishes precariousness from precarity.[1] Precarity refers to the unequally distributed conditions of vulnerability, positioning some populations and individuals as more vulnerable than others.

Butler recognizes that some people are seen as having greater value and others are rendered invisible. She calls this idea "grievability," meaning that we recognize some lives as worthwhile and therefore, if lost, grievable, while others are not seen or recognized and therefore not grievable (Butler 2009). She explains, " . . . we respond with outrage to lives that are injured or killed and which we already perceive as lives" (Butler 2008, para. 20). In pondering how lives are understood as grievable or not, she argues: "We do not ourselves manufacture the norms through which we come to perceive a life as a worthy life" (Butler 2008, para. 20); our understandings are framed by media and other social forces. She argues that we must recognize our universal egalitarian precariousness in order to figure out our moral imperative to respond to the injustices. Kasmir (2018) explains:

> Butler sees the potential for emancipation in embracing the common circumstance of precariousness, as against the unequal fate of precarity. She renounces politics that aim at achieving stability for select groups and instead favors an egalitarian precariousness for all as a liberating moment.
>
> (pp. 2–3)

Butler's ideas, in a general sense, parallel many others in the social sciences that argue for a much more dynamic understanding of the lives of others, of context, of histories, of the ways people are socialized to believe certain things and not others, etc. These help us to develop an understanding of our moral obligations to engage conditions of precarity that may be played out very differently than in our own lived experience. Perhaps this is nowhere more important than in education.

Precarity in Educational Spaces

Research related to precarity in education covers a wide range of conditions, from neoliberal policies, entrenched poverty, populist politics, and the global pandemic, among others. The effects of neoliberal educational reforms in recent decades have played a decisive role in advancing the conditions of precariousness through limiting access to funding and other resources for some schools relative to others, and for promoting a market-based approach to education over concern for student experience and learning (Ewing 2018; Lipman 2011; Noddings 2006; Weiner 2011). The intensification of neoliberal education reforms in recent decades has also had consequential impacts on teachers, leaving them feeling de-professionalized and constrained in their curricular decision-making amid legislation mandating increased testing (Cody 2019). It has also spawned job instability and worsening conditions of work in education (Blair 2018).

Experiences of exacerbated poverty, intertwined with neoliberalism, and now the global pandemic also deepen the experiences of precariousness for not only educators but also students and their families. Since May 2020 in the US, an additional eight million people – including two and a half million children – have fallen into poverty, mostly impacting children of color (Children's Defense Fund 2021). Globally, the number of children in poverty has soared to 1.2 billion due to COVID-19, and the proportion of children without access to education and/or healthcare has increased from 47% to 56% (UNICEF 2020). Poverty impacts health, food security, shelter, and other basic human needs, which can push educational priorities to the side as families become preoccupied with daily survival.

In addition, the recent rise in political extremism and rhetorical narratives of exclusion has further undermined a social safety net and sent clear messages of who belongs and who does not, creating greater divisions that have spilled over into increases in violence and hate crimes (Rogers et al. 2017). Narratives targeting immigrants, people of color, religious minorities, women, LGBTQIA+ communities, and others dehumanize large segments of the population and send messages that there is no place for them in the society (Huber & Muoz 2021). These kinds of negative forces have taken shape in educational settings in forms such as movements to narrow curriculum and to not teach racial histories (George 2021; Goodson & Schostak 2021) while also giving rise to coalition building among schools and communities to push back toward greater equity and inclusion (Huckaby 2019; Warren 2018).

As the coronavirus pandemic of 2020–2021 has ravaged the globe, schools in many locations throughout the world have been forced to close completely or pivot to online instruction, which has magnified disparities related to the digital divide (Narodowski & Campetella 2022; Bishai 2022) and also to the ability of teachers to effectively adapt given either their knowledge and skills or the mandates of a scripted curriculum – which constrains their ability to act independently (Pressly & Ha 2021; Lizana & Vega-Fernadez 2021). In locations where teaching has continued, teachers have had to find ways to adapt their curricula and pedagogies to new modalities while keeping students engaged in the learning process from a distance, often with limited support (Goodson & Schostak 2021; Bishai 2022). The gap between families who have access to educational technology – including reliable internet connections – and those who do not has come into sharper relief. This is reflected not only in families' socioeconomic class differences but also across whole school systems, with some countries and communities all but shutting down. Some students across the globe have missed a year or more of formal education, while others have continued undeterred, adapting relatively easily (Narodowski & Campetella 2022).

Educators have experienced increased stress related to heavier workloads, extended hours, and the absence of a clear way forward (Lizana & Vega-Fernadez 2021). In addition, many educators feel threatened by digital technologies replacing teachers and the gutting of the relational nature of teaching (Kirk 2020; Brewer & Lubienski 2019). They express a diminished sense of professional identity while students face a narrowing of the curriculum that feels less relevant to their daily lives now and into the future and often leaves them less engaged in the learning process (Fine 2018; Jones & Sheffield 2018).

The experience of education is integral to how people make sense of themselves and the changing world around them (Freire 2000; Zeichner 2013; Ladson-Billings 2021; Anderson, Herr, & Nihlen 2007), which unfolds not only within formal schooling but also in nonformal spaces and through lived experience more broadly (Coombs & Ahmed 1974).

Given the contemporary conditions of precariousness, educators are being called upon to think differently and more expansively about education (Fine 2018; Kumashiro 2020; Stovall 2020; Way et al. 2018). While many of the educational approaches related to social justice education and critical pedagogies may be useful, we must consider how our current era of precarity calls for new ways of thinking about our reflective, pedagogical, and activist orientations (Zembylas 2019).

Overview of the Chapters

The chapters in this timely volume engage with many, although not all, of the ongoing and contemporary conditions of precariousness to focus on how it is understood and experienced by an array of local actors across the globe who are involved in educational processes in schools and beyond. It brings together a wide range of issues, from popular organizing around racial and gender injustice, to the symbolic violence emanating from populist politics, and the global coronavirus pandemic, implicating precarity in relationship to education, broadly conceptualized. We see how identity development is challenged and also foundational to how we learn and teach, how curriculum and pedagogies change when responding to external forces, and how engaging in activism is a necessary educational praxis in pushing back. The chapters include the experiences of refugees, university students, youths, adult learners, teachers, and community organizers on three continents. Each chapter in this volume is grounded in rich data that provide nuanced and detailed understanding. The authors use a variety of research approaches, including historical analysis, autoethnography, self-study, participatory action research, portraiture, narrative inquiry, ethnography, and a range of other interview-based and observational study methodologies.

Together, the chapters in this volume – as a response to the current layering of precarious conditions – challenge us to work toward an ethical imperative, engaging us in deep inward reflection as a basis for re-envisioning practice and a more interconnected, humane, and just society. In so doing, we cultivate an understanding of how reflection, praxis, and activism are entwined and necessary to move beyond the fault lines of the current era in whatever form it might take. The chapters are organized in three sections: Precarious Entanglements: Situating the Self; Educational Practice in Precarious Spaces; and Pushing Back Against Precarity.

The chapters in Part I – Precarious Entanglements: Situating the Self – are reflective analyses around educators' and students' shifting identities of race, ethnicity, class, gender, and religion; personal and professional transitions; and systems of privilege and oppression. Together, these chapters suggest the importance of critical reflection and self-examination in shaping a sense of identity. This grounding provides a solid foundation on which to understand and engage in educational practice (Part II) and action for systemic transformation (Part III).

Zuniga Fuentes (Chapter 2) engages in a reflection of her life as it relates to her Latinx identity over time, revealing changes in how society, through its institutions, values and devalues language of descent and its implications for identity and belonging in a culturally pluralistic society. She speaks to the kinds of social and political pressures that destabilize a sense of self, creating tension around being the Latina she wants to be in an American society.

Jaber (Chapter 3) shares her experiences as an Arab American woman teaching at a white-majority school in the US and the experiences of Arab American Muslim girls attending this school. She examines how they balance their efforts to integrate into the school community and mainstream society while maintaining their identity at the intersection of race/ethnicity, religion, and gender. For Jaber, the experience of doing the research with the young women provides a window into, and a mirror for, better understanding her own educational history.

Wang and Goldstein (Chapter 4) explore the fragility of ethnic identity as Chinese American college students traverse the spaces of home life, K-12 schooling, university experience, and in traveling to their ancestral homelands. In each space, the tensions of identity construction vary, including the experiences of racial stereotyping, balancing parental pressures, being the only minority group in early years to being part of a much broader diverse community at the university, ultimately culminating in a more complex transnational hybrid identity. As with the other chapters about identity, we see it evolving over time and in different spaces.

Catlett and Proweller (Chapter 5) reflect on their own identities as Jewish women and their positionalities of privilege relative to race. They focus on how power, privilege, and oppression have shaped their lives and inform their work with young Jewish teen girls in a social justice program. This chapter explores two layers, among them the researchers' approach to their own social justice work relative to their positionalities, and engaging girls in unpacking their own understandings of systemic oppression as they undertake social change work in their communities.

Across these four chapters, we see that reflecting on one's own positionality is necessary before one can learn to recognize how others' lives are similarly or differently impacted by precarious conditions. The authors bring to the surface the complex, layered, and dynamic nature of precarity, including how others experience it. This process of reflection is necessary for teaching toward an understanding of precarity.

The chapters in Part II – Educational Practice in Precarious Spaces – explore how educational processes intersect with the current experiences of precarity, highlighting the imperative of creating affirmative and inclusive educational spaces that respond to people's lives. Precarious conditions force us to rethink how we educate.

New research engages how the pandemic has made the practice of education precarious and a site for new ways of life. Derrah, Clark, and Ballou (Chapter 6) reveal how Japanese university students grapple with the

pandemic, which has eliminated the socialization function of higher education that has traditionally included engaging with the work world to gain
life experience outside of the university and to network in hopes of establishing oneself in a career. While the pandemic also allowed the students
to find new value in family time and to develop hobbies, ultimately, they
are lamenting losses in their educational experience, which will likely have
long-term effects.

Educational spaces are increasingly precarious for students and teachers
due to challenges created by policies and politics. In Chapter 7, Waly examines how low-income students of color grappled with the outcome of the
2016 election in the US, which made them vulnerable, and how their teachers shifted their teaching from prioritizing the curriculum to the well-being
of the students. Here, we see how schools that were once a safe space for
students of color became less safe with the rise of populist politics in the US.
Teachers were then compelled to adjust their practice to counter these new
precarious experiences.

Frkovich and Carter-Richardson (Chapter 8) offer vignettes that show
the challenges they face in their own work as educators in both wealthy
and low-income educational spaces, and how discourses related to race and
social class in education are both necessary and driven underground. The
chapter highlights the ways that educators are kept from working in the best
interests of their students in both wealthy and low-income educational spaces
and highlights the power of subversive discourse as a safe and available tool
for resistance.

Finally, in Chapter 9, Aljaffery explores the experiences of refugee students during their migration journeys and in US high schools. The arduous
refugee journeys became stories of chasing dreams toward a bright future
with the help of some of their teachers. The author shows the confluence of
parent support, school structures, and teacher knowledge that enable the
development of a sense of belonging, which provides a foundation for a
new way of life.

Educational practice, as these chapters demonstrate, involves an intention-
ality in how pedagogy and curriculum are engaged, as educators and learners
are confronted by precarious conditions, often layered one on top of another.
As we have seen, teachers come to understand that there is a relationship
between sociopolitical dynamics and practice that they need to account for
in order to address the challenges that precarious times present for different learners. The conditions of precarity prompt educators to change their
mindsets as part of rethinking how to approach pedagogy and curricular
change. Changed mindsets and practices invite a new relationship between
challenge and possibility.

In Part III – Pushing Back Against Precarity – we highlight the educational work of activists and within social movements. These kinds of
approaches are necessary for pushing back against precarity in that they get at
a deeper understanding of structures of inequities, which are the foundation

for precarious conditions and hold out the promise of solidarity, collective agency, and social structural transformation. When we conceive of education broadly, we understand the importance of the learning that is possible when involved in activism – learning happens inside schools, in organizations, and in community processes as we collectively push back against precarity and create a more equitable foundation for life.

González and Snyder (Chapter 10) focus on a US university social justice-oriented study abroad program to Buenos Aires that turned into an online course due to travel restrictions during the COVID-19 pandemic. The authors interrogate how transnational feminist pedagogy can be adapted to an online modality to facilitate undergraduate students' learning about social injustice and social movements for change both locally and globally. They also reveal the importance of reflecting on one's own practice in order to deepen their work.

In Chapter 11, O'Donnell, John, and Valdivia examine how popular education, unfolding through Popular Education Training Workshops in Buenos Aires, helps learners who are facing injustice and trauma in their lives to leverage their pain and work to transform their lives and the lives of girls and women facing similar struggles. Trauma, when made public, is part of a process to move beyond it. The "difficult knowledge" (Britzman 2000, p. 27) of gender-based violence is engaged through trauma-informed pedagogy to support girls' and women's healing, building community and empowering women and girls as change agents.

Thapliyal (Chapter 12) explores the activist narratives of women educators in the *Movimento dos Trabajhadores Rurais Sem Terra* [Landless Workers Movement] in Brazil who participated in the struggle for itinerant schools, as they envisioned their right to education and agency. Engagement in educational activism politicizes and transforms the conditions of precarity. The struggle over these schools, including their successes and failures, reveals how they came to understand the structural foundations of the precarious conditions in public education for landless peasant families.

In Chapter 13, Suárez examines the alliance among the League of Revolutionary Black Workers, Black student activist groups, and community activists in Detroit in the 1960s as they worked toward community control of public secondary schools. As Suárez points out, forging varied alliances that meet at the intersection of race and class is central to the pursuit of educational justice. As racial reckoning and race-related precarity is elevated in today's public discourse, this analysis of activism in 1960s Detroit offers a deeper understanding of the potential of coalition building for educational reform and social change in more contemporary movements such as Black Lives Matter.

The chapters in this last section collectively highlight the importance of praxis (Freire 2000) – critical reflection leading to informed activism – and social movements as spaces of possibility in confronting both new and ongoing conditions of struggle (Au & Hagopian 2018; Rincón-Gallardo 2019;

Ginwright 2016; Warren 2018). Overall, these four chapters convey the importance of engaging with activism, radical pedagogies, and social movements as strategies essential to education for children, youths, and adults – not as an "extra" activity beyond a formal curriculum, but as a core necessity for life. It is important to recognize the interrelationship across schooling, education outside of formal schooling, and social processes, and to reconceptualize learning and teaching as not limited to one space. For example, classrooms can be spaces where "difficult knowledge" (Britzman 2000, p. 27) can be taken up because it is integral to necessary learning processes that are foundational to life.

The concluding chapter provides an overview of how various notions of precarity are taken up in educational spaces across the chapters in this volume. While precarity presents as layered and unpredictable challenges, it can also offer an invitation for proactive engagement of positive change. We identify ways of rethinking precarity as a space of possibility, highlighting the importance of simultaneous engagement in reflective, pedagogical, and activist practices in the contemporary moment.

Conclusion

This text overall lends itself to a broader understanding of how precarity, as it has intensified in recent years, is experienced in increasingly destabilizing ways, and how educators have engaged with its impacts. We can see more clearly what is new, often overlooked, worthy of attention, and therefore, worth acting upon. This new clarity is an invitation to engage multidimensionally. Prescribed curricula and conventional pedagogical practices are not sufficient. Collectively, the chapters call for us to reflect critically and situate the self in a nuanced understanding of precarious contexts and dynamics, to rethink pedagogical processes and the purpose of curricular content, and to push back against the many precarious social conditions we face today. In challenging times, education both within and beyond formal schooling should be understood as a necessary grounding for living a purposeful life.

Note

1. While she distinguishes the two concepts in her argument, most literature does not. We use the terms interchangeably, although the distinction that we are not equally exposed to precariousness is important to bear in mind.

References

Ahmed, Nabeela. 2020. Everyday and Everywhere Bordering and Precarity Under COVID-19. *SPERI Blog*, May 13. Sheffield Political Economy Research Institute (SPERI).http://speri.dept.shef.ac.uk/2020/05/13/everyday-and-everywhere-bordering-and-precarity-under-covid-19/

Anderson, Gary L., Kathryn Herr, and Ann Sigrid Nihlen. 2007. *Studying Your Own School: An Educator's Guide to Practitioner Action Research*, 2nd edition. Thousand Oaks, CA: Corwin Press.

Au, Wayne, and Jesse Hagopian. 2018. How One Elementary School Sparked a Citywide Movement to Make Black Students' Lives Matter. In Dyan Watson, Jesse Hagopian and Wayne Au (eds.), *Teaching for Black Lives* (pp. 22–31). Milwaukee, WI: Rethinking Schools.

Bishai, Martha F. 2022. Innovation in a Time of Making Do: COVID-19 and the Digital Divide Through the Lens of a Mobile Phone Mathematics Program in South Africa. In Karen Monkman and Ann Frkovich (eds.), *Belonging in Changing Educational Spaces: Negotiating Global, Transnational, and Neoliberal Dynamics* (pp. 256–275). New York: Routledge.

Blair, Eleanor J. 2018. *By the Light of the Silvery Moon: Teacher Moonlighting and the Dark Side of Teachers' Work*. Gorham, ME: Myers Education Press.

Brewer, T. Jameson, and Christopher A. Lubienski. 2019. Introduction: Teaching as a Profession in an Age of Privatization: Issues, Advocacy, and Approaches. In Christopher A. Lubienski and T. Jameson Brewer (eds.), *Learning to Teach in an Era of Privatization: Global Trends in Teacher Preparation* (pp. 1–14). New York: Teachers College Press.

Britzman, Deborah P. 2000. If the Story Cannot End: Deferred Action, Ambivalence, and Difficult Knowledge. In Sharon Rosenberg, Roger I. Simon and Claudia Eppert (eds.), *Between Hope and Despair: The Pedagogical Encounter of Historical Remembrance* (pp. 27–57). Lanham, MD: Rowman and Littlefield.

Butler, Judith. 2004. *Precarious Life: The Powers of Mourning and Justice*. London: Verso.

Butler, Judith. 2008. *Judith Butler, 2008 Commencement Speaker, Grinnell College*. www.grinnell.edu/news/judith-butler-2008-commencement-speaker

Butler, Judith. 2009. *Frames of War: When Is Life Grievable?* London: Verso.

Casas-Cortés, Maribel. 2021. Precarious Writings Reckoning the Absences and Reclaiming the Legacies in the Current Poetics/Politics of Precarity. *Current Anthropology* 62(5): 510–538. DOI: 10.1086/716721

Children's Defense Fund. 2021. *The State of America's Children 2021*. Washington, DC: Children's Defense Fund.

Cody, Anthony. 2019. Canaries in the Classroom: The Teaching Profession in Trouble. In Christopher A. Lubienski and T. Jameson Brewer (eds.), *Learning to Teach in an Era of Privatization: Global Trends in Teacher Preparation* (pp. 113–126). New York: Teachers College Press.

Coombs, Philip H., and Manzoor Ahmed. 1974. *Attacking Rural Poverty: How Nonformal Education Can Help*. Baltimore, MD: The Johns Hopkins University Press.

Ewing, Eve. 2018. *Ghosts in the Schoolyard: Racism and School Closings on Chicago's South Side*. Chicago: University of Chicago Press.

Fine, Michelle. 2018. *Just Research in Contentious Times: Widening the Methodological Imagination*. New York: Teachers College Press.

Fine, Michelle, Cory Greene, and Sonia Sanchez. 2016. Neoliberal Blues and Prec(ar)ious Knowledge. *The Urban Review* 48(4): 499–519. DOI: 10.1007/s11256-016-0365-x

Freire, Paulo. 2000. *Pedagogy of the Oppressed*, 30th edition. New York: Continuum International Publishing Group.

George, Janel. 2021. Critical Race Theory Isn't a Curriculum. It's a Practice. The Furor Over CRT Removes a Valuable Tool From Teachers' Hands. *Education Week*, May 26.

www.edweek.org/leadership/opinion-critical-race-theory-isnt-a-curriculum-its-a-practice/2021/05

Gerstel, Naomi. 2000. The Third Shift: Gender and Care Work Outside the Home. *Qualitative Sociology* 23: 467–483.

Ginwright, Shawn. 2016. *Hope and Healing in Urban Education: How Urban Activists and Teachers Are Reclaiming Matters of the Heart.* New York: Routledge.

Goodson, Ivor F., and John F. Schostak. 2021. Curriculum and Coronavirus: New Approaches to Curriculum in the Age of Uncertainty. *Prospects* 51: 29–45. https://doi.org/10.1007/s11125-020-09523-9

Harvey, David. 2003. *The New Imperialism.* Oxford: Oxford University Press.

Hochschild, Arlie, and Anne Machung. 2012. *The Second Shift: Working Parents and the Revolution at Home,* 2nd edition. New York: Penguin Books.

Huber, Lindsay P., and Susana M. Muoz (eds.). 2021. *Why They Hate Us: How Racist Rhetoric Impacts Education.* New York: Teachers College Press.

Huckaby, Francyne. 2019. *Researching Resistance: Public Education After Neoliberalism.* Gorham, ME: Myers Education Press.

Jones, Denisha, and Jesse Hagopian. 2020. *Black Lives Matter at School: An Uprising for Social Justice.* Chicago: Haymarket Books.

Jones, Steven P., and Eric C. Sheffield (eds.). 2018. *Why Kids Love (And Hate) School: Reflections on Difference.* Gorham, ME: Myers Education Press.

Kasmir, Sharryn. 2018. Precarity. In Felix Stein, Sian Lazar, Matei Candea, Hildegard Diemberger, Joel Robbins, Andrew Sanchez and Rupert Stasch (eds.), *The Cambridge Encyclopedia of Anthropology.* http://doi.org/10.29164/18precarity or www.anthroencyclopedia.com/entry/precarity

Kirk, David. 2020. *Precarity, Pedagogy and Physical Education.* New York: Routledge.

Kumashiro, Kevin. 2020. *Surrendered: Why Progressives Are Losing the Biggest Battles in Education.* New York: Teachers College Press.

Ladson-Billings, Gloria. 2021. *Culturally Relevant Pedagogy: Asking a Different Question.* New York: Teachers College Press.

Lipman, Pauline. 2011. *The New Political Economy of Urban Education: Neoliberalism, Race, and the Right to the City.* New York: Routledge.

Lizana, Pablo A., and Gustavo Vega-Fernadez. 2021. Teacher Teleworking During the COVID-19 Pandemic: Association Between Work Hours, Work-Family Balance, and Quality of Life. *International Journal of Environmental Research and Public Health* 18(7566): 1–11. https://doi.org/10.3390/ijerph18147566

Lorey, Isabell. 2015. *State of Insecurity: Government of the Precarious* (Aileen Derieg, Trans.). London: Verso.

Mason, Olivia, and Nick Megoran. 2021. Precarity and Dehumanisation in Higher Education. *Learning and Teaching* 14(1): 35–39. DOI: 10.3167/latiss.2021.140103

Means, Alexander J. 2018. *Learning to Save the Future: Rethinking Education and Work in an Era of Digital Capitalism.* New York: Routledge.

Means, Alexander J. 2019. Precarity and the Precaritization of Teaching. In Michael A. Peters (ed.), *Encyclopedia of Teacher Education* (pp. 1–5). Singapore: Springer. https://doi.org/10.1007/978-981-13-1179-6_117-1

Narodowski, Mariano, and Delfina Campetella. 2022. Creative Destruction in School Education during COVID-19. In Karen Monkman and Ann Frkovich (eds.), *Belonging in Changing Educational Spaces: Negotiating Global, Transnational, and Neoliberal Dynamics* (pp. 68–84). New York: Routledge.

Noddings, Nel. 2006. *Critical Lessons: What Our Schools Should Teach.* Cambridge, UK: Cambridge University Press.

Perry, Brea L., Brian Aronson, and Bernice A. Pescosolido et al. 2021. Pandemic Precarity: COVID-19 Is Exposing and Exacerbating Inequalities in the American Heartland. *Proceedings of the National Academy of Sciences of the United States of America (PNAS)* 118(8): e2020685118. https://doi.org/10.1073/pnas.2020685118

Pressley, Tim, and Cheyeon Ha. 2021. Teachers During a Pandemic: United States Teachers' Self-Efficacy During Covid-19. *Teaching and Teacher Education* 106. https://doi.org/10.1016/j.tate.2021.103465.

Rincón-Gallardo, Santiago. 2019. *Liberating Learning: Educational Change as Social Movement.* New York: Routledge.

Rogers, John, Megan Franke, Jung-Eun Ellie Yun, Michael Ishimoto, Claudia Diera, Rebecca Cooper Geller, Anthony Berryman, and Tizoc Brenes. 2017. *Teaching and Learning in the Age of Trump: Increasing Stress and Hostility in America's High Schools.* Los Angeles, CA: UCLA's Institute for Democracy, Education, and Access.

Sassen, Saskia. 2013. *Expulsions: Brutality and Complexity in the Global Economy.* Cambridge, MA: Belknap Press.

Schapp, Anders, Kathi Weeks, Bice Maiquascha, Edwina Barvosa, Leah Bassel, and Paul Apostoldis. 2020. The Politics of Precarity. *Contemporary Political Theory.* DOI: 10.1057/s41296-020-00435-z [Epub ahead of print.]

Scott, Janelle, and Jennifer Jellison Holme. 2016. The Political Economy of Market-Based Educational Policies: Race and Reform in Urban School Districts, 1915 to 2016. *Review of Research in Education* 40: 250–297. www.jstor.org/stable/44668624

Standing, Guy. 2016. *The Precariat: The New Dangerous Class.* London: Bloomsbury Academic.

Stovall, David. 2020. Knowing: Willingness, Fugitivity, and Abolition in Precarious Times. *Journal of Language & Literacy Education* 16(1): 1–7.

UNICEF. 2020. *Impact of COVID-19 on Multidimensional Child Poverty.* https://data.unicef.org/resources/impact-of-covid-19-on-multidimensional-child-poverty/

US Department of Education (USDOE), Office for Civil Rights. 2021. *Education in a Pandemic: The Disparate Impacts of COVID-19 on Students.* www2.ed.gov/about/offices/list/ocr/docs/20210608-impacts-of-covid19.pdf

Warren, Mark, and David Goodman. 2018. *Lift Us Up, Don't Push Us Out!: Voices From the Front Lines of the Educational Justice Movement.* Boston: Beacon Press.

Way, Niobe, Alisha Ali, Carol Gilligan, and Pedro Noguera. 2018. *The Crisis of Connection: Roots, Consequences and Solutions.* New York: New York University Press.

Weiner, Lois. 2011. Neoliberalism's Global Reconstruction of Schooling, Teachers' Work, and Teacher Education. Chapter 21 in Steven E. Tozer, Bernardo P. Gallegos, Annette M. Henry, Mary Bushnell Greiner and Paula Groves Price (eds.), *Handbook of Research in Social Foundations of Education* (pp. 308–318). New York: Routledge.

Williams, Jamillah Bowman, Lisa Singh, and Naomi Mezey. 2019. #MeToo as Catalyst: A Glimpse Into 21st Century Activism. *University of Chicago Legal Forum* Article 22: 371–393. https://chicagounbound.uchicago.edu/uclf/vol2019/iss1/22

Zeichner, Kenneth M., and Daniel P. Liston. 2013. *Reflective Teaching: An Introduction,* 2nd edition. New York: Routledge.

Zembylas, Michalinos. 2019. The Ethics and Politics of Precarity: Risks and Productive Possibilities of a Critical Pedagogy for Precarity. *Studies in Philosophy and Education* 38: 95–111. https://doi.org/10.1007/s11217-018-9625-4

Part I

Precarious Entanglements

Situating the Self

2 No Hablo Español

Contributions to the Loss of the Spanish Language Among Latinxs in the United States

Erica Zuniga Fuentes

Introduction

> "Attacks on one's form of expression with the intent to censor are a violation of the First Amendment. *El Anglo con cara de inocente nos arrancó la lengua.* Wild tongues can't be tamed, they can only be cut out."
>
> Gloria Anzaldúa (2012, p. 76), "How to Tame a Wild Tongue"[1]

For many Latinxs living in the United States, the Spanish language is a significant component of both personal and cultural identity. While the Latinx population as a whole is increasing and among the fastest growing in the United States at an estimated 58.9 million people (U.S. Census Bureau 2018; Ennis, Rios-Vargas, & Albert 2011), the percentage of Spanish-speaking Latinxs is declining (Krogstad & Lopez 2017). This chapter explores the social and cultural conditions that may be contributing to the loss of the Spanish language among Latinxs in the United States.

Drawing from a brief history of United States-Mexico relations as a foundation for understanding, we further aim to raise the inquiry of what it means to be Latinx in the United States – that is, how do Latinxs negotiate their identity and feelings of belonging? Additionally, how might Latinxs navigate negative perceptions, racist attitudes, and linguistic terrorism, and in what ways might this contribute to the loss of the Spanish language? I believe many Latinxs may experience a colonized mentality that may lead them to abandon Spanish – either out of fear for survival and safety or as a result of internalized racism.

"Sana, Sana, Colita de Rana. Si No Sanas Hoy, Sanarás Mañana"

The above title is a popular proverb in Latin American folklore that roughly translates to, "Heal, heal, little frog's tail. If you don't heal today, you'll heal tomorrow." This saying is recited by adults to children that have just hurt themselves, in an effort to cheer them up after a scraped knee or bruised arm. Although a simple poem, there is symbolism that comes from the

DOI: 10.4324/9781003258223-3

metamorphosis of a frog that can be paralleled with the Latinx community; with time, the thing that causes your pain will be gone, and though you will ache, you will move forward.

Growing up in a predominantly Hispanic/Latinx neighborhood in San Antonio, Texas, my grandparents lived about a mile away from my family; so, my two sisters and I often found ourselves socializing at their kitchen table most days after school. I was close to my grandparents and liked to ask them questions about what life was like when they were young. I remember one particular story my grandfather shared with me; he grew up in a neighboring rural town and was educated in a one-room schoolhouse with children of various ages. Even in his elderly years, he could still recall a painful and confusing incident as a young Latino boy; a fellow student claimed she had heard him "laughing in Spanish." He was punished – spanked by his teacher with a wooden paddle. Ultimately, my grandfather never finished school. He worked the farmland with his parents until he was old enough to enlist in the U.S. Army. I have always wondered if he did not finish school because of his experience with anti-Latino violence at school, which one could assume was encountered many times beyond this incident.

My grandfather was a descendant of the Canary Islanders that arrived in the region of Bexar County, Texas, in 1731. At the time, present-day San Antonio was emerging as a colonial Spanish settlement, and Spanish was becoming the language of the region as the indigenous population declined due to conflict, displacement, and disease from European colonizers. In spite of the past, my grandfather was proud of his mestizo heritage, of Spanish and indigenous blood, and the ancestry of his family as one of the "founders" of this particular area where many descendants still reside. I found it sadly ironic that he was made to feel like he did not belong in a place where he had always belonged, relatively speaking.

Although I was completely immersed in Latinx culture and surrounded by the Spanish language, I did not consider myself a native speaker in any way. I could pick up on phrases and do some rough translations when necessary but found myself resisting the work needed to reach the fluency of holding a full conversation and remained completely beyond my abilities through adulthood. I often felt embarrassed, playfully teased as a "coconut" (meaning, "brown on the outside, white on the inside") for lacking this skill, but as a youth, did not put much effort into making any lasting changes.

When I left my predominantly Latinx community for college in a rural east Texas town, I was constantly asked where I was from – and not just from, *really from* – as if I didn't belong *there*. I was told that my English was perfect and how "lucky" I was that affirmative action was a thing schools were doing now. It became a struggle to accept my identity as a Latina, and I often found myself shying away from my culture in order to fit in with my surroundings.

What they didn't know was that my family tree has deeper roots in the United States than the United States itself; we have been living on the same lands for centuries, and the exotic place I was from, and not just from but *really* from, was just a three-hour drive away. It was then that my former identity was clouded – was I proud to be Latina, or not? Had Spanish been assimilated out of me or assassinated? The importance of these memories has always stayed with me and inspired what would be the foundation of this chapter – what does it mean to be Latinx in the United States? What contributes to the loss of the Spanish language among Latinxs in the United States? Are their stories like mine – one of shame or survival? One of self-hatred or self-preservation?

Although this crisis of identity was a personal struggle to confront, I argue that these feelings are similarly experienced among many Latinxs and grew from a history of oppression. Rather than establishing a set of traditional research data, I grew my research from the memory of my grandfather as well as my own personal experiences, provoked by the quiet rage I felt from the xenophobic, anti-Latinx rhetoric from Donald J. Trump during both his campaigns and presidency. Much of this was a journey in both self-discovery and self-acceptance; while today I would critique my past dismissive attitudes toward the Spanish language as shameful, I can now comfortably assert that the negative feelings and resentment I felt stemmed from a "colonized mentality." I no longer harbor these past negative judgments or viewpoints and fully embrace a new, positive mindset of myself and my culture as I look toward the future, "*Si no sanas hoy, sanarás mañana.*"

History of United States–Mexico Relations (1519–1848)

This short history of imperialism between the United States and Mexico serves as a prologue to the next section and as a foundation for what led to the resulting attitudes toward Latinxs (particularly Mexicans/Mexican-Americans) living in the United States today.

To begin, Spanish conquistadors launched their "exploration" of Mexico in the early sixteenth century; in 1519, Hernán Cortés and his army over-threw Montezuma II, the emperor of what was the region's strongest and most powerful empire: the Aztecs. European diseases such as smallpox and salmonella killed over 80% of the population (Callaway 2017). The remaining were enlisted to assist Spain in the conquering of Mexico; those who did not were enslaved. Mexico would remain a Spanish colony for the next 300 years.

Social and economic injustices led Mexico to rebel and officially wage war on Spain in 1810. After a long, costly war (in both blood and finances), Spain surrendered to Mexico in 1821.

Mexico struggled in its early years as an independent nation, as the financial recovery from the war for independence proved to be a major challenge. However, the land that they had come to own was fertile, and Mexico wished to use the land to attract growth and gain global stability.

At the time, the region of what is now Texas was vastly unpopulated; wishing to expand the number of residents living in some of the less populated rural areas of Texas, Mexico offered land grants to U.S. citizens seeking to own land. There were conditions to the land grants, which required those accepting land to formally become Mexican citizens, abide by Mexican laws, convert to Catholicism, and agree to not own slaves (Foley 2014).

However, once living on the land, the settlers rapidly came to defy and dismiss the conditions they had agreed to – convinced that as Americans, they were superior to their Mexican hosts – and therefore did not see reason to respect or comply with the terms of the land grant. The concern for Anglos, as Foley (2014) writes, was that "Although the Mexican government had banned slavery, Anglo Americans were determined to exercise their constitutional rights (in a foreign country) to own them" and that "white people would be the equivalent to 'slaves' under Mexican rule (which denied them their God-given right to own slaves)" (p. 27). Eventually, the racial ideologies and negative stereotypes of Mexicans held by Anglo Americans, combined with the dispute on slavery, escalated tensions between the Mexican government and Texas residents – both Mexican and Anglo American alike – which led to the Texas Revolution in 1835. Still in recovery from their war for independence just years prior, power and resources had been scarce for Mexico, while Texas was experiencing exponential progress (ironically thanks to the growing population provided by the land grants). Ultimately, Mexico could not sustain a new war, which led to the secession of Texas from Mexico in 1836. This region came to be known as the Republic of Texas and remained an independent nation for nearly ten years, until the United States annexed Texas in 1845 as its 28th state (Novas 2003).

After the acquisition of Texas, the United States continued to stress the "destiny" of westward expansion; President James Polk, wishing to acquire a possibly gold-filled California, proved an aggressive instigator of these efforts, offering to purchase California territory from Mexico for 25 million dollars. Although Mexico was in financial crisis, the proposal was offensive and ill-received, and it was ultimately rejected. It was then that President Polk convinced the U.S. government to approve funding in 1846 to battle Mexico for the territory, with hopes to instead forcefully seize the land. An exhausted Mexico, still in recovery from its fight for independence from Spain and unforeseen loss of Texas – all within the last 36 years – did not have the financial resources, infrastructure, or support to win yet another battle. At that moment, Mexico had little choice but to reach an agreement with the United States.

Soon, on February 2, 1848, the Treaty of Guadalupe Hidalgo was signed. In this treaty, 55% of Mexico's land was lost to the United States, which included a large percentage of present-day California, Arizona, New Mexico, Utah, Nevada, Colorado, and Wyoming. This one document would affect thousands of Mexican citizens, now given just one year to make a difficult decision – either maintain their Mexican citizenship and relocate south of the Rio Grande or stay on their established properties and accept a new citizenship with the United States. The border had crossed them; now was the time to decide what nation they would call home.

However, the Treaty of Guadalupe Hidalgo was not heeded or enforced as initially agreed upon between the United States and Mexico; without knowledge or consent, the United States altered the terms of the treaty to work against Mexico and its citizens. As Novas (2003) notes:

> Article IX of the Treaty of Guadalupe Hidalgo specifically provided that Mexicans living in the new U.S. territories would have the right to retain their property. In utter disregard for Mexican tradition and the Treaty of Guadalupe Hidalgo, the Anglos who settled in droves in the newly acquired territories ousted Mexican grantees from the most desirable properties (those near water) and then claimed that they had the right to homestead vacant lands.
>
> (p. 75)

Although the initial agreement stated that Mexicans who decided to stay and become U.S. citizens maintained the right to their land and property, this was not the case, and Mexicans were displaced from their established homesteads, much of which families had exchanged ownership over through verbal agreements instead of paper documentation. Because of this, Mexican families could not provide legal proof that they owned their own properties, which made them susceptible to Anglo settlers' commandeering as the land did not technically have legal owners (Foley 2014).

As if there were not enough insult to the injury, gold had been discovered in California on January 24, 1848, less than ten days before the Treaty of Guadalupe Hidalgo was to be ratified. Impeccably terrible timing for Mexico, as this discovery could have drastically changed the course of Mexico's history and laid the foundation for global wealth and power. Instead, the United States flourished as a result of the California Gold Rush of 1848, which would forever change the geographical and residential layout for both California and the United States, as well as for those that flocked to the new frontier in search of gold and new beginnings.

These events – from the Aztecs to the Gold Rush and beyond – illustrate how Mexico and its people have been forced into oppression – preyed upon, intimidated, exploited, and abused – over the last several centuries. I provide these moments in history not merely as a timeline of events, but to demonstrate the pattern of perceived inferiority Latinxs (for this chapter, specifically Mexican and Mexican-Americans) have had to navigate for over 500 years. I want the readers to understand the history of how Latinxs came to be seen as lesser-than in the United States, and how so much of Latinx existence has involved perpetual loss by force.

Identity and Loss of Language

Understanding the history of the United States-Mexico relations is vital to recognizing how this impacts Latinxs in the United States today. Dating back to the Spanish conquest, through Mexican independence, the annexation of Texas, and a war with the United States, Mexico and its people have often been disregarded as second-class. Sadly, extensive research has shown that "perpetual inferiority" exists in the minds of many white Americans, meaning that they "believe that Latinos pass down a set of inferior cultural practices, which they are incapable of changing and adapting, from one generation to the next. Thus, the mechanism by which whites attribute fixed negative characteristics to Latinos is through heritability" (Lacayo 2017, p. 569).

In an environment that negatively perceives Latinx people as a menace to the United States (Chavez 2013) – whether that be socially, culturally, politically, economically, or even physically as a mere presence – it is then that members of the Latinx community internalize these negative stigmas within themselves and work toward eliminating those perceived ideas, even if it means negating oneself or one's previously constructed identity in favor of "Americanizing." Rather than unpacking the racist and xenophobic history of the United States, it is more beneficial to the current power hierarchy to place the blame of any national struggle – lack of employment, national debt, crime, welfare needs, a struggling America – on the backs of Latinx peoples, insisting that Latinxs are criminals taking "all" the jobs, living on welfare with free access to healthcare, not paying taxes, and are the threat to "making America great again"[2] (Dovidio et al. 2010).

In speaking about the negative perceptions about Latinx in the United States and how this impacts Latinx identity, Bucholtz and Hall (2007) argue: "One of the greatest weaknesses of previous research on identity, in fact, is the assumption that identities are attributes of individuals or groups rather than of situations" (p. 376). For example, a Latinx living in a low-income neighborhood is circumstantial in that, perhaps, Latinxs' lack of access to quality education due to racial discrimination and/or investment in their local schools inhibits them from obtaining a higher-paying job, which would have supported a move to a middle-class neighborhood – and helped them gain additional opportunities for social and economic advancement as a result of that new status. However, from a social standpoint, others may view this person of color as unintelligent, unwilling to learn, lazy, or even incapable of attempting to achieve a life beyond the one the person is currently living, without consideration of circumstances (Foley 2014).

The 2016 presidential election of Donald Trump was largely built upon the slogan "Make America Great Again." A major talking point on the campaign trail and agenda toward immigration policy was building a border wall on the United States-Mexico border, an estimated $21.6 billion project that he insisted Mexico would fund (Ainsley 2017). Many firmly believe that this medieval wall would somehow save the United States from perilous decline, after fearmongering tactics from Trump, insisting that:

> When Mexico sends its people, they're not sending their best. They're not sending you. They're not sending you. They're sending people that have lots of problems, and they're bringing those problems. . . . They're bringing drugs. They're bringing crime. They're rapists.
>
> (Schwartz 2015, para. 3)

As Neil Foley (2014) writes, "many Americans fear that this 'silent invasion' of Latino newcomers will overwhelm American culture and transform the United States into a 'third world' country" (p. 4). Generally, there seems to be a deep level of disbelief that Mexicans (and Latinxs as a whole) refuse to assimilate, linguistically and culturally, and are overall a drain to our national resources reserved for "real" citizens of the country, including the ideology that all Latinx people are illegal immigrants that are here to "take" jobs that non-Latinxs are seemingly entitled to have – except, of course, the jobs that require hard manual labor for little pay.

As mentioned in the previous section, many Latinxs were indigenous to the land and were absorbed into what is now part of the United States under the Treaty of Guadalupe Hidalgo, and they had been living on the same lands for generations prior to being terrorized into vacating their homes (Foley 2014). However, the descendants of these native peoples have since had to endure the socially constructed identity of the stereotypical "illegal alien" rather than that of native. That is, one that does not appear to belong in the United States and is still often perceived as a threat to society and "American" culture (whatever that may be, taking into consideration that the term "American" is interpretive and not culturally, socially, or historically one prescribed ideal), even in today's time (Emeka & Vallejo 2011). Chavez (2013) writes on these fears, stating:

> their social identity has been plagued by the mark of illegality, which in much public discourse, means that they are criminals and thus illegitimate members of society undeserving of social benefits, including citizenship. Latinos are an alleged threat because of this history and social identity, which supposedly makes their integration difficult.
>
> (p. 4)

The disconnect that exists between the assumed identity of Latinx living in the United States is present in institutions such as the American education and legislative system, constructing modes of structural repression that function to sustain superiority among non-Latinxs within the perceived social, psychological, cultural, and historical hierarchies (Bonilla-Silva 2018).

English-Only Ideology and Pressure to Assimilate

Culture is about shared meanings, and language is the foundation for which meaning-making and reciprocal exchanges between cultures can happen. I believe one contributor to the loss of the Spanish language among Latinx is generational assimilation; as each person slowly acclimates into mainstream social and cultural ideologies, English becomes the primary language, and the use of Spanish fades. Vanishing relationships with immigrants as each generation is Americanized[3] (Perez & Hirschman 2009), as well as intermarriage with non-Spanish-speaking Latinx or non-Latinx people, may also contribute to the loss (Lopez, Gonzalez-Barrera, & López 2017). As children are born, the language spoken in the home is their primary language, and once in school, formal education will either strengthen or challenge that primary language. As they grow up, whatever language feels most like "home" or most comfortable to their inner being becomes a part of who they are, their identity (Flores-González, Aranda, & Vaquera 2014). I will argue that some might choose to abandon their home and/or their language in hopes of "fitting in" with the culture of English-only favoritism, which leads to the regression of their first language and – with that – the vanishing of heritage and culture.

Padilla (2004) explains this phenomenon in direct correlation with this notion:

> Survival instincts coupled with an unquestioned acceptance of liberal ideology promoting pursuit of individual well-being pushes us to claim a White identity. Yet a critical analysis of that pursuit reveals some flaws in the goal. Most fundamentally, that goal asks us to forfeit our cultural and ethnic identity. Another flaw is that it assumes that even if one wanted to "pass" for purposes of obtaining White privilege, the privilege would follow. Even if Latino/as self-identify as White, they cannot control how others see them. So long as they are viewed as Latino/a, they will not obtain the White privilege that they crave. Here lies the greatest risk of all, as one could lose one's ethnic and familial identity without ever achieving one's desired identity, thus leaving an untethered soul who fits in nowhere.
>
> (p. 18)

The loss of the Spanish language among new generations of Latinx Americans is not only a cultural loss of heritage but also impactful on the individual from the standpoint of personal identity; as Bucholtz and Hall (2007) note, "language, as a fundamental resource for cultural production, is hence also a fundamental resource for identity production" (p. 382). Language is, therefore, observed outwardly as a part of culture in everyday life but internalized on an individual level that influences identity. Experienced socially, language is a powerful tool that can lead one to identify as either a part of a group or norm or as an outsider apart from this group or norm. However, if only one dominating culture (in this instance, American culture, paired with the English language) is lacking tolerance for the other (i.e., Latinx or Mexican-American culture, paired with the Spanish language), there is little room for which thoughts, feelings, and ideas can successfully be communicated between the two. As a result, there is no value given by the dominating culture to a language that does not have the social structure or social capital to positively support it, which leads some Spanish speakers to Americanize themselves into belonging (Bauer-Wolf 2017); those that continue to speak Spanish, however, may feel out of place culturally, suffering from an internal identity struggle in direct, binary opposition with the American way of living.

In an attempt to dissolve the Latino/a identity, an effort is made to "Americanize" those that are not already considered the idealistic version of what an "American" is. This configuration is seen in U.S. schools, in which the "desired effect of 'Americanizing' students was to socialize and acculturate the diverse community. In essence, if schools could teach these students English and 'American' values, then educational failure could be averted" (García 2001, p. 49). This is based on the assumption that "ethnicity and nationality [as identities] are permanently coextensive or co-determining" (Alcoff 2006, p. 21). Fearing that Latinos/as are concealing a secret allegiance to their "primary" culture/country or origin, "Americanization" is a constructed strategy to reproduce and reinforce the non-Latino/a power structure, as exemplified by the English-only movement, which is a form of characterized colonialism (Macedo 2000). Colonialism brings forth the ideology that the dominating culture is superior and devaluing of the cultures that are not within the same level of social, cultural, and national origin hierarchy.

The hostility toward Latinxs for existing, in both white and non-white spaces, illustrates the reasoning behind individuals choosing to abandon their Latinx roots, culture, and language in favor of survival, in favor of being treated as human beings and not as pests that need to be removed and exterminated.

Although speaking Spanish is seemingly forbidden for Latinx peoples (even conversing among themselves), it is widely accepted for a white individual to not only speak Spanish but exploit the culture. As Carris (2011) writes:

> In white public space, whites, and white ways of speaking, are invisibly normal. Conversely, racialized populations are visibly marginal and the objects of linguistic monitoring. . . . [W]hites in the USA are afforded a social and linguistic liberty to "police" linguistic practices of racialized individuals and even participate in the very practices they monitor.
>
> (pp. 475–476)

The popular song *Despacito*, featuring Justin Bieber, a young white Canadian male singer, is an example of this. *Despacito* was written in collaboration with a Puerto Rican songwriter and singer, Luis Fonsi, and a Puerto Rican rapper,

Daddy Yankee, and, according to Billboard Music, it "Ties for Longest Run at No. 1 in Hot 100's History" and ties in "the longest command in the chart's 59-year archives" (Trust 2017, para.1). In white spaces for white audiences, Spanish is not an issue if spoken by a white person; however, in both white and non-white spaces, speaking Spanish by a Latinx is policed and shamed (Delgado & Stefancic 2011; Foley 2014). This is also true for a Latinx speaking English with a detectable accent. In an analysis regarding the linguistic freedom that Anglos have over Latinx people, Carris (2011) writes about how "*La voz gringa*" (p. 475, italics in original), a non-Spanish-speaking white's use of Spanish, contrasts with that of a Spanish-speaking Latinx:

> *La voz gringa* evokes a social identity of privilege, affluence, and entitlement, and an empty-headedness associated with the disorderly use of Spanish attributed to whites in positions of power. In the USA, the powerful have long used language to discriminate against Spanish and perceived Spanish-sounding speakers.
>
> (p. 485)

As demonstrated by Carris (2011), foreign languages are a positive, enriching skill for whites and do not need to be corrected or held to high standards to be legitimized in our culture; however, speaking English as a second language is mandatory for Latinx members, and doing so imperfectly or with an accent leads to ridicule and discrimination (p. 475).

Ultimately, Latinxs are experiencing a heightened level of social and cultural anti-being, and struggles with personal identity can be linked with the English-only, anti-Spanish sentiment. Morales (2018) completes this idea of "linguistic terrorism" (p. 144) well, arguing that:

> [T]o advance the idea that Latinx immigrants are unassimilable intruders, it is equally imperative for us to adopt a unified stance against increasingly looming threats of anti-Latinx violence, stoked by the white supremacist populism of Donald Trump. Still much can be said for the strategic embrace of the idea that, on an ideological level, and perhaps at the level of consciousness itself, a Latinx awareness can provoke a needed re-examination of long-held assumptions about self, identity, and nation. . . . For some, the 'linguistic terrorism' or intolerance of foreign languages . . . that goes along with American xenophobia seems to have an expiration date: the ugly intolerance and physical violence toward Spanish speakers should dissipate as Latinx become fluent in English by the second generation and as their use of Spanish outside of informal code-switching diminishes over time.
>
> (pp. 143–144)

A deeper examination of my own identity and the "linguistic terrorism" Morales speaks of and how I truly perceived myself and my heritage was brought to light after Donald Trump won the presidential election in 2016; I felt that the *Make America Great Again* campaign slogan radicalized right-wing Anglo America into believing that the United States was taking back a country that had somehow been stolen from them by minorities. There is a lack of acceptance for the idea that the United States never has been, nor ever will be, a purely white America (Foley 2014) but desperately wants to attain this by whitening brown communities.

As mentioned earlier in this chapter, my grandfather had deep roots in the land before the United States was an independent nation, and although he could speak fluent English and was indeed a citizen, his preferred language was Spanish, and he used it often in our predominantly Latinx community. Yet, he existed in a space where Latinxs were not welcome, where there were negative consequences for even the perception of *laughing* in a language that was not English. Whether he realized it or not, my grandfather recognized that Spanish was a dangerous language, and took action to prevent future harm to his children and grandchildren. The linguistic terrorism that he experienced prompted my grandfather to speak English at home, unlike his upbringing or social interactions; consequently, his children primarily speak English, and grandchildren almost exclusively speak English. In my experience, it is frustrating in the sense that Spanish feels both familiar and foreign, all at the same time; as if I am staring at a friend's face whose name I can't remember.

For me, as well as many others that share stories similar to my own, English-only efforts have stripped Latinxs of Spanish as a heritage language and have damaged the social and cultural relationship between generations. Not being able to speak among relatives or other members of the community that did retain the language was an internal crisis that drove me into self-hatred for the inability to perform my Latina identity as well as confusion for whether or not I was even an authentic Latina or *Latina enough* to begin with. Only now, as I research and attempt to articulate these findings in relation to my lived experiences, do I understand that the hatred that I felt for myself was generational trauma, imposed from a history of colonization and oppression toward Latinx people and Spanish by association.

Internalized Racism, Whiteness, and Belonging

Internalized racism, as noted by Hipolito-Delgado (2010):

> has been defined as the acceptance of stereotypes or beliefs that paint one's racial group as subhuman, inferior, incapable, or a burden on society (Padilla 2001). Internalized racism oftentimes has adverse effects on the physical health, mental health, and identity development of people of color.
>
> (p. 319)

Internalized racism, therefore, is the by-product of existing in a racist society (Hipolito-Delgado 2010). Wanting to "become white" is the result of being conditioned to believe that being white equates to being good; pure; wholesome; and, ultimately, American. In being *non-white* by comparison, one might instead view oneself as the opposite – bad, corrupt, harmful, and un-American. This may lead to feelings of self-hatred, guilt, and shame of oneself and/or one's culture and feeling like an outsider or "foreign," regardless of citizenship status (Flores-González 2017; Golash-Boza 2006). This internalized racism pressures many to shed their Latinx roots, in hopes of being viewed and accepted as an American and belonging to American culture. Thus, Latinxs wanting to experience the "American Dream" are pressured to "pass" and/or assimilate in order to be perceived as less Latinx and more American, allowing access to spaces and places that may have previously been prohibited. As Dovidio et al. (2010) note, "White is the prototypical image of American" (p. 64); in that sense, wanting to be "American" is synonymous with wanting to be white – being non-white is the equivalent of being non-American.

Many individuals experience this need to be socially accepted and culturally validated, myself included. As mentioned in the introduction, I, too, battled with my own perceived inferiority, which, in turn, motivated me to be "less" of who I actually was – a bicultural Latina – and more of who I "needed to be" in order to thrive in every aspect of my life, especially with regard to educational advancement. For example, attending a predominantly white university in rural Texas felt hostile at times, and I wanted desperately to fit in and feel at peace. Wanting to be perceived as "more white than other Latinos" in order to be accepted and have access to greater opportunity was a mentality I did not fully understand or even acknowledge I struggled with, until graduate school. As such, I resisted efforts to learn Spanish that I had been accustomed to hearing in everyday life growing up in San Antonio, Texas, with a large population of Latinx people that are fluent in Spanish. I thought that, by not knowing Spanish, I would not be seen as "Mexican" (which internalized racism would suggest carries a negative connotation of foreigner or outsider) but as an "American" – a sacrificial rite of passage. Being a part of the dominant culture would, in turn, spare me from being associated with the dominated. In reality, I am both American and Latina – I do not, in any way, need to prove that I belong. My experience is not unique (Flores-González 2017).

Padilla (2004) describes the internal racism that one may encounter as a Latinx living in the United States:

> Despising all things native to ourselves causes unhealthy behavior, including self-loathing and participation in the perpetuation of negative stereotypes. Latino/as may be conditioned to believe that other Latino/as – particularly recent immigrants – are taking jobs away from U.S. citizens, or are unfairly taking advantage of U.S. social services.

Additionally, we may refrain from using Spanish in professional settings because it will betray our heritage, or we may believe that Whiter is better.

(p. 16)

This internalized self-loathing leads to elimination by assimilation; in this sense, the loss of language stems from the inability to speak Spanish due to assimilation through the generations, starting with the individuals who wish to separate themselves and/or their families from the stigma that comes with being a Latinx in the United States (Estrada, Tsai, & Chandler 2008). Here, I argue that for many, the loss of the Spanish language is gradual, generational, and intentional; this erosion is an effect of one's environment, and the pressure to abandon the language and the culture stems from negative social conditioning, which contributes to the loss over time.

[T]he oppressive shame Latinx may feel over their inability to speak English in the first generation dissolves into another, subtler shame over inability to speak Spanish when visiting their ancestral homeland, or, perhaps more shamefully, in encounters with Latin American native Spanish speakers in professional settings.

(Morales 2018, p. 144)

Opposite of the desire to desert former home and heritage to embrace life as an "American," there is a secondary point of view, a different "America" that consists of low-paying service jobs, segregation, and the pressure to eliminate one's accent in order to live with dignity. Latinxs, although tied to the United States since at least the 1800s, are still seen as foreign, as unwanted, and as un-American in contrast to the social norm of white monolingual English speakers. The mistreatment Latinxs endure can lead to one wanting to assimilate, that is, to lose one's culture and identity, in hopes of a better life (Alamilla, Kim, & Lam 2010).

Ultimately, being a proud Latinx in the United States is dangerous, not merely because of the violence that comes from sustaining one's Latinx culture but also because of what sustaining that Latinx culture means to "American" culture.

Conclusions and Final Thoughts

Recuérdame

Disney Pixar's *Coco* released in November 2017 to an overwhelmingly positive audience (Unkrich & Molina 2017). Praised for capturing the mystical tradition of *Día de los Muertos*, a celebration of loved ones who have passed, *Coco* also introduced a glimpse into the Mexican culture that many residing in the United States might not have been familiar with or might not have wanted to explore at all. Although Disney itself has a complex past of exploiting and/or stereotyping the marginalized (Gagnon 1998), it nevertheless remains a globally recognizable brand and mammoth in the film industry, consistently breaking box office records. For a film that focused on a Mexican tradition to be so well received with Latinx and non-Latinx audiences alike is a momentous step in the right direction toward a more positive, inclusive culture. I will admit, upon seeing the opening scenes of *Coco* at my local theater, I cried. Never before had I felt so seen in mainstream media – it brought an overwhelming sense of pride, even considering that, for a short period of time, I thought I was supposed to be someone else. There was pure joy in that moment, and I won't ever forget how it made me feel: to be *celebrated as a community* – not as stereotyped caricatures – a people with rich cultures and traditions, embraced by families across generations.

Among the songs created for *Coco*, many of which code-switch (performed in both English and Spanish), one stands out as a significant contributor to the story arch: "*Remember Me*," or, in Spanish, "*Recuérdame*" (Anderson-Lopez & Lopez 2017). When listening to the lyrics of the song, I felt there was this bigger meaning, or perhaps a dual meaning, of remembering ourselves. Remembering myself and who I am; I don't have to bury parts of myself as I'm living, even if pieces of myself – my identity, my heritage, my culture – have faded away. *Un día de la muerta*, a day to celebrate myself as I am, and as I might have been in another life. I believe in many ways, this sweet lullaby is symbolic of the challenges the Latinx community faces. It evokes a feeling of peace from the anxiety felt by the pressure to "forget" what we know about ourselves, our heritage, our legacy. It is representational, in the sense that many Latinxs battle both separation and loss on a constant basis; from ongoing linguistic terrorism and erasure of culture, to the very real physical separation of families at the Mexico-United States border (Acevedo 2019), Latinxs are not free to simply be. This film was groundbreaking in that Latinxs were represented as *people* and not criminals.[4]

I do hope that after witnessing the injustices the Latinx community has endured within the United States – catapulted into the spotlight after the election of Donald Trump, exacerbated by the separation of immigrant families – non-Latinx Americans will be mindful of the prejudice and conscious of the bias Latinxs must regularly navigate. In spite of the ongoing challenges and beyond the questioning of what it means to be Latinx in the United States, Latinxs will continue to resist the erasure of our culture and recognize ourselves as authentic members of the society, promoting a more equal and multilingual nation where Latinxs are unafraid to belong as they are.

Notes

1. Used with permission from Aunt Lute Books.
2. Campaign slogan of Republican Donald Trump in the United States 2016 presidential elections, "Make America Great Again" or "MAGA," prompted debate about what era of American history is being referenced, and for whom this past had benefited.

3. Along with Perez and Hirschman (2009), I use the term "Americanized" (inclusive of the related Americanize, Americanization, Americanizing) to mean the assimilation of the Latinx community into dominant, mainstream communities with Americanized identities.

4. . . . except the character *Héctor*, for getting into trouble for trying to "cross the border" from the spirit world to the living world "illegally," which is a separate commentary in its own on the militarization of borders and what belonging means, but I digress.

References

Acevedo, Nicole. 2019. Why Are Migrant Children Dying in U.S. Custody? *NBC News*, May 29. Accessed June 2, 2019. www.nbcnews.com/news/latino/why-are-migrant-children-dying-u-s-custody-n1010316?cid=public-rss_20190530

Ainsley, Julia Edwards. 2017. Exclusive–Trump Border "Wall" to Cost $21.6 Billion, Take 3.5 Years to Build: Internal Report. *Reuters.com*, February 9. www.reuters.com/article/us-usa-trump-immigration-wall-exclusive/exclusive-trump-border-wall-to-cost-21-6-billion-take-3-5-years-to-build-internal-report-idUSKBN15O2ZN

Alamilla, Saul G., Bryan S. K. Kim, and N. Alexandra Lam. 2010. Acculturation, Enculturation, Perceived Racism, Minority Status Stressors, and Psychological Symptomatology Among Latino/as. *Hispanic Journal of Behavioral Sciences* 32(1): 55–76.

Alcoff, Linda Martin. 2006. *Visible Identities: Race, Gender, and the Self*. New York: Oxford University Press.

Anderson-Lopez, Kristen, and Robert Lopez, lyricists. 2017. Remember Me. *Coco*, Lee Unkrich and Adrian Molina, directors, Walt Disney Studios Home Entertainment. https://youtu.be/ImutnoiBixY

Anzaldúa, Gloria. 2012. *Borderlands: The New Mestiza = La Frontera*, 4th edition. San Francisco, CA: Aunt Lute Books.

Bauer-Wolf, Jeremy. 2017. Feeling like Impostors. *Inside Higher Ed*, April 6. www.insidehighered.com/news/2017/04/06/study-shows-impostor-syndromes-effect-minority-students-mental-health

Bonilla-Silva, Eduardo. 2018. *Racism Without Racists: Color-Blind Racism and the Persistence of Racial Inequality in America*, 5th edition. Lanham: Rowman & Littlefield.

Bucholtz, Mary, and Kira Hall. 2007. Language and Identity. In Alessandro Duranti (ed.), *A Companion to Linguistic Anthropology* (pp. 369–394). Malden, MA: Blackwell Publishing.

Callaway, Ewen. 2017. Collapse of Aztec Society Linked to Catastrophic Salmonella Outbreak. *Nature* 542(7642): 404.

Carris, Lauren M. 2011. La Voz Gringa: Latino Stylization of Linguistic (In)authenticity as Social Critique. *Discourse & Society* 22(4): 474–490.

Chavez, Leo R. 2013. *The Latino Threat: Constructing Immigrants, Citizens, and the Nation*, 2nd edition. Stanford: Stanford University Press.

Delgado, Richard, and Jean Stefancic (eds.). 2011. *The Latino/a Condition: A Critical Reader*, 2nd edition. New York: New York University Press.

Dovidio, John F., Agata Gluszek, Melissa-Sue John, Ruth Ditlmann, and Paul Lagunes. 2010. Understanding Bias Toward Latinos: Discrimination, Dimensions of Difference, and Experience of Exclusion. *Journal of Social Issues* 66(1): 59–78.

Emeka, Amon, and Jody Agius Vallejo. 2011. Non-Hispanics With Latin American Ancestry: Assimilation, Race, and Identity Among Latin American Descendants in the US. *Social Science Research* 40(6): 1547–1563.

Ennis, Sharon R., Merarys Rios-Vargas, and Nora G. Albert. 2011. The Hispanic Population: 2010. *United States Census Bureau.* Accessed April 22, 2018. www.census.gov/prod/cen2010/briefs/c2010br-04.pdf

Estrada, Emily P., Yung-Mei Tsai, and Charles R. Chandler. 2008. Assimilation and Discriminatory Perceptions and Experiences: The Case of Hispanics in the United States. *The Social Science Journal* 45(4): 673–681.

Flores-González, Nilda. 2017. *Citizens But Not Americans: Race & Belonging Among Latino Millennials.* New York: New York University Press.

Flores-González, Nilda, Elizabeth Aranda, and Elizabeth Vaquera. 2014. "Doing Race": Latino Youth's Identities and the Politics of Racial Exclusion. *American Behavioral Scientist* 58(14): 1834–1851.

Foley, Neil. 2014. *Mexicans in the Making of America.* Cambridge, MA: Belknap Press/Harvard University.

Gagnon, Monika K. 1998. Race-ing Disney: Race and Culture in the Disney Universe. Unpublished Dissertation, Simon Fraser University. www.collectionscanada.gc.ca/obj/s4/f2/dsk2/ftp03/NQ37702.pdf

García, Eugene E. 2001. *Hispanic Education in the United States: Raíces y Alas.* Lanham, MD: Rowman & Littlefield.

Golash-Boza, Tanya. 2006. Dropping the Hyphen? Becoming Latino(a)-American through Racialized Assimilation. *Social Forces* 85(1): 27–55.

Hipolito-Delgado, Carlos P. 2010. Exploring the Etiology of Ethnic Self-Hatred: Internalized Racism in Chicana/o and Latina/o College Students. *Journal of College Student Development* 51(3): 319–331.

Krogstad, Jens M., and Mark H. Lopez. 2017. Use of Spanish Declines Among Latinos in Major U.S. Metros. *Pew Research Center*, October 31. www.pewresearch.org/fact-tank/2017/10/31/use-of-spanish-declines-among-latinos-in-major-u-s-metros/

Lacayo, Celia O. 2017. Perpetual Inferiority: Whites' Racial Ideology Toward Latinos. *Sociology of Race and Ethnicity* 3(4): 566–579.

Lopez, Mark H., Ana Gonzalez-Barrera, and Gustavo López. 2017. Hispanic Identity Fades Across Generations as Immigrant Connections Fall Away. *Pew Research Center*, December 20. www.pewhispanic.org/2017/12/20/hispanic-identity-fades-across-generations-as-immigrant-connections-fall-away/#

Macedo, Donaldo. 2000. The Colonialism of the English Only Movement. *Educational Researcher* 29(3): 15–24.

Morales, Ed. 2018. *Latinx: The New Force in American Politics and Culture.* New York: Verso.

Novas, Himilce. 2003. *Everything You Need to Know About Latino History.* New York: Plume.

Padilla, Laura M. 2001. But You're Not a Dirty Mexican: Internalized Oppression, Latinos, and Law. *Texas Hispanic Journal of Law & Policy* 7: 59–113.

Padilla, Laura M. 2004. Internalized Oppression and Latino/as. *Diversity Factor* 12(3): 15–21.

Perez, Anthony D., and Charles Hirschman. 2009. The Changing Racial and Ethnic Composition of the US Population: Emerging American Identities. *Population and Development Review* 35(1): 1–51.

Schwartz, Ian. 2015. Trump: Mexico Not Sending Us Their Best; Criminals, Drug Dealers and Rapists Are Crossing Border. *RealClear Politics*, June 16. www.realclearpolitics.com/video/2015/06/16/trump_mexico_not_sending_us_their_best_criminals_drug_dealers_and_rapists_are_crossing_border.html

Trust, Gary. 2017. Luis Fonsi, Daddy Yankee & Justin Bieber's "Despacito" Ties for Longest Run at No. 1 in Hot 100's History. *Billboard.com*, August 28. www.billboard.com/articles/columns/chart-beat/7942306/despacito-hot-100-number-one-ties-record-luis-fonsi-daddy-yankee-justin-bieber

Unkrich, Lee, and Adrian Molina, dir., *Coco*. 2017. Burbank, CA: Walt Disney Studios Home Entertainment, 2019. Disney+.

U.S. Census Bureau. 2018. *Facts for Features: Hispanic Heritage Month 2018*. www.census.gov/newsroom/facts-for-features/2018/hispanic-heritage-month.html

3 Invisibility and Hypervisibility of Arab American Female Students in Times of Heightened Anti-Arab and Anti-Islamic Sentiment

Sawsan Jaber

Introduction

It was Monday, November 16, 2015, two days after an ISIS bombing in France in a historically white school district with a growing demographic of students from a variety of minoritized backgrounds, particularly Arab American students. I was interrupted by another teacher while teaching my first period class. She placed her hand on my shoulder and asked me in front of my students, "How do you feel after what *your* people did in France?" I quickly realized she was referencing an ISIS bombing that had taken place over the weekend. Overcoming my disbelief in the implications of this question that was asked of me in front of my students, my mind reeled with questions: If my scarf as a Muslim woman and brown skin as an Arab led her to see me as a terrorist, what did she project on students who looked like me? The intersectionality of being Arab and Muslim meant that not only was my skin color differentiating me from my colleagues, but so was my hijab as an outward symbol of my faith. How would I unpack the comments made by this teacher with my students through critical conversations in a context I knew was not friendly to such conversations? How would I address "the elephant in the room" as the only Arab American Muslim woman in the district? What did it mean for my Arab American Muslim female students and how they were experiencing school?

This is unlikely an isolated incident and served as a springboard to analyze the lived experiences of Arab students who represent a demographic that has increased by 611% in a six-year period in the district. A new mosque in the area is a large driver of the growth of the Muslim Arab community. Muslims tend to live close to mosques due to religious obligations to pray five times a day along with the encouragement to pray in mosques. In the last two years, the mosque could no longer physically accommodate the growing community, so in addition to building an extension, a youth center, and extending the parking lot to accommodate more than five thousand worshippers at one time, the community helped to fund another mosque in a neighboring city that could accommodate similar numbers. These markers

DOI: 10.4324/9781003258223-4

were signs of a community that was growing exponentially in numbers in a short amount of time.

My own experiences as the only educator of color in the entire district are indications that phobias of Arab and Muslim bodies are tangible and could also be a part of the experiences of Arab and Muslim students in the district. Paris (2012) discusses how peer and educator misunderstandings of a student's culture can impact day-to-day events for them in classrooms and beyond, including detrimental impacts on adolescent identity formation. The lack of acceptance of student identities often causes them to abandon their pride along with their cultural and linguistic diversity as a result of the lack of inclusivity (Paris 2012). The acknowledgment and acceptance of those identities are essential to the pluralism that is required for students to build bridges between home identities and school (Paris 2012); students need to be empowered to take pride in their minority identities while developing the skills to be successful in their current and future environments (Ladson-Billings 2014). In my case, not only did it cause me to abandon cultural and religious markers, it also resulted in the dissonance between myself and my parents creating tremendous tension at home.

In order for educators to be able to connect Arab and Muslim students' home lives with their school lives to avoid tensions that are created when that disconnect is present, they need to understand Arab and Muslim communities: family values, norms, and people's experiences (Banks 2017; Ladson-Billings 2014). As a Palestinian American of refugee parents, I could relate to feelings of invisibility among teachers and peers from K-20. I grew up in a very traditional Palestinian home in the United States. My parents, the epitome of failed citizenship (Banks 2017), wanted to make sure we never forgot our religious and cultural origins, goals that were not unusual for many Palestinian Americans who were displaced due to decades of occupation in their home country (Abu El-Haj 2015). Like many of my students in the district, I attended public school during the week and Saturday school that was focused on Arabic and Islamic studies, until my parents could afford to move to a state with private, full-time Islamic schools. What that led to was a feeling that I did not really belong in any context (Abu El-Haj 2015). My parents did not understand the invisibility I felt as a Palestinian Muslim female because the intersections of my identity in the United States were considered "problematic" with bipartisan support of the state of Israel and growing anti-Islamic sentiment post-9/11 (Bajaj, Ghaffar-Kucher, & Desai 2016). They did not grow up in the United States, so they could not relate to how those growing sentiments impacted how I was viewed by educators and peers as a student in a classroom. Fear of Arabs and Muslims is attributed to historically systemic efforts of politicians and media to paint them as foreigners and exacerbated by accompanying perceptions of their presence as illegal (Aroian 2012; Bajaj, Ghaffar-Kucher, & Desai 2016; Kunst et al. 2012). Those stigmas and portrayals of the media defined my experiences and would prove to define those of my students as well.

My identity deemed me a "terrorist" on both fronts, Palestinian and Muslim; the intersectionality of those identities added to the complexities of my experiences (Crenshaw 2001). To most, I was also considered male dominated as an Arab female that fit the stereotype of being married young. My cultural and linguistic pluralism (Paris 2012) was being threatened by my teachers and peers because they did not acknowledge my Arabic tongue nor the richness of the Arab culture that I felt compelled to leave at the school room door each day. But my presence was highly visible when it came to bullying (Bajaj, Ghaffar-Kucher, & Desai 2016) and "special attention" given to me by my peers, teachers, and later my colleagues. I cannot recall the number of times I felt defensive when explaining who I was or where I came from or the confusion when my home country was nowhere to be found on the world map (Banks 2017). This was coupled with the fact that I never had the opportunity to see myself represented accurately through any of the texts we engaged with in the classroom. I was immersed in a culture of assimilation, an environment that did not recognize or acknowledge my cultural and linguistic pluralism and viewed me and other diverse students through a deficit mindset (McVee 2014; Rudman 2004; Takacs 2003). Of course, I could not name these phenomena then. Little did I realize that I would struggle to name them as an adult as well. In most educational settings, students like me are inadvertently encouraged to replace native cultures and languages, elements they bring from home, with a culture and language considered superior in order to be successful and assimilate (Gutiérrez 2008; Kunst et al. 2012; Kuttner 2016; Paris 2012). This continued through my undergraduate coursework – teachers in literature courses, women's studies courses, and history courses continuously made incorrect assumptions about who I was and what my story was. To many of them I was a young mother victimized by an arranged marriage. They did not realize that my presence in their classroom invalidated those assumptions and stereotypes.

The single-story view of me as an Arab Muslim woman extended into my professional role when that teacher walked into my classroom and associated me with an international terrorist group because of my headscarf. In this role, I was called a "terrorist" by a student who was relaying a message from his father. I had numerous parents pull their children out of my classroom because they "could not have someone like her teaching our kids." Incidents like this one lead me to question the experiences of my Arab and Muslim students who are facing similar situations in a time fueled with anti-Arab and anti-Islamic hate, contributing to the growth of these sentiments on a national scale (Bajaj, Ghaffar-Kucher, & Desai 2016). With the existing fear of Arabs and Muslims attributed to historically systemic efforts of politicians and media to paint them as foreigners and exacerbated by accompanying perceptions of their presence as illegal (Aroian 2012; Bajaj, Ghaffar-Kucher, & Desai 2016; Kunst et al. 2012), a stigma that Bajaj, Ghaffar-Kucher, and Desai (2016) deem responsible for the rise in hate crimes against anyone perceived as Muslim, I have to ask: How much of this was true in this school, and how was it impacting my Arab Muslim female adolescent students? To what extent did the experiences of these young girls mirror my own? I feel compelled to explore further how Arab adolescents are impacted when faced with the tensions of homes that are intent on preserving their culture and religion with those of a school that promoted assimilation (Gutiérrez 2008; Kunst et al. 2012; Kuttner 2016; Paris 2012) through its lack of acceptance of anyone who differed from the historical demographic of Caucasian on a day-to-day basis. I will be sharing some of that research in this chapter.

Research Design

Amid heightened Islamophobia where many Muslim students in schools mask their identities by assimilating or feeling they cannot learn because they were not socially accepted (Aroian 2012; Bajaj, Ghaffar-Kucher, & Desai 2016; Kunst et al. 2012), the stories of these students needed to be captured in a way to tell their story, and in a way, to tell mine. To better understand and capture the lived experiences of the Arab females in this particular context, I used a qualitative approach to focus on the social context and the perspectives of the participants in depth (Merriam & Tisdell 2015). This approach supported the process of finding parallels in the experiences of the female participants that mirrored some of my own. Through semi-structured interviews (Merriam & Tisdell 2015) focused on in-depth stories of the participants (Delgado & Stefancic 2013) and field observations during lunch times and passing periods (Merriam & Tisdell 2015), I was able to uncover the realities of the participants' daily experiences. The questions throughout these interviews and the process of data collection were guided by research confirming that in the current American context, Muslim and Arab American students are often bullied because of their ethnicity and religion (Bajaj, Ghaffar-Kucher, & Desai 2016) and that they are believed to threaten traditional American ways of life (Bajaj, Ghaffar-Kucher, & Desai 2016).

The four female participants in this chapter were a part of a larger study that focused on male and female experiences, as well as the perspectives of their parents and their teachers. After looking at the data and analyzing them for themes, I found myself reflecting on how many of my lived experiences are mirrored through the experiences of the girls; therefore, I focused on the experiences of these four Arab Muslim girls within this historically predominantly white school in the Midwest with the purpose of highlighting the complexities of the intersections of being Arab, Muslim, and female in precarious school contexts that have existed since I was a student in elementary school in the late eighties. Despite the more than 20-year age difference between myself and my students, it quickly became evident throughout my larger study that there was a level of universality in the experiences of Arab Muslim girls in the public sector that led to the development of a sense of double consciousness (Bruce 1992), a result of a need to belong (Ferráns & Selman 2014).

For the larger study, the data collection process was focused on two main channels of information: participant interviews and observations. These sources provided authentic accounts of the lived experiences and students' perceptions about their specific experiences in the school (Merriam & Tisdell 2015). However, for this study, the data were analyzed for common themes among the female participants alone. I highlighted commonalities between my experiences and those of my participants.

All the four female participants I will focus on here took part in the larger study and were selected on the basis of their self-identification as Arab Muslims. Muslim females are required by their faith to wear a headscarf and dress modestly, physical signs of difference that add to the complexities of their experience in American public schools. Like me, all the girls were of Islamic faith, came from Palestinian backgrounds, and were first-generation Americans with parents who were either immigrants or refugees of Palestine. The primary home language was Arabic, but students felt most comfortable speaking English as became apparent when I offered to conduct the interviews in either language since I spoke Arabic as well. A homogenous participant sample – all had the same faith, came from the same culture, spoke Arabic and English, and identified as Muslim Arab Americans – allowed me to capture students' experiences in depth (Merriam & Tisdell 2015). I have chosen a sample that mirrors many traits of my own (see Table 3.1.).

Table 3.1 Participants

Participant (pseudonyms)	Description
Eman	Seventh grade, Palestinian American Muslim, very quirky, she has a quiet spunk. Parents are divorced and she feels caught between mom and dad; dad is a refugee (forced out of his home) and mom is an immigrant (made a choice to move to the United States). Athletic. Intentionally she associates only with girls who are white during school, wears shorts in school; she academically struggles in school but works hard to do well.
Rana	Seventh grade, Palestinian American Muslim, receiving special education services. She is introverted, intentionally associates only with girls who are white during school. Reports lots of tension at home; wears shorts and changes clothes in school without her parents' knowledge. Both parents are immigrants.
Rayanne	Seventh grade, Palestinian American Muslim, athletic but no longer participates in sports. Mother is an immigrant; father is a refugee. She wears hijab but also wears name brand clothes that adhere to Islamic dress code. Spends informal time with students she considers social outcasts. Is academically strong.
Shams	Eighth grade, Palestinian American Muslim. Both parents are immigrants. She wears hijab, is an honor student and in honors-level classes, loves to read. She does not care for name brands, is introverted, has Eurocentric physical features, and got along with everyone before wearing hijab.

Findings

Much of what came to the surface during this study is in line with what scholars like Ladson-Billings (2014), Mitchell (2009), and Paris (2012) have argued regarding historic beliefs evident in the American culture that place the onus of responsibility on students to acclimate and adapt. Listening to the experiences of the girls helped me name and understand the complexities of my own experiences decades later. At no point in my journey of self-understanding and self-identity did I have the support of parents, educators, or peers to overcome direct threats to the intersections of who I was. As a Muslim hijabi, those intersections were worn visibly on my head. Similar to our current context, people at school did not understand the experiences of students who grew up in homes with Palestinian refugees as parents; they did not understand the shared traumas those students endured and the fear of parents that their children would forget their homeland, its language, it culture, or its history. On the other hand, my parents at home could not understand the experiences of attending American public schools and the overwhelming pressures by teachers and peers to assimilate. Ultimately, this created a sense of duality that I needed to be someone else in school, a person that I could not essentially take home. This duality was something that I could immediately recognize and name in my students, but it shocked me that I was 40 and only beginning to see it in myself.

It shocks me as I write this and realize that the sense of duality became a staple even in my professional career. With a feeling of always being othered, even as an adult, I was cautious of how much of myself I could share and extremely cautious of how I carried myself when around colleagues, all of whom were Caucasian.

The impacts of this duality were detrimental to my identity construction and social-emotional well-being as it would prove to be for the girls in this study. Kunst et al. (2012) highlighted how this directly leads to students struggling to find their voices in the classrooms they are a part of for a good portion of the day. Students like Shams, Rayanne, Rana, and Eman contribute to the idea that they could not be themselves in their context because if they revealed who they were, their identity would not be accepted in their social context. The fear of rejection resulted in a tension between two personas, a home persona and a school persona, that were often at odds with each other.

Duality as a Result of Non-Acceptance

Learning in this precarious context led the Arab American female students to share perceptions that their cultural and linguistic pluralism was not valued among teachers and peers. Rayanne said, "They will never really understand us." Rana echoed this saying, "I share very little because no one gets us." Students described only being able to share what was considered the norm with other students, or letting go of essential cultural and religious values to be able to "fit in." They described feelings of being "a different person" at home and at school, a sense of duality.

Disowning of Names to Assimilate

In early conversations, the four girls purposely mispronounced their names when asked. They rationalized this by admitting it was the way peers and teachers pronounced their names and correcting it would draw more negative attention. Modification of a name disempowered students and forced them to disassociate themselves with the most basic, yet foundational, aspect of their identity. Eman shared, "people don't know how to pronounce my name, and I don't feel comfortable using it the way you say it in Arabic." The other girls made similar statements about their names; two said that they were embarrassed when I pronounced their names correctly in front of their peers. The girls did not feel that they belonged in the school context even when they verbally indicated they did even as simply as claiming their own names. The tension between wanting to feel included and the reality that they were not included was something that was difficult for them to explicitly name.

In reflecting on the name stories of the girls with particular focus on one of the girls, Eman completely modified her name to a white name with the intent that it would help, noting "more people accept me." I recalled being a third grader in Ms. Ebenstein's class in Brooklyn and wishing I could say my name was Crystal when she asked me what my name was. Ms. Ebenstein never took the time to pronounce my name correctly and did not address students when they made fun of me and called me things like Selsun Blue or Sensen, clearly mocking my name. By fourth grade, I adopted the disposition that a minor modification to my name was something I could accept. I was Susan throughout middle school in any context where I was minoritized. I continued to use this name as an adult in many scenarios. I realize now that it was one of my first memories of subconsciously giving up pieces of who I was in order to assimilate. I could never take Susan home just like I felt I could not bring Sawsan to school. The experiences of the girls really resonated with my own.

An Implicit Denial of Culture and Religion Adding to the Sense of Duality

The duality was evident in what the girls chose not to share. Feelings of being further alienated because of who they were kept them from socializing in the way most adolescents do. They admitted to only sharing parts of themselves to which they felt most in their context could relate. As a Muslim growing up in America and attending public schools, one of the first realities we face is the number of holidays others celebrate in comparison to the two holidays we celebrate as Muslims, Eid Al-Adha and Eid Al-Fitr. The commercialization of American holidays even in the public sector always made it difficult for those not celebrating not to feel left out. What made this harder was schools not making an effort to clarify those distinctions for other students, especially at the younger ages. Why were some students celebrating while others were not? What other holidays existed within populations of students in schools that we could recognize and learn about? Since those conversations were usually not happening in classrooms, many Arab and Muslim students either gave in to celebrating non-Muslim holidays in performative ways in order to belong or kept their own celebrations a secret, adding to that sense of duality and the double consciousness that was a result of their reality.

When the girls were asked how traditional their families were, Rayanne responded, "We are very traditional. On Eid [purposely mispronounced] we go to the mosque, and pray and we go see our family. We go to our family's houses and we eat." When I followed up by asking how many of your traditions you share with your non-Arab peers and teachers, she said "None, I stand out enough with my hijab." All of the girls echoed similar sentiments highlighting that they did not feel comfortable enough to share their whole selves in the school environment. Eman said, "I do not invite friends to my house because of the things we have hanging on the wall [cultural relics and religious verses from the Quran]. I feel like people won't understand the Arabic, or the food, or anything." Both Eman and Rayanne alluded to a sense of double consciousness that was born out of a tension and dissonance between what they could share at school and at home.

The intersections of being Arab, Muslim, and female posed different types of threats in the context of the school. The girls felt a burden in explaining their otherness, causing them to repress their cultural and religious identities and focus only on commonalities with their peers. They described feeling conflicted between their parents' desire for them to preserve their cultural and religious values, and pressures to assimilate in order to fit into what they described as a school environment that did not accept their pluralism. Shams, a blond-haired, blue-eyed girl explained how her relationship with peers changed when she decided to wear her hijab after sixth grade:

> I had many friends when I was in elementary school and in middle school. You know everyone kind of split into their own groups and like you have like your own clique I guess, and I put on my hijab and like it hasn't really been the same because like when people look at me when I first put on my hijab they thought I was American or something because of like my hair color and how I look. But then when I put it on, they were like oh my god did you convert or something, and I obviously did not convert, I've been Muslim since I was little. But like when people see me, they see a Muslim girl, and I don't think they really get to like understand or know me as well as like before I put on my hijab.

Because Shams was white passing, she did not realize that her headscarf would create a barrier between her and her peers. Up until that point, she was able to fit in with the majority of her peers at school; her hijab was the marker that caused her to feel othered. Despite this outcome, she said, "Islam is a part of me" and "I would never change my hijab for anyone," but also said, "I wish I could be more trendy," highlighting an example of a clear sense of duality with which the girls were struggling.

Again, this took me back to my nine-year-old self. Like many girls in my family, I went through puberty at an age much younger than most girls. This meant that religiously I was required to wear my hijab and begin to dress more modestly. I was always more mature than most girls, but I was also carefree and adventurous. Being raised in a religious home, I had no doubts about my desire to wear my scarf with the first sign of my period, but I also worried about how I would be received in school and about how my hijab may hinder my physical activities. I was worried about how it would change my relationships with my Italian friends next door. Although I could not name it then, I knew that it alienated me from others when my relationships with the adults who were responsible for me at school also changed. They did not understand why the scarf was mandatory. Ironically, 30 years later, my youngest daughter struggles to wear her hijab and feels like she is disappointing God. She fears the repercussions of her peers and her teachers who already make fun of her name, exclude her in team sports in Ramadan, and spit in her food when she takes a Palestinian food to school for lunch. She worries about how much more violent the aggression would get if she added the hijab as another layer. I could not help but notice and note that for generations and in different pockets of public schools around the country, Muslim Arab girls were having similar experiences and not much had changed, nor had there seemed to be an urgency among schools to make school cultures more welcoming to them. Similarly, decades later, immigrant parents still feel the pressures of ensuring that their children know their homeland, culture, and religion despite significant pressures for them to assimilate. Both extremes cause the girls to feel like they cannot really fully belong to either context.

The tension was the same today as it had been 30 years prior, and the participants felt those pressures in multiple ways: When asked if Rayanne downplayed aspects of her identity, she voiced a desire to keep up with trends so her peers knew "hijabis can be trendy too" and so she did not feel "different" and "alone." She highlighted the internal struggle of cultural and religious expectations at odds with what was considered the "norm." I followed up asking if keeping up with trends helped her feel a stronger sense of belonging; she felt it did not matter and clarified by saying, "No matter what I do, I will be different to everyone here because of my hijab." This, again, highlighted the tensions and sense of duality that emerged due to the lack of systemic understanding and acceptance of the girls' cultural and ethnic identities.

The fear of facing a similar outcome to that of Shams is what prevented Eman and Rana from putting on the hijab despite their recognition that they should wear it and that their parents promoted the hijab at home. Rana said, "I'm not accepted without it. Can you imagine if I put it on?" Eman reverberated with visible disappointment in herself, "The pressure to put it on at home is always there, and I want to. But I can't seem to do it." The tensions between what they felt they wanted to do versus what they felt they could do were tangible. Their sentiments echoed with those of my daughter. Despite the fact that there was a much larger Arab Muslim community in America today than when I had grown up, the challenges of the girls to cover manifested in more violent and aggressive ways, keeping them from feeling comfortable practicing their faith or sharing their culture with their peers.

The girls were clearly two different personas at home and at school. Rana admitted she sometimes carried a change of clothing in her backpack because she felt her modest clothing was questioned by her peers, especially in summer months. She said, "I'll try to fit in with the way I dress. I wear shorts and fight with my mom when I get dressed, but I'm tired of fighting with my mom over my clothes." So, she decided the solution was to change in school to avoid conflict with her parents at home. Rana and Eman confirmed there was tremendous tension at home regarding the girls' clothing. While religion and culture demanded the girls dress modestly, the fashion trends sometimes dictated they dress differently. They felt that if they did not dress on trend, they would be "made fun of" and "excluded."

Duality Magnified Due to Parents' Lack of Advocacy

Although all four girls did not feel included enough in school to wear their cultural and linguistic pluralism with pride, the data indicated the girls' experiences and conflicts were much more severe due to obligatory religious physical identifiers making their otherness more apparent. When Eman was asked whether she felt her relationships were changing as she got older, she responded, "Yes. Like say there is a party they [friends] can go to, and I can't because my dad won't let me because of religious reasons. It would be nice to have friends that, like that can relate to me but also that are different." When asked if they feel their identity is accepted in school, the girls reported daily incidents of bullying, and Eman shared a personal story in tears. "I was targeted every day for two months. Students on my bus would throw paper balls when I got on and like they would scream Allahu Akbar and hide." I asked her if she reported it to her parents or to anyone in school. Eman said that she told the Dean and,

> She told me to write on a piece of paper what happened, and she said that I should call the police or something like that, and then she said she would call my parents. She never did. When I went to her again she said it was not bullying because they were different kids every day.

Although in Eman's eyes, this was impacting her every day and diminishing her desire to go to school altogether, the school administration did not feel it was severe enough to warrant their attention. When asked if she told her parents, Eman said they told her to "ignore the kids." She cried as she voiced her frustrations about how "they don't understand." Eman said that when she cried to her father, he thought she was being "weak." It was clear that these microaggressions (even though there was nothing micro about them) had been framing her school experiences from the very start of her day every day, and she felt frustrated having to face them alone. Eman said that her only defense mechanism to deal with these problems long term was to "try to fit in as much as possible so they stop noticing me." She also said that she felt she could no longer bring these problems home since her parents could not understand – thus, again adding to the tensions the girls were facing that were leading to a sense of duality.

This is where our experiences differed slightly. The most direct aggression I had ever faced as an adolescent student was to be told to "go back to my country" by other students who could not understand how someone with a hijab could be American. It never failed to take my breath away initially, but with time, I almost expected it no matter where I went. However, I could relate to the girls through the experiences of my daughters. As a parent, I find myself advocating for my daughters in school when a teacher made my eldest daughter apologize for 9/11 and asking for schools to make more intentional efforts to create opportunities for students to learn about each other and interact in more authentic ways so that they would no longer make fun of my daughter's name or spit in her ethnic food. But even then, I realized that I was able to advocate for my girls in ways that my parents and the parents of the participants could not. I realized how that could alleviate some of the tensions for my daughters, since I could relate to their experiences in ways my parents could not.

Although many of the girls showed positive relationships with peers and teachers and outwardly seemed to adapt to the dominant culture, these relationships were built on commonalities that did not allow them to share differences. False perceptions of inclusion based on surface-level acceptance of the "other" were highlighted. Students described their experiences as differing from everyone else and attributed this feeling of difference to their culture and religion. They reported having limited representation within their role models at the school, with me being the only teacher of color, leading them to suppress much of who they are. When asked who they felt were role models, all four girls said they could not relate to anyone but me. Shams said, "You teach me how to be a proud Muslim girl." Rayanne said, "I don't feel like I need to explain things to you." This was another limitation of the support they could be receiving to embrace their differences as assets.

Their feelings were masked by a semblance of belonging that was actually assimilation. The girls felt this identity suppression was magnified by their parents placing the burden of self-advocacy and teaching others about their culture and religion on the girls. Eman reiterated that in her bus incident, her parents asked her to talk to the school administration and did not get involved when the administration opted not to address the problem. Shams said, "My mom thinks they will never change, so she doesn't bother." It was evident that their parents were not able to navigate the unfamiliar landscape of public school as American immigrants, leaving the girls to face these problems on their own, even though they felt that doing so would alienate them further. Similarly, Rayanne exhibited a level of anger that was evident in her conversation about how she felt educating others. Rayanne said, "I am tired of the discrimination, and when a Muslim does something wrong, everyone hears about it and never forgets, but if a White person does something, nobody pays attention. I don't want to teach anyone." The effects of this responsibility are detrimental to student success and to full involvement in educational experiences. The failure of educators fulfilling the role of learning about these students and educating themselves about who they are directly led to students struggling to find their voices in classrooms of which they were a part (Kunst et al. 2012). All the girls contributed to the idea that they cannot be themselves, because if they revealed who they are, they would not be accepted.

Duality: Invisibility Versus Hypervisibility

What became apparent through the interviews of the girls when asked about my informal observations was that they felt invisible when it came to the school meeting their needs, creating safe spaces where they could socialize and participate, and including accurate representations of Arabs and Muslims beyond single story, stereotypical views in curriculum – all elements that surfaced through microaggressions and a lack of accommodation for these specific students. On the contrary, the girls felt hypervisible when it came to bullying and othering, especially when they wore visible signs of their cultural and religious diversity such as the hijab or not adhering to the mainstream trends with their dress. They were clearly weighed down by the duality; they yearned for social acceptance of their identities by both teachers and peers, but were left trying to navigate the precariousness of this exclusionary context alone.

Furthermore, the duality of being invisible at times and hypervisible at other times caused the girls to react in two ways. Two girls, Rayanne and Shams, became introverted and focused on academics, abandoning the prospect of building authentic and meaningful friendships with school peers, or trusting relationships with teachers, both of which are integral aspects for an adolescent's healthy social and emotional development (Howe & Lisi 2013). They wore their hijab with pride and did not care for fashion trends that compromised religious and cultural expectations. Furthermore, they forfeited participation in social events. Rayanne and Shams only shared their cultural and linguistic pluralism if they were asked, not voluntarily. Shams said, "If they ask me, I answer. But no one usually cares to ask, they just assume."

On the other hand, Rana and Eman tried as hard as they could to assimilate, adhering to fashion trends and refusing to wear their headscarves. These girls refused to socialize with other Arab students or other minoritized students during the school day with the hope that immersing themselves in social circles with white students would eventually result in being accepted by them. The girls attended social events and dressed to fit the norm. The price for social inclusion was not sharing any part of their beliefs or lives that highlighted their differences. Thus, the girls would not invite white peers to their homes for fear their peers would see "how different" they were. Rana and Eman admitted they were not forthcoming with their parents because there was much of which they knew their parents would not approve.

Conclusion: Fostering Inclusivity for Arab Muslim Students

Not recognizing the identity of Arab students, in particular the young women in this context, clearly created conflicts for the students when determining who they are in this complex space. It caused students to invalidate and suppress entire intersections of their identity, leaving them feeling like they did not belong to their ancestral cultures nor to American society. The acknowledgment and acceptance of multifaceted identities is essential to the pluralism required for students to build bridges between home and school identities (Paris 2012). Although students need to take pride in their diverse identities while developing skills to be socially and academically successful in their current and future environments, these girls were not given the opportunity to do so. When inequitable systems are prevalent, as was the case with the Arab students in this school, students are consumed with fitting in as opposed to finding their voices and using them to build their capacity and change their context; this ultimately strips them of their identity (Bajaj, Ghaffar-Kucher, & Desai 2016).

The data analysis revealed a tension that students were feeling between who they were expected to be at home and who they were expected to be in school. One that felt too familiar in my reflections of my childhood experiences in my own adolescent academic journey. This tension resulted in a sense of duality for the participants that manifested itself in various ways. The reality was an outsider observing these students would see evidence of students who appeared to be doing fine in what educators consider healthy student behaviors; however, the qualitative conversations revealed a social-emotional strain and a series of choices students had to make on a daily basis that were indicative of a tension that ultimately led to a sense of duality as a result of not feeling included. Students described their experiences as those that differed from everyone else's and attributed the differences to their cultural and religious diversity.

The experiences of the girls are indicative of a tension they had to navigate between not being able to bring their cultural and linguistic pluralism to school and share it with various members of their school community with the choice of abandoning those intersections, subconsciously giving birth to a sense of duality and double consciousness that allowed them to survive their school contexts. That data collected in this study indicate that the girls perceived that very little support was offered by the school, parents, and/or community to help them alleviate some of the clear impacts of this tension and that other stakeholders were often the cause of the tension.

These students yearned to belong and assimilate because they felt it was the only way to gain acceptance and came to understand that they would never be socially accepted. The intersectionality of being Arab, Muslim, and female positioned them in ways that made them susceptible to a sense of double consciousness. This particular school environment was a less friendly context for Arab and Muslim girls, especially those wearing the hijab, an outward symbol of their diversity. The girls reported the most aggressive reactions from students and teachers, citing their hijab and gender as reasons for the difference in treatment between them and others. Girls who did not wear the hijab spoke about the lack of inclusivity and fear of other students' reactions as the main reasons why they cannot wear the hijab.

Paris (2012) advocated for a fluid understanding of different cultures and a change in instructional practices that explicitly engage questions of equality and social justice. By these standards, educators are obligated to create safe spaces and build students' repertoire of tools to develop their strength to self-advocate, be civically engaged, and empower them to change the status quo (Paris 2012). In this context, the girls succumbed to the tension to assimilate by creating a pseudo-self that was more acceptable to the mainstream. It was the only way they felt they could coexist with their peers without adults understanding or advocating for them.

Misunderstanding students' identities clearly affects day-to-day events in classrooms and beyond, including their identity formation. The Muslim Arab American female students yearned to fit in to the point they could not recognize the aggression and harm being directed at them. Global demographic shifts that increase populations of color cause white members historically in power to feel threatened and insist on the assimilation of students of color while simultaneously preventing their assimilation by acting as gatekeepers to inclusion. Lack of acceptance caused many of the girls to abandon the cultural and religious values they determined to be socially undesirable, causing changes in mindsets and values or causing them to ignore their social needs to fit in and isolate themselves from school peers as a mechanism for survival. Furthermore, the abandonment of pride in their cultural and linguistic diversity as a result of the lack of inclusivity also resulted in dissonance with parents, creating tension at home and the birth of duality of personas, the struggle between who they were at home and who they were expected to be in school, as they navigated the two spaces.

When tracking the impacts of these tensions in my own life as an adult, it occurred to me – two years ago as I was presenting to a large group of educators at a conference on how to meet the specific needs of Arab and Muslim students – that due to my own experiences as a child, I had suppressed my own identity even in the professional spaces I had occupied until that point. That sense of double consciousness was so strong, it almost became a permanent part of who I was. Like the girls, the sense of duality was so ingrained in who I was, it was only then that I realized it was born as a result of nonacceptance. At one point, I had disowned my name too; I implicitly denied my culture and religion, and I felt like that nonacceptance was magnified because my parents did not understand. I too felt invisible when it came to teachers and peers making authentic efforts to know me and make me feel seen, understood, and ultimately included, but I felt hypervisible when I was being othered and often misunderstood. Presenting these data to that crowd, that epiphany caused me to be overcome with emotion. That sense of duality in that moment felt like a trauma I had endured that I could not trace the source of to any specific incident or person. It took doing my PhD and hearing the lived experiences of these four girls for me to realize what I too had faced. It was in that moment that I had to learn to love myself and all of my intersections and share my whole self in all spaces unapologetically. It was also at that moment that I had vowed to do everything in my power and with my privilege to ensure that I dedicated my life's work to ensuring that I could help students name these aggressions and work through them at much younger ages.

References

Abu El-Haj, Thea Renda. 2015. *Unsettled Belonging: Educating Palestinian American Youth after 9/11*. Chicago: University of Chicago Press.

Aroian, Karen J. 2012. Discrimination against Muslim American Adolescents. *The Journal of School Nursing* 28(3): 206–213.

Bajaj, Monisha, Ameena Ghaffar-Kucher, and Karishma Desai. 2016. Brown Bodies and Xenophobic Bullying in US Schools: Critical Analysis and Strategies for Action. *Harvard Educational Review* 86(4): 481–505.

Banks, James A. 2017. Failed Citizenship and Transformative Civic Education. *Educational Researcher* 46(7): 366–377.

Bruce, Dickson D. 1992. WEB Du Bois and the Idea of Double Consciousness. *American Literature* 64(2): 299–309.

Crenshaw, Kimberlé Williams. 2001. The First Decade: Critical Reflections, or a Foot in the Closing Door. *UCLA Law Review* 49: 1343–1379.

Delgado, Richard, and Jean Stefancic. 2013. *Critical Race Theory: The Cutting Edge*, 3rd edition. Philadelphia: Temple University Press.

Ferráns, Silvia Diazgranados, and Robert Selman. 2014. How Students' Perceptions of the School Climate Influence Their Choice to Upstand, Bystand, or Join Perpetrators of Bullying. *Harvard Educational Review* 84(2): 162–187.

Gutiérrez, Kris D. 2008. Developing a Socio-Critical Literacy in the Third Space. *Reading Research Quarterly* 43(2): 148–164.

Howe, William A., and Penelope L. Lisi. 2013. *Becoming a Multicultural Educator: Developing Awareness, Gaining Skills, and Taking Action*. Thousand Oaks, CA: Sage Publications.

Kunst, Jonas R., Hajra Tajamal, David L. Sam, and Pål Ulleberg. 2012. Coping With Islamophobia: The Effects of Religious Stigma on Muslim Minorities' Identity Formation. *International Journal of Intercultural Relations* 36(4): 518–532.

Kuttner, Paul J. 2016. Hip-Hop Citizens: Arts-Based Culturally Sustaining Civic Engagement Pedagogy. *Harvard Educational Review* 86(4): 527–555.

Ladson-Billings, Gloria. 2014. Culturally Relevant Pedagogy 2.0: a.k.a. the Remix. *Harvard Educational Review* 84(1): 74–84.

McVee, Mary. B. 2014. "Some Are Way Left, Like This Guy, Gloria Ladson-Billings": Resistance, Conflict, and Perspective Taking in Teachers' Discussions of Multicultural Education. *Peace and Conflict: Journal of Peace Psychology* 20(4): 536–551.

Merriam, Sharan B., and Elizabeth J. Tisdell. 2015. *Qualitative Research: A Guide to Design and Implementation*. San Francisco: John Wiley & Sons.

Paris, Django. 2012. Culturally Sustaining Pedagogy: A Needed Change in Stance, Terminology, and Practice. *Educational Researcher* 41(3): 93–97.

Rudman, Laurie. A. 2004. Social Justice in Our Minds, Homes, and Society: The Nature, Causes, and Consequences of Implicit Bias. *Social Justice Research* 17(2): 129–142.

Takacs, David. 2003. How Does Your Positionality Bias Your Epistemology? *Thought and Action, The NEA Higher Education Journal* 2003(Summer): 27–38. http://qa16.nea.org/assets/img/PubThoughtAndAction/TAA_03_04.pdf

4   Searching for Belonging

How Transnationalism Influences Chinese American College Students' Ethnic Identity Construction

Yan Wang & Beth L. Goldstein

Introduction

Chinese Americans have historically been perceived as perpetual foreigners (Tuan 1998; Lee 2015) in the US, despite their residence in this country for many generations. The persistently asked question – "where are you from?" – reminds them of their situational foreignness. While the larger society tends to write a Chinese identity on people of Chinese descent, this chapter queries how Chinese Americans themselves –university students in particular – negotiate their ethnic identity.

Identity is not place-bound. Transnational movement as manifested in physical state boundary crossing certainly impacts people's sense of self. However, the "cognitive and imagined elements of transnational livelihoods" (Levitt & Waters 2002, p. 9) also influence how people construct their identities as they engage, directly or indirectly, with transnationalism.

This chapter focuses on Chinese American college[1] students to explore how transnationalism enacted in physical and symbolic forms influences their ethnicity construction as they move from their familial home space to educational spaces of school and university, and to a space of their homeland. They shift from expressing ambivalence about who they are toward embracing a hybrid identity – Chinese American. However, the various stereotypes they combat in each space sharpen the precarity of their identity negotiation.

Through examining home, educational, and homeland spaces, we ask the following two questions: 1) How do Chinese American college students negotiate their ethnicity as they move between multiple spaces? 2) What role does transnationalism play in their ethnicity construction? We argue that students experience the power structure in each space in ways that significantly influence their self-perception. The transnationalism that permeates each space pushes them to renegotiate their ethnicity.

Theoretical Framework

Scholars argue that space, instead of just representing geographic locations and physical entities, is strongly influenced by culture and politics locally and globally (Agnew 2011; Massey 2005). Therefore, rather than "becom[ing] a

DOI: 10.4324/9781003258223-5

kind of neutral grid on which cultural differences, historical memory, and societal organization are inscribed" (Gupta & Ferguson 1992, p. 7), space has a distinct identity driven by the spatial distribution of hierarchical power relations (Gupta & Ferguson 1992). This understanding of space recognizes its socially and culturally constructed nature; for example, a home is not simply an objective construction of a building but a subjective construction of the conversations, cultures, etc. happening in the building that define the unique nature of the home space. In this research, we utilize this concept of space to understand Chinese American students' construction of identity as they navigate political, cultural, and social messages about being ethnic Chinese across the spaces of home, school, university, and China. We thereby study identity through mobility and meaningful relations, including subordination and exclusion (Georgiou 2010, p. 19).

Transnational movement inherently involves moving from one space to another, crossing national boundaries. Narrowly defined, the concept has referred to the physical movement of people between a land of origin and a land of settlement. However, transnationalism is also understood more broadly. Basch, Schiller, and Szanton Blanc (1994) define transnationalism as:

> the process by which immigrants forge and sustain multi-stranded social relations that link together their societies of origin and settlement, . . . an essential element of transnationalism is the multiplicity of involvements that transmigrants' [*sic*] sustain in both home and host societies.
>
> (p. 7)

We use transnationalism not only as a framework that manifests itself in physical movement across nations and in the ways people maintain and are constrained by social relations across these nations but also in a symbolic dimension as manifested in people's lives academically and culturally. Symbolic transnationalism pertains to people whose daily lives include a flow of items, cultural values and practices, language, and sense of connection linked to their family's home country, even though they may never actually set foot in their country of origin due to lack of monetary resources, desire, or legal means to travel (Aranda 2006; Espíritu & Tran 2002; Wolf 2002). Research on transnationalism documents how immigrants' lives are impacted and how transnationalism has challenged the meaning of the nation-state (Basch, Schiller, & Szanton Blanc 1994); shaped parenting (Sánchez & Machado-Casas 2009); and influenced children's construction of identity, gender, and sense of place (Levitt 2001; Sánchez & Machado-Casas 2009; Menjívar 2002). For people of Chinese descent, especially those from privileged backgrounds, transnationalism impacts their sense of self (Li 1994; Gabriel 2011; Ong 1999; Fong 2011). Previous studies have also explored how transnationalism influences the second generation (Kibria 2002; Louie 2004; Liu 2015). Second-generation students become situated between different and competing generational and locational points of reference, including those of their parents and their grandparents as well as their own, both real and imagined (Wolf 2002). Parents and grandparents utilize mores from their country of origin to assert power in evaluating the second generation's ethnic authenticity. The intergenerational and locational tensions push the second generation to negotiate beyond existing spaces by transforming and creating new spaces for themselves (Espíritu & Tran 2002).

The extensive studies on transnationalism commonly look at two macrospaces that people cross, namely, their country of origin and country of residence – spaces of the state. Studying more microspaces, such as home and educational spaces, provides insight into how daily and often conflictual encounters with transnationalism shape the development of personal hybrid identity. Our focus on college students addresses the formative importance of college years for students' identity construction (Evans, Forney, & Guido-DiBrito 1998). In this era of higher education internationalization, the campus environment offers explicit curricular opportunities for academic transnationalism, along with less-scripted opportunities for cross-national and cross-cultural interpersonal interchange. Diverse college student populations provide Chinese American students with new ways of interacting with their peers and fresh understanding of who they are. Therefore, situated in two theoretical constructs of space and transnationalism experienced in physical and symbolic forms, we examine how Chinese American college students resolve ambiguity, impositions, and precarity to reach for an emergent identity they can embrace.

Methodology

Drawing from a larger study of Chinese American college students' understanding and performance of Chineseness, this chapter included 13 traditional-aged Chinese American college students (ten females, three males) attending a Midwest university in the US between 2014 and 2018. All participants had enrolled in Chinese (Mandarin) language classes in college and came from families where at least one parent was of Chinese descent. Most participants are second generation (all three men – Jack, Ben, and John – and four of the women – Emma, Cindy, Amy, and Ava). Linda and Angel are 1.5 generation; Peilin, Elizabeth and Sophia are 2.5 generation; and Alice is 3rd generation. Alice, Sophia, and Amy are biracial.

Research data included two interviews with the 13 student participants, plus interviews with nine parents, ten friends, and five siblings. In addition, data were also collected through informal interviews with the student participants (impromptu conversations), and language class observations. Wang interviewed each student at least twice using semi-structured protocols; interviews lasted 40 to 90 minutes. The interview questions asked about experience growing up as ethnic Chinese in the US, family dynamics, school experience, university life, and visits to China. Parent interviews focused on the dynamics of home space; friends gave insight into educational and social spaces; and siblings commented on ethnicity negotiation across spaces. Interviews with parents, siblings, and friends lasted 40 to 120 minutes. Wang conducted at least one classroom observation 50 minutes in length for each participant, with a focus on class participation and interaction with peers. Home visits coincided with parents' interviews. Informal interviews with participants occurred during meals together and graduation ceremonies. Wang, who is from China, taught Mandarin at this university. She taught most of the Chinese American students in this research before the study, not during it. Wang's Chinese identity both connected and distinguished her from the participants. The classroom, home, and social interactions – recorded as field notes – not only helped build rapport between the field researcher and the research participants but enhanced the overall validity of the study.

Participants chose their preferred language during the study, either Mandarin or English. Audio-recorded interviews were transcribed verbatim by Wang, who is fluent in both Mandarin and English. Data were analyzed thematically using the MAXQDA software. Three stages of coding were conducted. First, each transcription and field note were read to identify topical threads. Topical threads were clustered to form axial codes. Finally, the clustered coding was condensed to form larger themes across the data (Creswell 2013).

Findings

The three spaces that Chinese American college students engage in – home, educational, and homeland – impacted their understanding of who they are, often in conflictual ways. As they move across spaces, they encounter different expectations and assumptions for their behavior, which complicates their identity search. The following sections present students' negotiation as it unfolds through each space.

Home Space: Embracing Ethnicity Through Language and Culture

All participants described how the environment their parents created at home differed from the dominant society, including elements such as food, decorations, and cultural practices. Chinese material culture in their home space established an initial base for their ethnicity. Alice mentioned the presence of ancient Chinese furniture in her home, either inherited from her grandparents or bought online. Sophia talked about the ancestral altar her grandmother set up in the house. Almost all participants mentioned "the Chinese elements" at home, such as brushwork paintings, calligraphy, and souvenirs. Eating Chinese food and celebrating Chinese festivals, such as the Lunar New Year and Mid-Autumn Day, were part of their lives growing up in the US and regular reminders of their Chinese heritage.

Maintaining Chinese Ethnicity: Speaking My Heritage Language

For the majority, their home language was either Mandarin, a dialect of Chinese such as Cantonese or Fujianese, or a mixture of English and Chinese (Mandarin or a dialect). The majority of parents either had limited proficiency to communicate with their children in English or expected their children to speak their heritage language because, as Emma's parents shared, they believe "不管你走到哪里，别人都会看到你是中国人" [no matter where you go, people would see you as Chinese]. However, the participants' fluency in their heritage language varied vastly. Some were fluent speakers, some barely understood it, and fewer were literate.

Because ethnic Chinese in the US often speak a language other than English and practice a culture that is incongruent with that of the dominant society, they are perceived as unassimilable and forever foreign (Tuan 1998). This perception poses a "social-psychological predicament that can arise from widely-known negative stereotypes about one's group" (Steele & Aronson 1995, p. 797), which they name stereotype threat. Steele (2010) argues that stereotype threat "is a standard predicament of life. It springs from our human powers of intersubjectivity" (p. 5). Imposing this perpetual foreigner stereotype on people of Chinese descent demonstrates the exclusionary and minoritizing power of the dominant culture's hegemony. However, what functions as a negative stereotype against people of Chinese descent in the dominant culture has value within their ethnic community. That students are differentiated linguistically and culturally from the dominant group has roots in the values of the parents in this study. Just as Emma's parents' perception of being treated as "forever Chinese" became an admonition to speak Chinese, other parents also expected their children to be fluent in Chinese and to respect inherited cultural practices and values. When Chinese Americans' linguistic ability is found otherwise, the validity of their ethnicity is challenged both within and outside of the Chinese community. While parents implied this in the interviews, Chinese American students experienced this stereotype threat explicitly when they socialized with people in other spaces, which will be discussed later.

Maintaining "Chineseness" Through Cultural Values: Tension Arises

While material culture practices helped enhance attachment to their ethnicity, other practices at home brought tensions between Chinese American students' Chinese and American identities. This, we would argue, reflects how transnationalism works symbolically. For example, Jack noted that his father constantly compared him with his peers in China to push him to study hard:

> 我爸就是有点特别，像中国那样，你说中国学生，像我这么大的，就是起来复习，吃早饭，上学，上完学去那个什么补习班，补习班回来再学习，然后就是整天就是学嘛。所以，

他就以为中国就是那样 (所以他要我也那样). [My dad is different; his way is like the Chinese way. He said that what Chinese students of my age do every day is to get up, eat breakfast, go to school, and go to after-school academic supplementary classes. All they do is study. My dad thought that is how Chinese students are (and he kind of asked me to do the same)].

Though Jack lived in the US, students' academic practices in China influence Jack's understanding of his own life and identity. He fought hard with his father, demanding respect for his American identity. That is, he argued that as an American, he should not have to study as hard as students in China. Similarly, Ben and Linda were constantly reminded by their parents of the intense academic competition in China as motivation to study harder in the US. Furthermore, fulfilling filial piety and respecting parental authority were also stressed in the Chinese American households, as parents strongly believed that defined what a Chinese person should do. Ben, Ava, Peilin, and Linda all shared the pain of balancing these "Chinese" home values with the American values from outside the home. Linda captured her angst balancing parental authority with the democratic parent-child relationship that she perceived in the US:

他就不让我 解释 '不行!'就他对那种, 然后我就受不了 . . . 有时候就是他不听我的, 因为他知道我的逻辑更,更那个, 更对, 他就怕我 [He would not allow me to explain. Simply "No." Like he is the one who is always right. I cannot accept this . . . sometimes, he insisted on his idea because he knew mine was right, and he was afraid that (accepting mine would undermine his authority)].

This generational difference not only generates tension between parents and children but creates a complex transnational space through parents' constant comparison of their lives "there" and "here." Emphasizing life "there" not only reminds students of the advantages of living in the US but transmits a message of conforming to these "Chinese" practices, which parents consider superior. Espíritu and Tran (2002) argue that parents' ethnic cultural practice was "transnational rather than ethnic" emphasizing "the power and appeal of both 'here' and 'there' in the construction of immigrant lives" (p. 391). In this case, students' preference to be "here" (e.g. not facing intense academic competition) allows parents to claim their power as the ultimate guardians of "authentic" cultural memory (Espíritu & Tran 2002, p. 391). Chinese parents use ethnic cultural practices to create a world that not only allows their children to live transnationally in a symbolic way but asserts parental authority to assess their children's Chineseness through parents' direct ties with their country of origin. This symbolic transnationalism consolidates Chinese American students' understanding of being Chinese in the US despite the tension it brought between parents and children. This echoes Wolf's (2002) assertion that "The 'family' seems to offer an extremely magnetic and positive basis of [Chinese] identity for many children of immigrants, yet it is also a deep source of stress and alienation" (p. 256). This is especially true for immigrant parents' control of their daughters.

Maintaining Chinese Ethnicity: Navigating Gender Roles

Patriarchy and its corollary of gender preference for males, which traveled from Home (their country of origin) to home (their resident country) with Chinese American students' parents and grandparents, has also pushed Chinese American women especially to navigate their identity transnationally. Espíritu and Tran (2002) share that Vietnamese women negotiated their identity under their parents' use of stories to "regulate the misbehavior of their children, especially their daughters, by linking such behavior to cultural betrayal" (p. 390). This is similar for Chinese American women in this study. Their parents used gendered child-rearing practices to assert their power in evaluating their daughters' authenticity as Chinese women. Sophia expressed her grandmother's constant reminders of her "unacceptable" behavior: "You can't be that loud you know; you got to be quiet. You are a girl. Be a girl" or "You can't make faces like that in public. That's not very lady-like." Several female participants complained about shouldering family chores and responsibilities and being taken less seriously than their brothers. Peilin said "Me and my sister would do a lot of the chores around the house and my brother would just be off. Maybe just take out the trash a few times, and that's it." The "son preference" is enacted as a transnational practice brought intergenerationally from China that impacts how young women experience being Chinese in the US. The patriarchal mores, which privilege men and boys and expect women and girls to respect and obey men, reinforce the stereotype of Chinese women as obedient, submissive, passive, domestic, and exotic (Uchida 1998). This stereotype functions as a subordinating threat to Chinese American women as they construct their ethnic meaning-making.

Ironically, Chinese American female students perceive themselves as vulnerable in ways that have been somewhat mitigated in China by its one-child policy. Peilin shared frustration about being denied the privilege girls in China now have:

> 她说在中国因为有独生子女政策，所以女孩也很受重视，可是因为她们在美国，不受这个政策的影响，她作为女孩就没受到重视。她说她的爷爷奶奶很看重他的弟弟，但是却不重视她和她妹妹 [She said because of the one-child policy in China, girls are valued as much as boys. However, because they are in the US, they are not restricted by this policy. She, as a girl, is not appreciated at home. She said her grandparents preferred her brother to her and her younger sister.]

(Field notes, 5/2/2017)

While it is not clear whether Peilin's family used transnational relocation as a strategy to avoid this policy or not, this one-child policy intersects with the "son preference" ideology at home to create a transnational space, which adds tension for Chinese American women's identity negotiation.

In summary, each participant's home space functions as a small island to distinguish the family from the outside society. In either tangible or symbolic ways, parents create a transnational space by embodying values and beliefs of "the Home" (country of origin) in their home space (place of residence). Parallel to Espíritu and Tran's (2002) discussion of "there" and "here" in immigrant parents' transnational child-rearing practices, the parents in this study agree with Wolf (2002), believing that "Home is morally superior to the home they now inhabit and constitutes the foundation for judging the behaviors as proper" (p. 285). That these values have immigrated to the Chinese American students' US home spaces in parent-child interactions, echoes Wolf's (2002) argument that "the fluid movement back and forth [between the place of origin and the place of settlement physically or emotionally] that persists as young people establish their identities . . . underscores that ethnic identity is formed not simply in one place, the US, but this process includes interactions with the [country of origin] on multiple levels" (p. 258). Therefore, stressing Home values such as family care, filial piety, female subordination, and parental authority are ways that parents not only try to instill ethnic culture into their children but enable them to "live a kind of transnational life at the level of emotions" (Wolf 2002, p. 285).

Parents' emphasis and sometimes implementation of these Home values creates intergenerational tensions; it also renders Chinese American students vulnerable in their identity construction, as they constantly balance being Chinese and being American. Because the majority of the participants come from a place where they are one of the few Asians, their understanding of being Chinese largely derives from their family dynamics. They have few outside resources or other Chinese to turn to for support.

Educational Space: K-12 Experiencing Alienation in K-12 Schooling

While family is the primary arena where Chinese American students learn to be Chinese, when they move to an educational space, the clashes between the values at home and school create tensions around being Chinese and being American. Furthermore, the dominant white environment, not only in student populations but in the values and beliefs that American education fosters, further impacts Chinese American students. Though we separated the home space from educational space in this chapter, this does not indicate that the two are independent of each other. On the contrary, they are closely linked as students move daily from their home space to an educational space.

Education has been applauded as the greatest factor in Americanizing immigrants, including its intentional imposition of white culture and minoritization of immigrants' culture (Mirel 2010). Although the public school system has changed from monocultural to intercultural education over time (Mirel 2010), education in the US remains dominated by white culture in ways that significantly shape students' ethnic identity development (Lee 2005). Ideas about what constitutes a good student, what is considered masculinity and femininity, and what language is proper center around whiteness, against which students of color are constantly judged (Lee 2005). Though often excluded from the black and white discourse, Asian American students also experience overt and covert racism in the educational space. Stereotypes that the dominant society imposes on Asian Americans marginalize and alienate them (Lee 2005; Lei 2003). Asian American boys are stereotyped as feminine due to their quiet demeanor (Lee 2005); Asian American girls are stereotyped as hyper-feminine and exotic (Uchida 1998). Asian American students are depicted as model minorities; their academic success is interpreted as nerdy or threatening (Lee 1996). It is often within schools that these stereotypes are made clear.

Within this political, social, and cultural dynamic in K–12 contexts, Chinese American students learn to either resist or conform to these stereotypes. While our research did not explicitly focus on their K–12 experience, students' negotiation in K–12 education emerged through their volunteered reflections and their parents' comments. Most participants shared struggles to fight racism and the model minority stereotypes. Yet, the pressure of this fight sometimes conflicted with family values that emphasized family over peers, filial respect, and diligence in studies. This conflict pushes Chinese American students away from celebrating their ethnicity in the educational space. Almost all participants recalled being called names, such as "Ching," "Chang," or "Konichiwa." They were often made fun of, such as "你的鼻子为什么会那么不高?" [How come your nose is not pointed?] (Amy) and "你眼睛特小" [Your eyes are so small] (Jack). Other participants were questioned about their food. Ava shared:

> I think [when we eat lunch at school] is like the biggest way I try to hide my identity because I spent all of my high school, like every time at lunch, getting questions about my food all the time, . . . I think I got so tired of it, so tired about [of] feeling self-conscious about the food I was eating. I was like, "Why cannot I just eat my food and you just not wonder what it is!" so I realize I tried to hide my Asian-ness through food.

Chinese Americans are stereotyped because of their appearance and food. The racialized environment of the K–12 educational space, where white unhyphenated American is the norm, propels Chinese American students to devalue themselves. Some chose not to bring Chinese food to school, and others dyed their hair or wore colored contact lenses to fit in.

The model minority stereotype additionally threatens how Chinese American students construct their ethnicity. Many participants recalled feeling alienated by both their peers and their parents. Amy recalled numer-ous occasions when peers shunned her for her devotion to study. Instead of believing Amy's good grades were due to her diligence, her peers were convinced her race made her smart; Amy recounted what she overheard, "她比我们聪明. . . . 她是个怪物" [She is smarter than us. . . . She is an alien]. While many people believe the model minority stereotype is a posi-tive perception of Asian students, it is, in fact, a hegemonic device to pit Asians against other minorities (particularly African Americans and Latinx Americans) and within the Asian community (Lee 1996). This can be seen from Linda's experience. Because she was not academically confident, Linda chose not to socialize with her Asian peers. She felt ashamed for not living up to the model minority stereotype:

> [他们]比我好，然后不能比那种，我总是觉得就是我不怎么聪明. . . . 考试也是，肯定不咋地 [They (those Asians in math, sci-ence and technology track) are smarter than me. I cannot compete with them. I always feel I am not smart. . . . I am not confident about getting good grade in tests].

This racialized perception of Asians has seriously damaged Linda's pride in being Chinese. To make things worse, her parents reiterated the empha-sis on academic performance, a value that travels transnationally through the spaces of Home, home, and school. Being pushed multiple times to achieve a higher ACT score, Linda was ambivalent about being Chinese. She shared:

> 那一段心情特别不好，觉得要是你是美国家庭吧，你要是考个32，他们就觉得够了，就不会逼你非得更高，我觉得要是美国人就好了 [During that period, I was very frustrated, thinking if I were born to an American family and got a 32 (on the ACT[2]), they would be OK with it and would not force me to get a higher score. I hope I can be an American].

In summary, Chinese American students' struggle in the K–12 space, where whiteness and nonimmigrant identities are designated as the norm, demon-strates the political identity associated with spaces (Massey 1999) through the spatial distribution of hierarchical power relations (Gupta & Ferguson 1992) on students' identity negotiation processes. At the same time, it indi-rectly reflects how symbolic transnationalism, manifested through stereotype threats and home values, contributes to their sense of being pulled between multiple identities. Moving from space to space is more complicated than code switching; rather, they are expected to be different people. They are expected to fit in with their peers at school and to conform to the Home values and practices.

Higher Educational Space: A Renewed Understanding
of Being Chinese

Often, in higher education, the student population is more diverse in terms of race, ethnicity, class, and nationality than in most K-12 schools. A diverse campus environment opens a new world for students to negotiate who they are. College is indeed an arena for students to explore ethnicity, race, sexuality, or other dimensions of identity (Inkelas 2004; Chan 2007). In addition, in college, students have more opportunities to engage in transnational border crossing manifested in the campus curriculum and in study abroad. With the recent emphasis on internationalizing higher education, American universities have brought more international students to campuses, sent more students on education abroad programs, and expanded curricular options. Student organizations, campus events, lectures, classroom discussions, hallway conversations, and peer interactions all provide important contexts for Chinese American college students to rethink, reconstruct, and redescribe their identity. This allows them intellectually and physically to participate in the globalized transnational movement.

While in K-12 education, most participants experienced a suppressed and ambivalent relationship to being Chinese, in college, many of them developed an appreciation of their Chinese ethnicity. Peer interaction and Chinese language classes play a vital role in their embrace of their ethnicity, as reflected in the following quotes:

> 可能我住的地方都是 Honors，他们对这种事情有兴趣，因为他们也知道中国跟美国的，international affairs，也很重要，所以他们说"哦，很厉害啊，说多一点吧。"因为他们也学新的东西，他们有很大的兴趣啊....他们问我也觉得很好啊。因为以前没有那么多人对这种事情感兴趣。[Maybe because my peers are all from the Honor's college, they are very interested in getting to know me. They know the international affairs between China and US are important. They encourage me to speak more about China, because they can learn new things. They have a lot more interest in it. . . . It's good that they ask me, because in high school not a lot of people were interested in these things.]

> (Amy)

> I feel like they [language classes] helped me enjoy, like, my ethnicity more, because, like, you know in high school, it was hard for me, because, you know, people always asked me like "Oh, can you speak Chinese like blah blah" and then I would not be able to say it. So now, like I want to, like you know, I can speak more and more. I can write more and more.

> (Angel)

Their peers' interest in their heritage and their increased fluency in Chinese bring pride in being Chinese.

The presence of international students, especially those from China, provides Chinese American college students with direct experience with Chinese nationals. However, these direct interpersonal experiences push them to eventually embrace a Chinese American identity. Jack remarked:

> 我是比较喜欢 ABC 这样的，我不跟那些中国来的人交往 . . . 我觉得男孩太蔫，然后又没什么本事 . . . 都是公子哥，. . . 没什么钱然后又假装他们有钱 . . . 中国来的女孩，maturity 比较少，就是比较小，她们就是喜欢那些小孩的东西，像毛绒玩具，在我看来就是 immaturity . . . 中国女孩就是觉得你有钱，她的 personality 就变了，然后我觉得这有点怪。因为那钱不是我的，那是我父母的钱，我并没有什么钱，像咱们这些人就是这样长大的" [I prefer to socialize with ABCs (American born Chinese); I don't socialize with students from China. . . . I think the boys are too listless. They are not capable of many things, and they are mostly playboys. They don't have the money but like to pretend they are rich. . . . Girls from China are not mature enough. They love kids' stuff, like stuffed animals. In my eyes, they are immature. If one girl finds out you are rich, her whole personality will be changed. This makes me feel weird, because it is not my money; it is my parents'. I don't have the money. This is the mentality we ABCs grow up with].

Here, instead of being stereotyped, Chinese American students stereotype students from China as "spoiled little emperors" (Short, Xu, & Liu 2012, p. 96). While the participants' perceptions of Chinese students may not be accurate (Fong 2011), this stereotype against peers from China pushes them to identify with American-born Chinese. Jack recognized the uniqueness of his hybrid identity. He noted:

> 因为我又是美国长大，我又是中国人脸，所以我觉得比较重要，就是两边都得明白 . . . 我觉得你得对 . . . 你得 understand 你的 heritage, 然后是 . . . I take great pride in being Chinese, right? 因为中国你有那么多历史，乱七八糟的，所以我还是对中国，就是我的 heritage 比较 proud, 可是我会 identify 自己是 American, 所以两边都有。
>
> [Because I grew up in the US, and I have a Chinese face, so I think it is very important to know both sides. . . . I think you have to . . . you have to understand your heritage, and then, I take great pride in being Chinese, right? Because China has such a long history, I am proud of China and my heritage. But I would also identify as an American, so I have both sides].

Transnationalism embodied in an academic space allows them to embrace their hybridity, both Chinese and American identity, as Jack said, "having both sides." Unlike in the spaces of home and K-12 schooling, where Chinese American students experienced transnationalism largely symbolically, in higher education, these students experienced transnationalism directly through exposure to foreign language curriculum and interaction with international students from China. This direct experience along with the diverse campus environment allows Chinese American students to integrate Chinese and American sides into their meaning-making of self. The development of a hybrid – transnational – identity becomes more salient when they visit their country of origin.

Ancestral Home: Redefining Heritage Identity

Directly engaging in transnational border crossing through visiting their place of origin further challenges Chinese American college students' understanding of who they are. Visiting their ancestral land gives them the experience of Home, albeit differently than their parents experienced it. At the same time, their Chinese "membership" is questioned as a result of stereotypes they encounter in China. Navigating these complexities brings tensions and readjustment to their location of identity.

Visiting their ancestral land, Chinese American college students felt a strong sense of Home that their parents have tried hard to cultivate within their US homes; exposure to similar food, shared values, and being surrounded by people who look like them all contribute to their feeling comfortable in their country of origin, as highlighted in the following comments:

> I just enjoyed kind of being around people that are kind of the same as me, you know, it's a nice comforting feeling and just knowing that that's where I am from and that's where my roots are, you know. It kind of gave me a sense of home.
>
> (Ava)

> 我觉得有家的感觉，在香港我会比较多 . . . 因为那边的学生啊，真的拼命（笑）厉害的，所以我觉得跟他们在一起有点，我觉得,可以了解我" [I have a stronger sense of Home in Hong Kong . . . because students there, who are also desperate about their study, can understand me (my devotion to study) when I was with them.]
>
> (Amy)

This sense of familiarity, ease, and home were also observed among Kibria's (2002) Korean and Chinese American students. It is a prevalent feeling people in the Chinese diaspora have when visiting their ancestral land (Li 1994; Liu 2015).

However, this also comes with an emerging sense of alienation. Similar to what Kibria (2002) found, the limited ability to speak their heritage language and to demonstrate cultural mannerisms performed through dress and demeanor contribute to this alienation. Most participants shared they received looks for how they spoke, how they looked, what they wore, and how and what they ate. The homeland trip made Chinese American students more aware of their differences from, than commonalities with, the Chinese. Their primordial notion of identity based on ties of blood or shared descent from a common ancestor (Dikotter 1992) seems over-ridden by contemporary cultural differences. In their ancestral homeland, Chinese American students experience the "foreigner" stereotype; they are expected to be able to speak Chinese fluently and conform to Chinese culture because they are perceived as "Chinese." Their body marks them as "Chinese," but their linguistic limitations and cultural knowledge exclude them from being "Chinese," whereas in the US, it is their linguistic and cultural practice that others them as perpetual foreigners. The same stereotype of being able to speak Chinese and practice a certain culture reflects how hierarchical power manifested in each space impacts students' ethnic identity construction. When they move from space to space, combating these politically laden stereotypes, they realize how precarious their situation is and how complicated it is to cultivate a secure sense of who they are; Ava sighed, "I cannot win. Everywhere I go, it's like 'your food is very Asian' or when I was in Taiwan, they will be like 'you are such an American'." Thus, the trip works to highlight marginality for Chinese American students in their ancestral homeland and illuminates their alienation in their country of residence. Though the heightened sense of their identity as Americans on the trip to their ancestral land was more significant than their being Chinese (Kibria 2002), it also pushes them to construct their identity beyond the nation-state.

The nationalism imposed on Chinese American students by the Chinese society, which is based on national heritage, adds another layer of estrangement. Despite the encouragement of people of Chinese descent to assimilate and pay political loyalty to their country of settlement, China still expects strong motherland nationalism from the Chinese diaspora (Louie 2004; Zhao 2018). China portrays them as "海内外中华儿女" [the daughters and sons of the Chinese nation at home and abroad] (Zhao 2018, p. 20). Chinese American students sensed this implied political loyalty when interacting with local Chinese, and they actively negated this affiliation, as Emma stated:

但是在中国，我就发现 "oh, I am not really Chinese," 我并不是 . . . 就是因为中国人平时，中国人觉得你不管是什么地方的中国人，哦，OK，中国人就觉得你的家乡是中国, 是大陆, 那你就是中国人，所以他们就把所有的华人都当做中国人，其实华人跟中国人不一样，对不对。像我是美国的华裔 [When I was in China,

I found out that "oh, I am not really Chinese." Chinese people tend to think no matter where you were born, China is your home country, and that is Mainland China. Then you would be Chinese. They consider all the people of Chinese descent Chinese. But people of Chinese descent are different from people in China, right? I am an American with Chinese heritage].

Denying the implied cultural, ancestral, and political connotations in this simple sentence, "You are Chinese," Chinese American students express a desire to separate their ethnic identity from nationality and political loyalty. Other participants developed an identity that transcends national borders, as evident in Amy's statement:

> 我会说 nationality 是美国的嘛，在哪里出生就是，但 identity 真的是很难，因为我是文化上是 Chinese, 但然后就是加了一点点，就几个 percent 美国人，但政府来说，我两边都不是。爱国主义 . . . 比较偏美国吧，但美国也有很多地方我是不同意的。然后身为一个基督徒，我觉得 patriotism 跟我是不太会，因为我是属于更高的那种，就是上帝的那种 laws 不是人的那种 laws, 我也不会把政府的领导人放的那么高，因为我知道人是有一个限度的 [I will say my nationality is America, because it was determined by where you were born. But it is hard to talk about identity. Culturally, I am Chinese. I perhaps have only several percentages of American culture. Politically, I identify with neither of the two countries. My patriotism . . . is toward America, but there are a lot that I disagree with what America has done. As a Christian, I feel like my patriotism is not [restricted by nation]. Mine belongs to a higher level. (I am patriotic) to the law of God not the human laws. I won't expect too much from the government leaders, because I know human has limitations].

Amy's dismissal of the nation-state further demonstrates her transnational identity. Her ambivalence about her identity, of being culturally Chinese, nationally American, and belonging to God highlights the complexities of identity. It challenges the ideologies of singularity – of singular loyalties, of singular national space, and of clear-cut borders – the bases on which the nation-state aims to sustain its power and legitimacy (Georgiou 2010, p. 26). Experiencing transnationalism in this direct and physical way, Chinese American students such as Amy develop an identity that transcends the "either-or" choice of being Chinese or American. They embrace an identity situated in the third space beyond China or the US (Bhabha 1994). They are not Chinese in the sense of what is expected from them by people in their ancestral land nor are they American in the way that American society perceives them. They become comfortable with embracing a hybrid identity as Chinese American, one that is unique and meaningful to them.

Conclusion

By exploring Chinese American college students' negotiation of ethnicity as they move from multiple spaces crossing home, schooling, higher education, and country of origin, this chapter highlights the significant roles that space and transnationalism manifested in physical and symbolic forms play in students' identity construction. They encounter pressure to be different people in different spaces, facing both intra-ethnic and external competing expectations. Intergenerational ethnic tensions between Chinese parents and children revolve around ways in which Home (place of origin) narrates home (residence) in values, practices, and allegiances. The stereotype threats and racism that target Chinese Americans simultaneously isolate them and sharpen their quest for identity. Within the more diverse physical and symbolic transnationalism in higher education, Chinese American students navigate their identity against the precarious dynamics of each space as they move from being ambivalent about their identity to more comfortably embracing hybridity through renegotiation and modification.

Notes

1. "College" in the U.S. context has the same meaning as "university" – referring to tertiary-level education. Both terms – college and university – will be used interchangeably.
2. The ACT is a US exam for university entrance. Thirty-six is the highest possible score.

References

Agnew, John A. 2011. Space and Place. In John A. Agnew and David N. Livingstone (eds.), *Handbook of Geographical Knowledge*. London: Sage. http://dharmageosphere.com/upload/space_and_place_L3.pdf

Aranda, Elizabeth M. 2006. *Emotional Bridges to Puerto Rico: Migration, Return Migration, and the Struggles of Incorporation*. Lanham, MD: Rowman & Littlefield.

Bach, Linda, Nina Glick Schiller, and Cristina Szanton Blanc. 1994. *Nations Unbound: Transnational Projects, Postcolonial Predicaments, and Deterritorialized Nation-States*. Langhorne, PA: Gordon and Breach Publishers.

Bhabha, Homi K. 1994. *The Location of Culture*. New York: Routledge.

Chan, Elaine. 2007. Student Experiences of a Culturally-Sensitive Curriculum: Ethnic Identity Development Amid Conflicting Stories to Live By. *Journal of Curriculum Studies* 39(2): 177–194.

Creswell, John W. 2013. *Qualitative Inquiry Research Design: Choosing Among Five Approaches*, 3rd edition. Thousand Oaks, CA: Sage.

Dikotter, Frank. 1992. *The Discourse of Race in Modern China*. Palo Alto, CA: Stanford University Press.

Espíritu, Yen L., and Thom Tran. 2002. "Viet Nam, Nuoc Toi" ["Vietnam, My Country"]: Vietnamese Americans and Transnationalism. In Peggy Levitt and Mary Waters (eds.), *The Changing Face of Home: The Transnational Lives of the Second Generation* (pp. 367–398). New York: Russell Sage.

Evans, Nancy J., Deanna S. Forney, and Florence Guido-DiBrito. 1998. *Student Development in College: Theory, Research and Practice*, 1st edition. San Francisco: Jossey-Bass.

Fong, Vanessa. 2011. *Paradise Redefined: Transnational Chinese Students and the Quest for Flexible Citizenship in the Developed World*. Stanford, CA: Stanford University Press.

Gabriel, Sharmani Patricia. 2011. "Migration of Chineseness": In Conversation with Ien Ang. *Inter-Asia Cultural Studies* 12(1): 122–131.

Georgiou, Myria. 2010. Identity, Space and The Media: Thinking Through Diaspora. *Revue Européenne des Migrations Internationales* 26(1): 17–35.

Gupta, Akhil, and James Ferguson. 1992. Beyond "Culture": Space, Identity, and the Politics of Difference. *Cultural Anthropology* 7(1): 6–23.

Inkelas, Karen Kurotsuchi. 2004. Does Participation in Ethnic Cocurricular Activities Facilitate a Sense of Ethnic Awareness and Understanding?: A Study of Asian Pacific American Undergraduates. *Journal of College Student Development* 45(3): 285–302.

Kibria, Nazli. 2002. Of Blood, Belonging, and Homeland Trips: Transnationalism and Identity Among Second-Generation Chinese and Korean Americans. In Peggy Levitt and Mary Waters (eds.), *The Changing Face of Home: The Transnational Lives of the Second Generation* (pp. 295–311). New York: Russell Sage.

Lee, Erika. 2015. *The Making of Asian America: A History*. New York: Simon & Schuster.

Lee, Stacey J. 1996. *Unraveling the "Model Minority" Stereotype: Listening to Asian American Youth*. New York: Teachers College Press.

Lee, Stacey J. 2005. *Up Against Whiteness: Race, School, and Immigrant Youth*. New York: Teachers College Press.

Lei, Joy. 2003. (Un)necessary Toughness? Those "Loud Black Girls" and Those "Quiet Asian Boys". *Anthropology & Education Quarterly* 34(2): 158–181.

Levitt, Peggy. 2001. *The Transnational Villagers*. Berkeley: University of California Press.

Levitt, Peggy, and Mary Waters. 2002. Introduction. In Peggy Levitt and Mary Waters (eds.), *The Changing Face of Home: The Transnational Lives of the Second Generation* (pp. 1–30). New York: Russell Sage.

Li, Hao Victor. 1994. From Qiao (僑) to Qiao (橋). In Wei-ming Tu (ed.), *The Living Tree: The Changing Meaning of Being Chinese Today* (pp. 213–220). Stanford, CA: Stanford University Press.

Liu, Shuang. 2015. *Identity, Hybridity and Cultural Home: Chinese Migrants and Diaspora in Multicultural Societies*. New York: Rowman & Littlefield.

Louie, Andrea. 2004. *Chineseness Across Borders: Renegotiating Chinese Identity in China and the United States*. Durham, NC: Duke University Press.

Massey, Doreen. 1999. *Power-Geometries and the Politics of Space-Time*. Hettner-Lecture 1998. Heidelberg: University of Heidelberg.

Massey, Doreen. 2005. *For Space*. London: SAGE Publications.

Menjívar, Cecilia. 2002. Living in Two Worlds? Guatemalan-Origin Children in the United States and Emerging Transnationalism. *Journal of Ethnic and Migration Studies* 28(3): 531–552.

Mirel, Jeffrey E. 2010. *Patriotic Pluralism: Americanization Education and European Immigrants*. Cambridge, MA: Harvard University Press.

Ong, Aihwa. 1999. *Flexible Citizenship: The Cultural Logics of Transnationality*. Durham, NC: Duke University Press.

Sánchez, Patricia, and Margarita Machado-Casas. 2009. At the Intersection of Transnationalism, Latina/o Immigrants, and Education. *The High School Journal* 92(4): 3–15.

Short, Susan E., Hongwei Xu, and Ying Liu. 2012. Little Emperors? Growing Up in China After the One-Child Policy. In Eric P. Kaufmann and W. Brandford Wilcox (eds.), *Whiter the Child?: Causes and Consequences of Low Fertility* (pp. 95–112). London: Routledge.

Steele, Claude M. 2010. *Whistling Vivaldi: How Stereotypes Affect Us and What We Can Do*. New York: W. W. Norton & Company. Kindle Edition.

Steele, Claude M., and Joshua Aronson. 1995. Stereotype Threat and the Intellectual Test Performance of African Americans. *Journal of Personality and Social Psychology* 69(5): 797–811.

Tuan, Mia. 1998. *Forever Foreigners or Honorary Whites? The Asian Ethnic Experience Today*. New Brunswick, NJ: Rutgers University Press.

Uchida, Aki. 1998. The Orientalization of Asian Women in America. *Women's Studies International Forum* 21(2): 161–174. https://doi.org/10.1016/S0277-5395(98)00004-1

Wolf, Diane L. 2002. There Is No Place Like "Home": Emotional Transnationalism and the Struggles of Second-generation Filipino. In Peggy Levitt and Mary Waters (eds.), *The Changing Face of Home: The Transnational Lives of the Second Generation* (pp. 225–294). New York: Russell Sage.

Zhao, Jian. 2018. 改革开放 40 年中国侨务政策的回顾 [Review of the Policies toward Overseas Chinese for the Past 40 Years]. *Journal of Overseas Chinese History Studies* 4: 14–22.

5 Reflections on Privilege, Oppression, and Possibilities in Times of Radical Change

Beth S. Catlett & Amira Proweller

As white, Jewish feminists with long careers as university faculty in the fields of the social foundations of education and women's and gender studies, we have been engaged in an ongoing critical interrogation of our professional identities and roles as educators and activists, as well as the place of our work in shaping a more just and humane society. In this current historical moment, the fault lines of injustice have been exposed in a variety of ways. For instance, we face an epiphenomenal public health crisis in the form of a global pandemic. This COVID-19 pandemic has heightened the visibility of structural inequities and institutional violence in the United States in very profound ways. These disparities that characterize our contemporary moment include systems of patriarchy, sexism, misogyny, and rape culture that are especially virulent and have become increasingly normalized and all-too commonplace in the 21st century. Our attention to these structures of gender inequality is compelled by current statistics that document the pervasive landscape of gender-based violence in the United States. For example, data demonstrate that one in three women in the United States experiences some form of contact sexual violence in their lifetime (Smith et al. 2017). In particular, 31% of teen girls have been victims of sexual assault or violence, and 77% of rape victims were known to their attackers (Illinois Coalition Against Sexual Assault 2017; National Women's Law Center 2017). These systems of gender inequity represent just one element of an extended set of interlocking structures of power, oppression, and privilege within which we are implicated and accountable.

In addition to systemic gender-based oppressions, especially virulent rhetoric and violent action has increasingly played out against a variety of marginalized communities, most notably for the purpose of this chapter, the Jewish community. The anti-Semitic mass murder at the Tree of Life Synagogue in Pittsburgh and other anti-Semitic assaults throughout the world evidence that Jews continue to be discriminated against and indeed are victims of the highest percentage of anti-religion hate crimes (Hodge & Boddie 2021; Rubin 2017). More specifically, the U.S. Department of Justice reports that of the number of incidents of religiously motivated hate crimes in the

DOI: 10.4324/9781003258223-6

United States in 2019, anti-Jewish attacks were the most common form of anti-religious group attack, with 953 cases (FBI 2019).

Within the context of these multilayered oppressions, we see that the current moment demands radical change, and further requires that we not remain static, but rather recommit ourselves to continuous learning and growth through critical interrogation of our own social locations and their unique complexities. Through focused inquiry into our positionalities within systems of power, privilege, and oppression, we anticipate deepening our self-knowledge and revisiting difficult but necessary conversations about how we are implicated in systems from which we benefit so that we can advance the cause of social justice in ways that are responsible and responsive to the challenges of this moment. In particular, we feel compelled to re-engage and deepen our introspection into the intersection of our privileges as white women within an American system of white supremacy. The focus here is not only on power and positionality but also on accountability. As Russo (2019) explores, this focus on the ways in which we are implicated in, and accountable for, our white privilege, holds the potential for building capacity for individual and collective social change, grounded in a recognition of accountability for privilege, its relationship to oppressive systems, and the harms it produces (Russo 2019).

Indeed, our positionalities as privileged white women, who also are impacted by systems of gender-based oppression, are layered over with our positionality as Jews, which extends out of a long history of Jewish persecution and discrimination. We take up the ways in which these intersecting identities and systems have shaped our social justice work in the university and the community. To this end, our chapter explores how our positionalities and self-inquiry align with, and are informed by, the work we have been asking young, Jewish teen girls to do in the context of their youth program, Research Training Internship (RTI). To say a bit more about the RTI program, for the last eight years we have been involved in research with Jewish teens who have participated in this out-of-school collaborative university-community social justice program. Each of the RTI program cohorts has been composed of a diverse group of Jewish, female or non-binary identified teens from different neighborhoods in a large midwestern metropolitan area. The participating youth come from reform, conservative, and orthodox denominations. Indeed, the program participants over the last many years have represented diverse Jewish identities and affiliations. RTI's strategic purpose is to engage the youth in building leadership capacities for critical dialogue about systemic privilege and oppression in their immediate communities, as well as in broader societal contexts (Catlett, Proweller, & Crabtree-Nelson 2019). While the program is focused on supporting the youth to explore how power operates societally and shapes their social identities, it is also a productive space for the youth to come to see and understand how they are implicated in intersecting systems of inequality and can work against systemic oppression with other teen and adult allies beyond the Jewish community. Meeting twice a month in three-hour sessions at the local partnership university, RTI program participants have had opportunities to engage in open and critical dialogue and to receive instruction in youth-led participatory action research (YPAR), in preparation for developing and implementing a culminating action research project intended to effect change relevant to their lives and their surrounding community. In this chapter, we center the research projects of two different cohorts: one focused on gendered violence and rape culture and the second on antisemitism, healing, and solidarity.

Recently, YPAR has emerged as a meaningful approach for studying and involving privileged youths in important social inquiry about complex social relations, in particular, how power and oppression function and the role that privilege plays in producing, sustaining, and normalizing social injustice and the consequences thereof (Case 2013; Stoudt 2009; Stoudt, Fox, & Fine 2012). As an approach that provides the youth opportunities to develop their capacities as critical researchers and decision-makers, YPAR empowers them to reshape institutions and systems that directly impact them and their communities. As such, YPAR undertaken with/by privileged youths holds great potential for making visible the ways in which privilege is necessarily connected to systems of power, privilege, and oppression; operates to protect privilege; and ultimately reproduces and sustains inequality. Moreover, it creates the context for privileged youths to develop a recognition and understanding of their accountability to move to a more critically conscious place from which to engage in acts of individual and collective radical social change (Stoudt, Fox, & Fine 2012).

Through this weaving of our self-inquiries and youth voice, our chapter centers on the importance of intergenerational partnership and responsibility for us. This work keeps us present to the urgency of this moment and holds us to our commitment to shepherd through generations yet to come into a world we would like to leave behind and they would like to step into for their futures. Furthermore, our chapter brings to the fore, both through our self-inquiry and young people's interrogations, the legacy of antisemitism and the long complex history of multiple identities marked by both privilege and oppression.

Methodologically, we ground our interrogation in data collected from a series of ongoing structured conversations between the co-authors about how intersecting systems of privilege and oppression operate in our lives. These conversations have generated rich insights informed by our academic backgrounds and disciplines, our personal experiences, and the ongoing work we have been doing with these youths. Drawing on the qualitative tradition of autoethnography (Johnson & Parry 2015; Magnet 2006; Grenier 2019), we intentionally engage in self-reflexive processes that take account of the inter-relationship across our biographies, lived experiences, and social identities (Fine 2018) in relationship to the social and cultural interrogations (Ellis & Bochner 2000) in which we engage with the RTIs. Our analysis draws on critical, intersectional feminist framings that compel us to examine how interlocking axes of privilege and oppression – as related to our identities, our experiences, as well as broader social structures – are integral to the fabric of our lives as white, Jewish feminist educators and activists (Crenshaw 1994; Hill Collins 1990; Okun 2010; Richie 2012). Additionally, this exploration engages with data from research conducted with participants in the RTI youth program, specifically, our research with the RTI cohorts from 2016–2017 and 2018–2019. In particular, we explore data that emerged from individual interviews with the RTI participants, field notes of program sessions, and written materials, including their YPAR reports.

In what follows, we first discuss our respective experiences that mark the ways in which intersecting systems of privilege and oppression, in particular, antisemitism and whiteness, pervaded our early lives. We then bring our own experiences to bear on our current professional lives, our work with the RTIs to engage in social inquiry about complex social relations, specifically, how power and oppression function, and the role that privilege plays in producing, sustaining, and normalizing social injustice.

Biographies, Experiences, and Identities

Our work around social justice and anti-racism in the academy is shaped in complex ways by several social identities linked to power, privilege, and oppression and – most salient for us at this sociopolitical moment of exacerbated precarity – our white and Jewish identities. Like Rubin (2017), and foundational to our worldviews, we often have queried, "white or other?" This question stems from a long history of the complex intersections of privilege and oppression among many Jewish people. As Rubin (2017) chronicles:

> It was soon after WWII, during the 1940s and 1950s, when Jewish people began to gain access to many institutional privileges of being White in America and soon became one of the most upwardly mobile (economically) of all of the European ethnic groups in the United States (Brodkin 2000). Post WWII, Jews were not really seen as a minority group in the United States by the larger society; they were simply seen as White (Singer 2008). According to Langman (1995), "[The notion] that Jews are White is relatively new and provides the irony that Jews, who have a long history of being oppressed by Whites as a non-White 'other,' are now grouped with the same Whites who have been their oppressors" (p. 4). . . . Singer (2008) also problematizes this concept when she states . . . I may be white, but I live in two worlds, and neither one totally accepts nor understands the other. . . . We remain a hidden minority amidst white privilege." (p. 51, as quoted in Rubin, p. 135)

The question becomes how do we as Jews live in this liminal space. Amira's recognition of living in this liminal space first unfolded as a child of one of very few Jewish families in a small community in the northeast where she came to her earliest understanding of outsider status, marginalization, and otherness. Christian hegemony surfaced early in her childhood experiences, in particular in public school. She vividly recalled events such as a conversation, in second grade, with a classmate who lived in the neighborhood, and adamantly insisted that Amira, as a Jew, was responsible for murdering Jesus Christ. She further experienced expressions of blatant antisemitism when a neighbor constructed a wooden swastika on the back of his shed that faced Amira's kitchen window. As a final example here, Christmas concerts and classroom activities around holiday time were often fraught. For instance, Amira once was asked to draw an angel in a class; she refused, the teacher insisted, and as a result, Amira's parents paid a visit to the school principal to explain that an angel was not part of Amira's Jewish tradition or upbringing and that the teacher's insistence deepened Amira's felt sense of marginalization in a largely white, Christian setting. This was one, among many instances, of Amira's parents visiting the school.

In contrast to Amira, Beth came to our early conversations absent of any awareness of concrete childhood experiences with antisemitism. However, as we were writing this chapter, Beth's husband shared a memory – for the first time – from their college years. When visiting Beth's family, he came upon Beth's father scrubbing a stone in the front of their house. When asked what he was doing, Beth's father shared that he was cleaning a swastika that had been drawn onto the stone. He then told Beth's husband (at the time, her boyfriend) that he didn't want his daughters to know, to be upset by this demonstration of antisemitism in their own community. In reflecting on this surprising revelation, it appears that Beth's parents went to significant lengths to insulate their children from awareness not only of the role that antisemitism played in their lives and in their proximate community but of the role that other systems of power – including racism and white and class privilege – played out in their lives as well. Beth grew up in a predominantly white, affluent suburb, where her sense of her own white and class privilege was invisible, internalized as normative, and left unquestioned. The values that her parents emphasized were Jewish community, family, education, hard work, and achievement. In addition, the Jewish ethic of Tikkun Olam, of repairing the world, and Tzedakah, of doing deeds of philanthropy and charity (Greenberg 1988), were central principles undergirding a Jewish sense of social responsibility.

Looking back at her family of origin experiences, Beth now is able to unpack analytic insights into the extent to which these foundational ways of being in her family and childhood community normalized the trappings of white superiority, white supremacy, and class privilege. That is, absent any explicit conversation in her family about intersecting systems of power, privilege, and oppression – and leading their lives in a segregated, predominantly white community – Beth has come to see how the context of her upbringing as white, Jewish, and upper middle-class in effect served to reinforce dominant discourses of charity and philanthropy that position privileged whites as saviors, benevolent actors serving those perceived as deficient and "less fortunate" (Catlett & Proweller 2011; Okun 2010). As several theorists have pointed out, while the intention of helping those who are underserved may on its surface be well-intentioned, many times white people with race and class privilege fail to understand how their privileged circumstances, alongside an absent awareness of their place in systems of oppression, run the risk of adversely impacting those they "serve." Indeed, taking on this position only acts to reproduce and reinforce intersecting systems of power, privilege, and oppression.

Paolo Freire, in *Pedagogy of the Oppressed* (2000), was one of the first to assert that "giving back" is not true generosity, but instead, a move to accommodate rather than dismantle structures of inequality:

> Any attempt to soften the power of the oppressor in deference to the weakness of the oppressed almost always manifests itself in the form of false generosity; indeed, the attempt never goes beyond this. In order to have the continued opportunity to express their generosity, the oppressor must perpetuate injustice as well. . . . True generosity consists precisely in fighting to destroy the causes which nourish false charity.
>
> (pp. 44–45)

In contrast, Amira remembers feeling so marginalized in her community that it is hard for her to tap into identities of privilege. For Amira, childhood memories were not as straightforward. She perceived and experienced difference early on, living in a working-class/lower-middle-class community that was diverse in terms of race and ethnicity, and being tracked in college preparatory courses in high school that were largely populated by white, middle-class youths. This educational tracking system was arguably Amira's first concrete recognition of a system of white supremacy, where white youths were placed into high achieving classes in preparation for college, while youths of color, many from lower-income backgrounds, were tracked in remedial classes or vocational programs (Oakes 2005). Thus, race and class privilege were evident to Amira, but in these early years, she did not necessarily have an analytic framework to challenge the apparent normative nature of these structural arrangements. Amira now asks herself how much she internalized these experiences of educational disparity as the norm, so much so that white superiority was perhaps seen as the standard and the ideal.

These childhood memories reveal to us how we have internalized the hegemony of whiteness and middle-class conventions as received wisdom – in a way that wasn't complicated or interrogated when we were children. Although disquieting, our self-reflexive process around these memories has bolstered our strong and ongoing commitment to interrogate these structures of privilege and inequality and has shaped our current academic work in particular ways. For example, we have over the years worked jointly on program development, implementation, and research on college students' community-based service learning. We work with our university students to unpack and debunk charity models of service that, notwithstanding our early formative experiences, we have come to understand hold substantial risk for reproducing power imbalance and social injustice (Green 2001). Moreover, this charity model of service learning privileges those doing the service relative to those having their needs served. This service model tends to present as apolitical in orientation and based in discourses of volunteerism, charity, and philanthropy. Our work in service learning with university students over the years, therefore, has been grounded in a commitment to holding ourselves accountable to interrupt these embedded structures – these charity models of service – in a manner that assists relatively privileged students in seeing themselves as allies engaged in the work of social change with rather than for others (Catlett & Proweller 2011).

Bringing Our Multiple Identities Together in Practice

Building on our commitments to interrupting conventional models of service learning with university students, we continue to reflect upon our childhood memories. Absent open or direct dialogue in our families about structures of inequality, we see the work we do now, not only with university students but also with Jewish high school-aged girls, as a way to create visibility and dialogue aimed at resisting these systems. We recognize the need to be intentional about facilitating dialogue with young people – in our case, with high school-aged Jewish girls – about internalized, interpersonal, and institutional systems of power (David & Derthick 2017). Furthermore, we are considering what our most salient intervention should be at this time when social inequities and strife have surfaced with great intensity. With this in mind, we seek to unearth and render visible the ways in which we are implicated in multiple systems of privilege, and how our experiences of oppression as Jews, can support our work to surface inequity and animate social justice. As RTI has evolved over these last eight years, the major goals of the program align well with what we have identified as our most important social justice work and contributions moving forward. In a manner very similar to our own self-study, our approach to the work in RTI is grounded in an understanding of the complexity of Jewishness, thus a basis for unpacking with the RTI interns privilege and oppression across a range of domains – gender, class, race, ethnicity, religion, sexual orientation, and ability, among others. Thus, a significant part of the interrogation that takes place in RTI involves focused discussion about these various intersections so the participants come to understand that the experience of oppression can be related to one identity while simultaneously experiencing privilege in relationship to a different identity. Such political education serves to illustrate how inequality shapes the lives of social groups differently as a consequence of how they are structurally situated.

Existing theory emphasizes that those who benefit the most from social, cultural, and economic advantage are generally not in the position of having to interrogate their own privilege (Catlett & Proweller 2011; DiAngelo 2018; Goodman 2015; Howard 2010; Swalwell 2013; Wise & Case 2013). Rather, individuals often reflect primarily on their marginalized identities, while their privileged identities more often than not remain invisible to them. Working with one of the early RTI cohorts, in 2015, we saw evidence of this dynamic, and theorized that these young people were beginning to "push at the margins of privilege" (Proweller et al. 2017). In other words, even if they were not yet able to fully articulate and examine the ways in which their privileged locations implicated them in systems that exclude others, the participants' narrative accounts suggested an emerging understanding of communities' hold on the affordances of privilege and the perils of such privilege in their own communities.

As described earlier, the RTI program centers on young people designing and conducting their own action research project. This process involves the participating interns in data collection and analysis that is then compiled into a written research report, an action project, and a public presentation of their research findings. In a YPAR research project conducted by one of the early program cohorts in which they collected and analyzed data from a survey they administered to over 200 Jewish youth in the Chicago area, the interns concluded that many young people felt pressure not to expose problems within their lives and communities. For example, a majority of research respondents identified a variety of mental health problems and concerns, and further indicated that they believed their parents were not listening to them, and were not taking these mental health issues seriously enough. Thus, this YPAR project helped the RTIs to surface the tendency of privileged communities to either deny or minimize the extent to which problems exist in their own communities. This reflects a deeply rooted investment in preserving and protecting an illusion of superiority that can be used to re-instantiate their power and privileged status.

Building on these formative understandings, a subsequent RTI cohort, in 2017, committed themselves to making privilege visible through a YPAR project focused on rape culture as a pervasive and problematic system shaping their lives and communities in particular ways. The RTI participants discussed, at length, the ways in which power, privilege, and oppression manifested in their daily lives, mirroring the broader social structure. In this instance, significant time was spent unpacking their own experiences of being stereotyped, objectified, and trivialized as young women, pointing to media constructions and cultural tropes that perpetuate dangerous expectations of idealized female perfection, that normalize traditional gender roles, and that disinvest girls of their voice and agency (Brown 2016; MacDowell 2017). What emerged from their conversations was an understanding that while rape culture is widespread, it is also invisible and normalized (Giraldi & Monk-Turner 2016). Not unlike other forms of systemic power, privilege, and oppression, rape culture is difficult to see and disrupt. As such, the program participants spent a great deal of time engaging in discussion about the extent to which rape culture is embedded in a variety of platforms that work together to condone and perpetuate gender-based violence, and began to name the different ways that rape culture manifests in their daily lives.

What the RTI participants came to realize was that rape culture has roots that run deep, and intervening in and ultimately disrupting rape culture and its consequences depends on seeing through its veiled manifestations down to its systemic bases and surfacing what traditionally has remained invisible in their own communities. Indeed, as we theorized on the basis of our work with the 2015 RTI cohort, and as resonated in particular with Beth and her childhood experiences, communities of privilege often exhibit significant investment in obfuscating social issues that could otherwise expose deeper problems within the community (Proweller, Catlett, & Crabtree-Nelson 2021) As such, too often we see privileged individuals and communities direct attention outward, which often translates into altruistic attitudes and charity models toward other communities that are constructed as deficient and in need of service (Mitchell 2008). These participating interns challenged themselves to engage in a critically focused interior investigation that highlighted engaging with their own community rather than an outward turn toward helping others in need.

Thus, the RTI participants decided to take up the topic of rape culture and its disruption in particular within the Jewish community in the context of a community Seder, a time-honored ritual meal celebrating the Passover holiday. The Passover story unfolds in the Passover Haggadah, a Jewish text that narrates the Jewish exodus from enslavement in Egypt, and is read around the Seder table. The interns committed themselves to this community Seder as a space for directing the interrogation lens toward their own community through an accustomed ritual familiar to their community. Their focus was on intervention and community accountability as a way to understand and expose the fundamental bases of gender-based violence in their own Jewish communities. In deciding to address the issue of rape culture in/through a rewriting of the Passover Haggadah, the RTI participants saw this as a way to hold privileged communities accountable for engaging in social justice work to end gender-based violence, stating in their research report:

> We chose to focus our Haggadah on rape culture because of how much it is integrated into our daily lives. Rape culture embodies many of the injustices that we have studied this year, and we feel that it is important to bring to light these societal injustices. The culture around unfair gender roles/expectations, sexual violence, and sexism in general is so integrated into our world, but our society and our Jewish community institutions are not doing enough to stop or address it. This Haggadah is not just a feminist analysis of our community. It is an invitation to those with privilege, resources, and power to join us in changing the rape culture around us.
>
> (RTI Participants 2017, p. 14)

Since the reading of the Passover Haggadah at the Passover Seder is a familiar communal activity, the RTI participants speculated that it would be a context within which Jewish community members from a variety of local synagogues and neighborhoods would be open and receptive to considering an issue that is more often than not shrouded in silence.

To extend this through line of our work as white, Jewish feminist educators – of identifying and exploring the ways in which privilege operates in our own lives and communities – we turn now to consider the most recent RTI action research project. In 2019–2020, the RTI participants decided "to explore whose voices were being left out in their own circles. As female-identified teens in a Jewish space, they were reflexive with their privilege and wanted to make such spaces more accessible" (RTI Participants 2020, p. 5). Their starting proposition was that straight cisgender community members would find the Jewish community more inclusive and welcoming than would nonhetero-sexual and non-cisidentified individuals. Through their survey and interview research, the interns uncovered that privilege and oppression, and indeed pro-cesses of marginalization, operate in their own communal spaces. Specifically, nonbinary and gender nonconforming people face many barriers to inclusion in Jewish communal spaces. Many women and LGBTQ+ people also found the Orthodox Jewish community notably non-inclusive. Moreover, the RTI research made particular note of the normalization of heterosexual privilege within the community. This normalization, the interns theorized, reflects a common theme among privileged identities to remain relatively unaware of the operation of power, privilege, and oppression and its consequences for those who have been historically marginalized (DiAngelo 2018; Goodman 2015; Howard 2010; Swalwell 2013; Wise & Case 2013). In their report, the interns conclude, "we believe it is incredibly important to recognize your privilege and realize that others might be marginalized within your community" (p. 9).

The RTI research discussed here reflects the significance of the work we do in partnership with young people to intentionally examine multiple intersect-ing systems of privilege and oppression that shape our lives and experiences, as well as investments in social change efforts. Our collaborative work over these last few years has been centered on the intersections of white privilege, gender oppressions, and Jewish identities. These systems and identities have emerged with particular salience for us as well as the young people with whom we work. Moreover, our work within the RTI program over these last years has also helped young Jewish women to see themselves as empowered agents of change, continuing the vital work of surfacing inequity and animating social justice that is arguably needed more than ever at this time.

Stepping Up and Working in Solidarity

In this chapter, we have taken the space and time to engage in reflective practice and self-study. As Michelle Fine (2018) suggests, as critical feminist educators we are called upon to map and untangle the biographies of our work and situate our research questions in our pasts, our present, and with a view toward the future. We're engaged in this process during a time of profound precarity and increasing instability. Indeed, at the writing of this chapter, we have just witnessed an unprecedented act of attempted insurrection incited by a sitting U.S. president. The rioters brought with them into the U.S. capital anti-Semitic and white supremacist tropes (Adkins & Burback 2021; Associated Press 2021) a glaring reminder of the incredible importance of our work and what yet remains to be done.

What we have come to understand even more deeply is that our work as white, Jewish, feminist social justice educators requires us to engage in an intentional and sustained way that centers reflective practice on cultivating awareness and consciousness about our own identities and positionalities within systems of inequality. We also remain committed to extending this awareness and consciousness to those with whom we interface both in our teaching and in our research. We understand that our work does not stop there – we must not, and cannot, stop at mere consciousness-raising. Rather, we see critical reflection and consciousness-raising as a threshold from which to step into action.

Drawing on our Jewish roots and feminist sensibilities, we look to animate our commitments and strengthen our resolve to be part of a collective movement to dismantle the master's tools (Lorde 2007). As white women with relative privilege, we recognize our accountability for dismantling oppressive systems, even, and especially, when we challenge systems from which we may benefit. Furthermore, as Jewish white women, we must guard against allowing the Jewish principle of *Tikkun Olam* – repairing the world – to, however inadvertently, re-instantiate a sense of white and/or Jewish superiority. That is, we must stay keenly aware of the harmful impacts of dominant discourses of volunteerism, charity, and philanthropy that position those of race and class privilege as benevolent actors serving those perceived as lacking sufficient strengths and resources (Catlett & Proweller 2011; Okun 2010).

Accordingly, and in a manner parallel to the RTI work we've discussed here, we are committed to guarding against directing our lens outward, and instead turn the mirror on ourselves and the communities in which we work and live. We are at a moment in which our resolve to work within privileged communities, and Jewish communities, is strengthened. Moreover, we continue to believe that one of our most powerful tools for this work is YPAR. As mentioned previously, YPAR has conventionally been used in working with historically marginalized youth, yet – more recently – has been utilized in anti-oppression work, in particular as a method that allows young people from privileged communities to identify and examine their place within intersecting systems of power, privilege, and oppression, as a starting point from which to push against unjust institutions (Stoudt, Fox, & Fine 2012). We draw on this methodology in working with privileged youth so that we can hold those in positions of relative power – like ourselves – accountable to interrupting unjust systems even, and most importantly, when we have benefited from those systems, too often at the expense of others. In doing this work, whether in the classroom or in our community-based research endeavors, we never want to lose sight of where our questions originate and to whom we are accountable (Fine 2018; Keating 2013).

Although a focused awareness of our privileged positionality is always important to foreground, at this moment of precarity we also have a heightened awareness of the ongoing, pernicious, and escalating antisemitism that characterizes our country, and indeed our world. Intersectional feminist thought (Crenshaw 1994) helps us to frame simultaneous examination of the entirety of our identities and social locations – holding and interrogating both our experiences of privilege, including white privilege, and Jewish oppression. Returning to our collaborations with young people in RTI, the 2019 cohort focused their YPAR project on antisemitism, individual and generational healing, and solidarity with other oppressed groups. In exploring experiences and impacts of antisemitism within their communities, the RTI research highlighted the "pain and trauma brought forth by antisemitism, both past and present, but [they] also wanted [their] research to uncover how Jews in Chicago have and gather resilience" (RTI Participants 2017).

As their research reflected, one way through which these young Jewish feminists thought about building resilience focused on building coalitions as an effective approach toward resisting oppression. One passage from their research report is illustrative of their commitment to solidarity and coalition building:

> For this project we talked to a lot of different people about the types of oppression that different groups face. We found that although anti-semitism is unique, it has much in common with other types of oppression. In conducting interviews about xenophobia, we talked to [an inter-faith community-based leader]. He said one thing that really stuck out: anti-semitism is "one of the fingers on the hand of xenophobia and white supremacy." This was a powerful moment of realization. We saw that anti-semitism and its victims do not stand alone
>
> (RTI Participants 2019, p. 23)

Through their research, the RTIs were able to build upon a strong foundation of feminist theorizing that emphasizes interconnectivity (Keating 2013). For instance, as Keating (2013) posits, opportunity arises from a recognition of difference while simultaneously enabling cultivation of what people hold in common. Indeed, the RTIs recognized some common features of antisemitism and xenophobia, among them fear of the "other" and targeted scapegoating. These tactics lay blame for social ills at the feet of one group as a way of deflecting institutional accountability. As the RTIs so powerfully articulated:

> There are many similarities and differences, but at the end of the day, all of our oppression is connected. We have a common interest in standing together and standing up for each other's rights. Fighting anti-semitism is fighting xenophobia is fighting racism is fighting Islamophobia. White supremacy attempts to separate us. It pits us against each other in a fight for our basic human rights. We must radically resist this separation, because the only way we can end all oppression is by fighting together. We are truly stronger when we are united
>
> (RTI Participants 2019, p. 24)

The RTIs recognize that all groups, and differently situated groups, need partners for collective resistance work. The building of diverse coalitions allows us, as white, Jewish feminists to position ourselves in solidarity, working with others in the struggle against systemic oppression and toward a more socially just society (Brown 2016; Kaba 2015, 2021). Moreover, this collective resistance work must be grounded in a commitment to working side-by-side with those most deeply impacted, because we all have vested interests in challenging and transforming systemic injustice (Russo 2019).

Conclusions and Implications for the Future

At this juncture, we continue to ask ourselves – what are our central imperatives? Our work over the years with the RTI program and the participating youth has strengthened and sustained our continued reflective practice as white Jewish feminist educators committed to an interrogation of the many axes of power, privilege, and oppression that characterize our experiences. We find ourselves committed to a continuation of a focused examination of our Jewishness, including attentiveness to experiences of antisemitism, as well as an ongoing critical interrogation of our whiteness and other axes of privilege, and how they can combine to strengthen our social justice work.

As white Jewish educators, we are mindful about being thoughtful, critical, responsible, and responsive in our work. Indeed, our partnerships with young people to create participatory action research projects has helped us see the rich potential of intergenerational relationships as a foundation for helping young people, and in particular female-identified teens, mobilize for activism. More specifically, YPAR as a methodology is centered on youth research that prompts social action. As discussed above, we saw this process in practice when the 2016–2017 RTI cohort researched rape culture and sought to bring their knowledge out into their own Jewish communities as a means of challenging rape culture and structures of gendered violence. In addition, we are attempting to support a particular orientation for this activist work, an orientation that draws on intersectional feminist framings

(Crenshaw 1994) to foreground an ability to grapple with cultures of power, and in particular cultures of power from which they very well might have benefited (Swalwell 2013; Swalwell & Spikes 2021).

We aim to partner with white Jewish feminist young people to turn the lens onto their own experiences, and their own locations of privilege and oppression, as a starting point. We draw inspiration from the work of Brown (2016) to support these young people to shape counter-narrative spaces that challenge the valorization of privilege. For instance, our role as adults is to create the conditions for conversations with young people about power, privilege, and oppression, in the interest of continuing to challenge existing structures. We are strategically mindful that a lack of attention to legacies of privilege can have significant consequences. It goes without saying that the precarity of our times makes things worse for people who are the most disenfranchised. For those in positions of relative privilege, failure to critically reflect on systems of power and privilege only serves to exacerbate the vulnerability of those who are most disadvantaged, and to reproduce and reinforce the power of those in positions of relative privilege (Russo 2019).

As Brown (2016) articulates so powerfully, "[s]tepping into the difficult work of feminist activism with girls is a complex, radical, boundary-crossing interruption of the way things usually go. It's also wildly creative and vitally necessary if we are to create the world we want and if we are to sustain that world over time" (p. 186). We are all – in these precarious times – necessarily entangled and reminded that it is more imperative than ever to remember that we cannot step back or look away. Indeed, working in partnership with young people to create the world we envision, it is critical to step up, build coalitions, and work in solidarity with those who share similar political visions and values. Through exposure and participation with differently situated individuals and communities, awareness of one's privilege and the implications for disenfranchised communities becomes that much more apparent. Along with the opportunity for deep learning across differences, bringing privileged youth into collaborative work with differently positioned young people can risk harm to marginalized peers if the privileged youth position themselves as saviors or spectators (Benjamin et al. 2021).

Mitigating this risk requires participating with different communities along the lines of shared values and commitments in social justice and social change work. It's about collaborative work, and often assuming supportive roles so that communities that have historically been on the social margins can lead the way in activism and advocacy toward structural change and collective liberation. It is imperative that as white Jewish feminist activists – youths and elders – we continuously ask ourselves, what are we accountable for, and to whom are we accountable. We can trace our accountability and next steps back to the legacy of the Talmud, a central Jewish text, which challenges us: "You are not obligated to complete the work but neither are you free to abandon it. Do not be daunted by the insurmountability of the world's grief. Do justly, now. Love mercy, now. Walk humbly, now" (Shapiro 1995).

References

Adkins, Laura E., and Emily Burback. 2021. Neo-Nazis, and Camp Auschwitz Symbols on Display at Capitol Riots. *Pittsburgh Jewish Chronicle*, January 8. https://jewish chronicle.timesofisrael.com/neo-nazis-qanon-and-camp-auschwitz-symbols-on-display-at-capitol-riots/

Associated Press (AP). 2021. Anti-Semitism Raised in Capitol Insurrection Raises Alarms. *U.S. News & World Report*, January 13. www.usnews.com/news/politics/articles/2021-01-13/anti-semitism-seen-in-capitol-insurrection-raises-alarms

Benjamin, Beth, Amira Proweller, Beth S. Catlett, Andrea Jacobs, and Sonya Crabtree-Nelson. 2021. Intersectional Feminist and Political Education With Privileged Girls. In Katy Swalwell and Daniel Spikes (eds.), *Anti-Oppressive Education in "Elite" Schools: Promising Practices and Cautionary Tales From the Field* (pp. 245–263). New York: Teachers College Press.

Brodkin, Karen. 2000. *How Jews Became White Folks and What That Says About Race in America*. Piscataway, NJ: Rutgers University Press.

Brown, Lynn M. 2016. *Powered by Girl: A Field Guide for Supporting Youth Activists*. Boston: Beacon Press.

Case, Kim A. (ed.). 2013. *Deconstructing Privilege: Teaching and Learning as Allies in the Classroom*. Abingdon, UK: Routledge.

Catlett, Beth S., and Amira Proweller. 2011. College Students' Negotiation of Privilege in a Community-Based Violence Prevention Project. *Michigan Journal of Community Service Learning* 18(1): 34–48.

Catlett, Beth S., Amira Proweller, and Sonya Crabtree-Nelson. 2019. Power and Negotiation in a University/Community Partnership Serving Jewish Teen Girls. *Journal of Community Engagement and Scholarship* 11(2): 19–30.

Crenshaw, Kimberle Williams. 1994. Mapping the Margins: Intersectionality, Identity Politics, and Violence Against Women of Color. In Martha Albertson Fineman and Roxann Mykitiuk (eds.), *The Public Nature of Private Violence: The Discovery of Domestic Abuse* (pp. 93–118). New York: Routledge. https://doi.org/10.4324/9780203060902

David, E. J. R., and Annie O. Derthick. 2017. *The Psychology of Oppression*. New York: Springer Publishing.

DiAngelo, Robin. 2018. *White Fragility: Why It's So Hard for White People to Talk About Racism*. Boston: Beacon Press.

Ellis, Carolyn, and Arthur P. Bochner. 2000. Autoethnography, Personal Narrative, Reflexivity: Researcher as Subject. In Norman K. Denzin and Yvonna S. Lincoln (eds.), *Handbook of Qualitative Research*, 2nd edition (pp. 733–768). London: SAGE.

Federal Bureau of Investigation (FBI). 2019. 2019 Hate Crime Statistics Table 1, Incidents, Offenses, Victims, and Known Offenders by Bias Motivation. *FBI, Uniform Crime Reporting, Criminal Justice Information Services Division*. https://ucr.fbi.gov/hate-crime/2019/topic-pages/tables/table-1.xls

Fine, Michelle. 2018. *Just Research in Contentious Times: Widening the Methodological Imagination*. New York: Teachers College Press.

Freire, Paulo. 2000. *Pedagogy of the Oppressed*, 30th edition. New York: Continuum International Publishing Group.

Giraldi, Ashley, and Elizabeth Monk-Turner. 2016. Perception of Rape Culture on a College Campus: A Look at Social Media Posts. *Women's Studies International Forum* 62: 116–124.

Goodman, Diane J. 2015. Oppression and Privilege: Two Sides of the Same Coin. *Journal of Interpersonal Communication* 18: 1–14.

Green, Ann E. 2001. "But You Aren't White": Racial Perceptions and Service-Learning. *Michigan Journal of Community Service Learning* 8(1): 18–26.

Greenberg, Rabbi Irving. 1988. *The Jewish Way: Living the Holidays*. New York: Summit Books.

Grenier, Robin S. 2019. A Sojourn Experience in the Land of Fire and Ice: Examining Cultural Competence and Employee Well-Being Through an Autoethnographic Exploration. In Sharon B. Merriam and Robin Grenier (eds.), *Qualitative Research in Practice: Examples for Discussion and Analysis*, 2nd edition (pp. 161–181). San Francisco: Jossey-Bass.

Hill Collins, Patricia. 1990. *Black Feminist Thought: Knowledge, Consciousness, and the Politics of Empowerment*. New York: Routledge.

Hodge, David R., and Stephanie C. Boddie. 2021. Anti-Semitism in the United States: An Overview and Strategies to Create a More Socially Just Society. *Social Work* 66(2): 128–138.

Howard, Adam. 2010. Elite Visions: Privileged Perceptions of Self and Others. *Teachers College Record* 112(8): 1971–1992.

Illinois Coalition Against Sexual Assault. 2017. *Sexual Violence Facts*. https://icasa.org/uploads/documents/Stats-and-Facts/sexual-violence-fact-sheet-2017.pdf

Johnson, Corey W., and Diana C. Parry (eds.). 2015. *Fostering Social Justice Through Qualitative Inquiry: A Methodological Guide*. Walnut Creek, CA: Left Coast Press.

Kaba, Mariame. 2015. Making Connections and Building Alliances to End Police and State Violence. Panel from DePaul University, Chicago, IL, February 11.

Kaba, Mariame. 2021. *We Do This 'Til We Free Us: Abolitionist Organizing and Transforming Justice*. Chicago: Haymarket Books.

Keating, AnaLouise. 2013. *Transformation Now!: Toward a Post-Oppositional Politics of Change*. Chicago: University of Illinois Press.

Langman, Peter F. 1995. Including Jews in Multiculturalism. *Journal of Multicultural Counseling and Development* 23(4): 222–236.

Lorde, Audre. 2007. The Master's Tools Will Never Dismantle the Master's House. In *Sister Outsider: Essays and Speeches*, revised edition (pp. 110–113). Trumansburg, NY: Crossing Press.

MacDowell, Paula. 2017. Girls' Perspectives on (Mis)representations of Girlhood in Hegemonic Media Texts. *Girlhood Studies* 10(3): 201–216.

Magnet, Shoshana. 2006. Protesting Privilege: An Autoethnographic Look at Whiteness. *Qualitative Inquiry* 12(2): 736–749. https://doi.org/10.1177/1077800406288617

Mitchell, Tania. 2008. Traditional vs. Critical Service-Learning: Engaging the Literature to Differentiate Two Models. *Michigan Journal of Community Service Learning* 14(2): 50–65.

National Women's Law Center (NWLC). 2017. *Let Her Learn: Stopping School Pushout for Girls of Color*. Washington, DC: NWLC. https://nwlc.org/wp-content/uploads/2017/04/final_nwlc_Gates_GirlsofColor.pdf

Oakes, Jeannie. 2005. *Keeping Track: How Schools Structure Inequality*, 2nd edition. New Haven, CT: Yale University Press.

Okun, Tema. 2010. *The Emperor Has No Clothes: Teaching About Race and Racism to People Who Don't Want to Know*. Charlotte, NC: Information Age Publishing, Inc.

Proweller, Amira, Beth Catlett, and Sonya Crabtree-Nelson. 2021. Feminist Activism and YPAR: Privileged Girls Interrupt Rape Culture. *Violence Against Women* 27(15–16): 3157–3175.

Proweller, Amira, Beth Cooper-Benjamin, Beth Catlett, Sonya Crabtree-Nelson, and Andrea Jacobs. 2017. White Feminists Not White Feminism: Political and

Psychological Resistance in Intersectional Education with Privileged Girls. Paper presented at the American Educational Research Association annual conference, San Antonio, Texas, April 27–May 1.

Richie, Beth E. 2012. *Arrested Justice: Black Women, Violence, and America's Prison Nation*. New York: New York University Press.

RTI Participants. 2017. *The Revenge of Dinah: A Feminist Seder on Rape Culture in the Jewish Community*, Research Training Internship (RTI) Report, May.

RTI Participants. 2019. *We the People*, Research Training Internship (RTI) Report, May.

RTI Participants. 2020. *#TogetherAgainstAntisemitism – An Exploration of Anti-Semitism in the 21st Century*, Research Training Internship (RTI) Report, May.

Rubin, Daniel I. 2017. Whiter Shade of Pale: Making the Case for Jewish Presence in the Multicultural Classroom. *International Journal of Multicultural Education* 19(2): 131–146. https://doi.org/10.18251/ijme.v19i2.1415

Russo, Ann. 2019. *Feminist Accountability: Disrupting Violence and Transforming Power*. New York: New York University Press.

Shapiro, Rabbi Rami M. 1995. *Wisdom of the Jewish Sages: A Modern Reading of Pirke Avot*. New York: Bell Tower.

Singer, Miriam J. 2008. A Hidden Minority Among White Privilege. *Multicultural Perspectives* 10(1): 47–51.

Smith, Sharon G., Jieru Chen, Kathleen C. Basile, Leah K. Gilbert, Melissa T. Merrick, Nimesh Patel, Margie Walling, and Anurag Jain. 2017. The National Intimate Partner and Sexual Violence Survey (NISVS): 2010–2012 State Report. Atlanta, GA: National Center for Injury Prevention and Control, Centers for Disease Control and Prevention.

Stoudt, Brett G. 2009. The Role of Language & Discourse in the Investigation of Privilege: Using Participatory Action Research to Discuss Theory, Develop Methodology, & Interrupt Power. *Urban Review* 41(7): 7–28.

Stoudt, Brett G., Madeline Fox, and Michelle Fine. 2012. Contesting Privilege with Critical Participatory Action Research. *Journal of Social Issues* 68(1): 178–193. https://doi.org/10.1111/j.1540-4560.2011.01743.x.

Swalwell, Katy M. 2013. *Educating Activist Allies: Social Justice Pedagogy With the Suburban and Urban Elite*. New York: Routledge.

Swalwell, Katy M., and Daniel Spikes (eds.). 2021. *Anti-Oppressive Education in "Elite" Schools*. New York: Teachers College Press.

Wise, Tim, and Kim A. Case. 2013. Pedagogy for the Privileged: Addressing Inequality and Injustice Without Shame or Blame. In Kim Case (ed.), *Deconstructing Privilege: Teaching and Learning as Allies in the Classroom* (pp. 17–33). New York: Routledge.

Part II
Educational Practice in Precarious Spaces

6 Shifting Fields

Japanese University Students' Habitus During the COVID-19 Pandemic

Richard H. Derrah, Phillip M. Clark & Kevin Ballou

Introduction

On January 15, 2020, the first case of COVID-19 was reported in Japan. The virus had begun its spread around the world in what was to be the most sweeping global pandemic in living memory. By the end of that month, Prime Minister Shinzo Abe convened an "Anti-Coronavirus Task Force," a body of policymakers meant to navigate the country through this unprecedented threat.

By January 31, 17 cases had been registered nationwide, though the rapid deterioration of social normalcy evidenced in Wuhan and other parts of the world indicated that without careful governance the infection might wreak disaster in a country that was, at the time, still scheduled to host tens of thousands of international visitors to the Tokyo 2020 Olympic Games. By the end of February, the government issued a blanket recommendation for the whole country to temporarily close elementary and secondary schools – a recommendation that was swiftly followed. Within days, the Summer Olympic Games were officially postponed.

On April 7, after a month of steadily rising infection rates, the prime minister declared a *hijou jitai* 非常事態 or "state of emergency" for six prefectures, which was announced to last one month. By April 16, the status was extended to all of Japan, and indefinitely. In principle, this meant very little in the way of lawmaking or the type of official lockdowns occurring elsewhere in the world – no binding legal restrictions were enacted. In practice, many businesses either shuttered their doors or began abbreviating business hours. University officials across the country, where the school year traditionally begins in April, were faced with the decision of how to proceed.

The governing body that oversees education in Japan is the Ministry of Education, Culture, Sports, Science, and Technology (MEXT). Strategies to combat the virus included MEXT distribution of cloth masks to schools, cancelling or postponing student field trips, and offering financial assistance at all education levels for students whose families faced sudden financial difficulties (MEXT 2020a). The ministry began compiling statistics on infections, focusing mostly on primary and secondary education (MEXT 2020b).

DOI: 10.4324/9781003258223-8

Though MEXT posted bulletins regarding online instruction, there were no recommendations to close universities. University officials were left to make decisions on their own.

Within this context, we place the current chapter. Here, we focus not on the choices of administrators, but how these choices affected Japanese university students, for whom, in April 2020, classes became wholly online environments. We describe the reported experiences of students, and how COVID-19 changed classroom spaces, instruction, and learning. We found that the majority of our participants felt keenly the absence of the expected social and academic interactions, though not without hope. By focusing with a "Bourdieusian" lens, we attempt to make sense of participant perspectives in a way accessible to those both familiar and unfamiliar with Japan.

In this chapter, we describe the response of one public and two private universities to the COVID-19 pandemic, including the ways that administrative decisions have affected student perspectives. In the following sections, we describe our conceptual framework based upon the ideas of sociologist Pierre Bourdieu, describe our methodology using Symbolic Interactionism, and introduce the setting and participants. In the section on findings, we excerpt participant voices from the data, and finally discuss the results, providing our conclusions.

Bourdieu's "Thinking Tools"

In this chapter, we call on Pierre Bourdieu's work on social reproduction, in particular invoking his primary "thinking tools" of *capital, field*, and *habitus* to provide a view of students' lived experiences. Each of these three concepts interacts with the others, and an understanding of all three is necessary for this interaction to be evident. While entire volumes have been written (by Bourdieu and others) on these concepts, for the purpose of clarifying how we have approached the data, we will here offer a somewhat simplified summary of the terms.

The most familiar of Bourdieu's concepts is *capital* (Bourdieu 1986), which can take various forms: *economic, social*, and *cultural*, as well as a fourth, meta-category – *symbolic capital* (Bourdieu 1990). Capital itself is currency, which may be particularly clear in the concept of *economic capital*. Economic capital in its simplest iteration consists of financial resources or assets that can be "immediately and directly convertible into money and may be institutionalized in the form of property rights" (Bourdieu 1986, p. 242). For our purposes, economic capital could be evident in the financial wherewithal of students (or their parents) to, for example, pay for tuition or class fees, rent, or food; to purchase regular Wi-Fi access; or indeed to own or have continual, unfettered access to a computer or other device of sufficient capability to access online courses.

Bourdieu's conception of *social capital* is, most simply, whom one knows. It has been defined as "a network of social connections which can be mobilized for particular purposes" (Nash 1999, p. 432). Social capital can and does provide (or hinder) access – to, for example, career opportunities in the form of acquaintance with recruiters, interviewers, or those in a position of power within the company to which a candidate might apply. Contact with peer groups, and, within these groups, the interactions of junior with senior students (*kōhai* and *senpai*¹), or even regular interactions with professors or advisors fall under social capital.

Bourdieu's conception of *cultural capital* has three forms: *embodied*, or internal, part of one's dispositions or *habitus*; *objectified*, in the form of things such as books or art; and *institutionalized*, or consecrated qualifications, such as an academic degree. Cultural capital can be conceptualized as an acknowledged level of competence, talent, or mastery of a consecrated or valorized ability – in certain contexts within Japan, for example, cultural capital could be accessed via fluency on the part of a native Japanese speaker in a foreign language (depending on that language's perceived prestige), or a relatively high score on the Test of English as a Foreign Language (TOEFL), or even a position on a distinguished sports team.

Symbolic capital overarches and informs the other types of capital, for symbolic capital is capital that has value only in as much as it is perceived or recognized to have value (Bourdieu 1986). Consider how, for example, an ability to sing well popular songs in karaoke may be considered a type of cultural capital but is an ability only valuable in certain situations. The skill may require work, time, and talent to develop, but it may only be recognized as worthy of praise within certain contexts, or *fields*.

Field, or *le champ*, can be conceptualized as field of play, an area of struggle for position and dominance. Bourdieu defined field as "the relations of force that obtain between social positions which guarantee their occupants a quantum of social force, or of capital, such that they are able to enter into the struggles over the monopoly of power, of which struggles over the definition of the legitimate form of power are a crucial dimension" (Bourdieu & Wacquant 1992, p. 230). The larger social field, the so-called *field of power*, would represent a society as a whole. There are, however, of course many subfields within any larger field, each of which comprises "an autonomous universe, a kind of arena in which people play a game which has certain rules, rules which are different from those of the game that is played in the adjacent space" (Bourdieu 1991, p. 215). In the context of this study, one can conceptualize the field of Japanese education, and, within this, the field of higher education, of private school education, of a particular school, of a certain department within the school, of first-year students within that department, of a major, even of a classroom. These fields would have their own sets of rules and expectations for the behavior of each person within them.

Finally, *habitus* is both a process and state, a "system of acquired dispositions" (Bourdieu 1990, p. 10) that one adopts (typically outside of conscious awareness) within a particular field. The habitus of a Japanese university student might consist, for example, of certain typical fashions, particular part-time jobs that would be considered commonplace or appropriate (café staff, cram school tutor), a limited variety of hairstyles or hair colors, or limited types of lunch (a bento box from home or a convenience store) shared with peers between lessons.

Bourdieu's concepts provide a framework for readers, both those familiar and unfamiliar with Japan, to access and perhaps more closely understand the fields of and within the Japanese universities that we consider, as well as the varied responses of those involved. To view student experiences in this light can move us toward understanding what is lost when such fields diminish in scope or size (e.g., a university classroom containing other students has an essential social aspect, which is dramatically altered when that same classroom becomes a video conference). In the following section, we briefly detail our methods and methodology.

Symbolic Interactionism

While numerous studies have used symbolic interactionism as a conceptual framework, in this chapter, we use symbolic interactionism as our methodology. We see this methodology as focusing on the meanings the participants develop through social interactions (Blumer 1969).

In symbolic interactionism, one posits that the real world exists but can only be known by studying the perspectives of people within that world. This stance coalesces with the objectives of our study as we seek to understand how our participants understand the Japanese university experience.

Symbolic interactionist methods are twofold and include *exploration* and *inspection*. In our study, *exploration* consisted of the data collection methods used including participant observations, informal conversations, responses, and other writings (Emerson, Fretz, & Shaw 1995). For the second step, *inspection*, we used two cycles of coding. The first cycle of coding identified data aligned with Bourdieu's thinking tools, excerpted via *in vivo* codes (direct quotations of participants).[2] In our second cycle of coding, or the coding of codes, we looked for connections that might explain the relationships between elements within the data (Hatch 2002).

Setting: Contexts and Participants

Our participants comprise both male and female students from one public and two private universities in western Japan. Japan's public universities are considered more prestigious, though there are a handful of private universities also considered top-tier (Ishikawa 2009, p. 168). We shall refer to the schools in this study as Gengetsu University (GU), Mikan University (MU), and Kansai State University (KSU).[3]

Gengetsu University is a large private university in Japan, ranked among the top private schools in the region. Data for this study were collected from 46 second-year students recruited from two classes in the Global Studies Department (GSD), one of the most competitive programs in the university.

The second university, Mikan University, is a private regional university with campuses spanning several prefectures. The 31 students in this study from MU represent four classes from the sociology department.

Finally, Kansai State University is a mid-sized public university with campuses in and around a large Japanese city. Data from KSU were drawn from 71 participants among three classes studying in healthcare-related courses.

The academic year in Japanese universities runs from April to March, with the first term from April to August and the second term from September. Gengetsu University's Global Studies Department began its spring 2020 term on schedule (although other university departments delayed their term for two weeks), but all courses were carried out online. Data collected from GU include student weekly blog entries and student reflective essays. The blog entries were open to any topic, while the reflective essays were on the topic of life during the COVID-19 pandemic. These were assigned in the last month of the spring term. All data from GU come from material both assigned and completed in English.

Mikan University was originally scheduled to start school in the first week of April, but was delayed until April 20, then again to May 7, ultimately beginning a month late. The sociology faculty, from which our participants were drawn, required some element of synchronous instruction conducted via Zoom as well as the hosting of all assignments on Google Classroom. Data collected from MU include questionnaire responses, student personal reflections on the COVID crisis, and researcher field notes. Researcher field notes were taken in English while other data collection was conducted in English or Japanese depending upon the primary language of instruction within the class.

Kansai State University also started later than scheduled and required teachers to post assignments on the university's online learning management system. KSU started May 7 and also conducted only 13 weeks of classes. Data collected include student open-ended responses to a questionnaire. All of the data collected at KSU were in English.

Quotations are almost entirely unedited to keep the natural idiom of the participants, though for clarity, in some cases grammar has been naturalized. Japanese responses were translated into English by the authors, and in cases of doubt, they were double-checked by native Japanese speakers of English.

Findings

In considering the data – and, before this, in forming questions for students to answer about the COVID-19 situation – we made efforts to avoid assumptions that all of the responses would be negative and wrought with angst.

While it would be easy to simply comb through responses for any negative reactions and hold these up as exemplars, there was no universal student experience or unanimous student viewpoint.

Opting Out

One reaction to the new online instruction came from students who selected to "opt out," at least temporarily, from university. This option included both formal declarations and informal action. In Japan, students have an option to take a temporary leave of absence (*kyūgaku* 休学), which is a relatively simple process. The student requests a conference with their faculty advisor and the appropriate paperwork is filed. In the MU department relevant to this chapter, the number of students taking a leave of absence in 2020 increased by 60%. In the Global Studies Department of GU, the number of students taking a leave of absence in spring 2020 more than doubled the number from spring 2019. Other students used the informal opt-out method, which is when students simply stop attending classes. One researcher at MU reported that with the onset of the pandemic, the number of students who stopped attending was more than double the usual number in just the first half of the academic year.

A more limited method of "opting out" includes students reducing how they interact within the online environment. At MU, students were requested to turn on their cameras when taking part in live online classes. However, for what the faculty considered personal, privacy, and economic concerns, teachers were asked not to make active cameras a requirement – resulting in some virtual classrooms consisting partially or entirely of small black squares with either ID numbers or names of hidden students. In many instances, the number of students who turned on their cameras gradually decreased over the course of the semester. At GU's Global Studies Department, the majority of students took classes in the "on-demand" fashion; however, for teachers who opted to teach live online lessons, no official policy regarding students' use of cameras was implemented. Once the process of all students keeping their cameras on became the norm, only in exceptional circumstances (e.g., technical issues) did students keep their cameras off. The official GSD policy on class attendance for the semester was that there should be no record kept of attendance at all. In contrast, MU required teachers to provide "make-up work" that students could complete at their own pace if the student reported an absence that was linked to an online issue such as poor Wi-Fi, or other computer problems. Opting out was facilitated by university policy, and students availed themselves of this in various forms in numbers far larger than was seen before the pandemic. Still, most students did participate, although they found that the university experience to which they may have expected to return (or which they hoped to begin) was markedly transformed. In the next section, we describe the reported student experiences.

"I Didn't Expect Such a Campus Life Would Be Waiting for Me"

For those students who did attempt to fully participate in the online learning environment, many were surprised at the university life that awaited them. Some first-year students wrote in blogs that their time "at" university was unlike what they had expected. "I often imagined my wonderful university life with new friends before this coronavirus spread," wrote one freshman, two months after classes had begun. "But I've never seen my classmates nor teachers."

Some students reported an increased time requirement to complete assignments. For some lecture-based classes, faculty recorded lectures and posted these videos online for students. One European exchange student receiving some instruction in Japanese stated that due to poor sound and video quality and without the opportunity to ask questions, she often had to listen to video lectures two or three times, a considerably longer time duration than the usual 90 minutes. Other students, as the semester progressed, remarked on how the unstructured time of on-demand classes produced an unwieldy amount of work. "I should have a lot of time," wrote one student, "but, there are too many tasks, and I cannot control them at all."

Japanese university lecture classes often adopt a format whereby students listen to a lecture, then write handwritten reports in response, culminating in a final examination. In typical practice, these reports are limited to a few per semester; however for spring 2020, many professors asked for reports to be submitted every week, perhaps as a way of "making up" for the missed time of face-to-face meetings. One student wrote of this: "I suppose (teachers are) not aware that when they decided to (collect) responses just to make sure if the students are actually taking the classes via weekly reports, THE OTHER TEACHERS ARE DOING IT THE SAME WAY so the wave of works are coming one after another and the worse thing is they all are due simultaneously" (emphasis in original).

Within the live online Zoom classes also, students had difficulties. "It's hard to answer," wrote one, "I don't know anybody here." A method used by some teachers to create a less intimidating, more intimate environment of small-group or pair-work involved the use of so-called "break-out rooms," a function of the Zoom application which allows a temporary separation of participants into smaller video chats. Instructor monitoring of these break-out rooms, however, was not as easy as monitoring traditional classroom interactions, and students often either spoke of topics unrelated to lessons or simply sat silently. One student reflected bitterly: "I especially hate the break-out room. It usually has a long silent time where nobody talks." Students quickly began to realize that interacting with their classmates and teachers, and attending classes at all, had taken on a new form.

Not Being There: Participating and Attending

In virtual classrooms, students sat quietly, non-talking heads in Zoom video conferences who appeared onscreen at designated class times, each student with an active camera framed within the tiny resizable square that was visible to others in the same session. There were no university chimes to signal transitions, no crowded hallways of other students milling their way to other classes. In the new "live" online lessons, a student's personal living quarters might be visible in the background – a poster of a boyband, an unkempt family shelf of magazines, and the typical flotsam of domestic life. Zoom, however, is a mobile as well as desktop application, and because of this, many students attended online classes via tablets or mobile phones. On rare occasions, one might notice in the background not a home or apartment but the ambient movements of the interior of a coffee shop, or the bustle of the student's part-time job. Zoom offered students, if not teachers, a freedom and easy mobility, a new way of being "present" for a class.

In one account from our field notes, we recorded a student attending class from one of Japan's many bullet trains – traveling, he said, to meet friends, as there were, after all, no strict legal lockdown measures in Japan that prohibited movement. In another instance, a student was visible secured into a seatbelt, the shadows of moving trees passing over her face as she attended an afternoon lesson while in transit. Other students walked down home hallways, or spoke asides to unseen companions with their voices unheard, courtesy of the Zoom self-mute function. Sometimes, ambient sounds and voices could be heard. One student attended every live online class from a local Komeda Coffee, a national chain that claims to provide a "neighborhood living room" (Komeda n.d.) for patrons. The draw to be out of the house and simply around people often seemed more powerful than concern over the distractions of a noisy coffee shop.

Administrators began to report to our email listservs numerous complaints, from both teachers and students, about the frustrations and limitations of the online environment, asking for opinions or possible solutions. Discussions began about where privacy began and common academic courtesy ended, often resulting in entreaties to both sides to simply "try to manage" (author field notes of email communication, 2020).

What followed echoed situations around the world. In Japanese media, the term *remohara* or "remote harassment" was coined to describe situations where online tele-workers or students felt diminished or threatened, often in cases where bosses, teachers, or classmates commented on their personal spaces at their homes (*Daigaku de toraburu* 2020). Some students who decided to keep their cameras on activated the "virtual background" function in Zoom, where they could choose from a number of digital images to fill in the space around them and leave their personal lives relatively unseen, whether stationary or mobile, at home or at a local café. In some cases, new contexts created new rules – in one university department, the administrators asked teachers not to require students to activate their cameras. Other departments urged the opposite, asking teachers of English oral communication to make sure student cameras were on, so that articulation could be monitored in pronunciation checks. In all cases, however, the virtual classroom created a context where students could suddenly attend classes while physically occupying a space nearly anywhere they wished. This inspired varying responses, as we will see in the next section.

"Staying Home Is Just Comfortable"

Perhaps inevitably, some students began to report that as the months progressed, they became accustomed to not attending physical classes. In some cases, what were once punishing commutes simply ended. "A good point," one student wrote, "is that I do not have to go to the campus. I go to the campus taking one hour forty-five minutes, so I get tired by this." By June, another student reflected: "Online classes are convenient. I don't have to commute to the university so I can get up late and I can even take classes on the bed." For others, living near campus with the anticipated benefits associated with school proximity resulted in disappointment: "I'm living by myself near (the) university, so I sometimes feel lonely."

Some students reported that the limitation to online classes allowed them to have time to develop interests outside school. Some found new hobbies, some spent more time on established hobbies. One wrote: "I find I can spend time more freely than ever. When I have no classes and assignments, I can learn for myself and can do some my hobbies. I miss my school, and at the same time, I love this online class semester. It is weird." Students reflected on how they used their time: "It is a good opportunity for me to reconsider my lifestyle and the things that I should do."

Among other silver linings mentioned by students was a rediscovery of "family time."

"After entering university," wrote one second-year student, contrasting the 2020 spring term with her freshman year, "I spent less time with my family and did not have enough time eating together. However, during quarantine, I had every single meal together with them." Another wrote, "The online classes contribute to the fact that a family can lunch all together."

Such resigned yet hopeful responses indicated a certain resilience in students that was reassuring. Yet, this new attitude of exploring personal interests and appreciating the safe harbor of home stood in contrast to other realizations, where students seemed to feel the vacuum left by an absence of a normal, outside-the-home social life.

"I Miss My Friends"

The move to a virtual environment was perhaps hardest on first-year students who were denied many of the opportunities usually afforded those entering university. One freshman lamented, "what was difficult about not being able to go to the campus? I don't know, because I have never been to the campus not even once." Many students commented on the inability to make friends: "My stress is not being able to make friends, so I feel alone even when I take the classes with classmates. I cannot enjoy the classes totally, I often get tense when the classes get started. Therefore, I want to go to (university) and want teachers to start face-to-face learning." Some even projected these feelings of loneliness and fear as haunting them beyond the end of the pandemic. "I'm afraid that in online classes my first impression is judged only by what's on the screen. I think about the disappointment my classmates might feel when we actually meet."

For older students with established friendships, separation impacted their social and academic lives. "GSD students have lots of assignments constantly. I often do them at campus with my friends while chatting. It helps me feel as if time goes fast. However, I do my assignments in my room alone on this semester. It isn't easy to stay focused on my works." Separation permeated students' daily routines. "I have been at home since the quarantine period. I didn't go anywhere nor met my friends. Then my lifestyle broke down. I always eat and sleep and eat and sleep again. Also, I cannot study without a quiet place, so I cannot start studying while my family is awake. Always I start studying after my family sleeps, so I start it at almost midnight. I am completely reversed day and night."

Separation from friends and the lost opportunities to make new ones affected students in multiple ways. Yet, it was more than a sense of loneliness: It was a loss of access to the experiences and advice of other students, which is fundamental to a successful Japanese university experience. At MU, students select one seminar class a term and a single seminar for their last two years of university. That seminar teacher is responsible for counseling the students, their graduation papers, job hunting, and numerous other vital aspects of the student's university life. The choice of a seminar teacher is not taken lightly, and the lack of advice regarding teachers – which ones are easy to talk to, helpful with graduation reports, or know how to navigate a job interview for a particular company – is detrimental to students. Separation has had a serious impact on students and affected them in ways they may not have imagined, from issues influencing future employment to a simple sense of happiness. As one student noted "I miss the ducks swimming in the lake of Kansai State University campus. I always saw them when I used the lake side road, and felt happy."

"I Don't Have Enough Money"

The economic impact of pandemic countermeasures filtered down in unexpected ways. One student wrote: "I didn't have a part-time job from March to July. I work at a restaurant. The restaurant is near [a] theater, so it is difficult to open without the shows. The [theater] decided to cancel the shows from March, so I didn't have a job since then." While part-time work opportunities declined, some students decided not to work at all, in order to avoid going out in public and risking exposure to the virus. Wrote another student: "Working at a family restaurant and a cram school was my job, but I stopped working at a family restaurant. That is because there is a risk of coronavirus infection. In addition, it takes an hour to go to the restaurant by train. Using a packed train also increases the risk of coronavirus. After that, my income decreased, but it did not influence my life so much because my expenses were not big compared with last semester."

Staying home seemed to limit the need for many things. "I like shopping," reflected one student, "and I always bought too much, using an excuse which I have many chances to go out before. However, I do not have to go out and I no longer need many things such as clothes and cosmetics. Therefore, I reduce my possessions and decided to live as a minimalist. Then I could purge my junk drawers and closets." Others saw expected savings diverted to offset the monotony of home life during the pandemic. "I thought I could save money, but I couldn't, because I couldn't work as much as before. I spent more than 30,000 yen a month before, but I spent much less than that in this semester buying clothes, cosmetics, and food, but I bought things for my life in this semester, such as books, or projector, or movies."

Beyond personal expenses, students with less financial support from family or other outside sources were concerned about their ability to stay in school. "I think the Japanese government should support students," wrote one student. "According to recent news, one in thirteen students are thinking of leaving their university because they can't do part-time job." Criticism was also directed at universities, viewed by many as providing a diminished experience with no reduction in tuition or fees. "The tuition fee is not changed. Many classes are shorter than before, but I should pay the same tuition." Mikan University, concerned about forcing students to spend prolonged periods in front of a computer daily, gave teachers the option to cut class time from the usual 90 minutes down to 60 minutes or less, as long as the teacher provided additional readings or other work.

"Some Freshmen Are Willing to Join Our Club, but I Haven't Met Them Yet"

An integral aspect of university for many Japanese students is *bukatsudō* 部活動, or involvement in club and circle activities. The different character of such activities from their equivalents in other countries has been discussed by various researchers (Cave 2004; Kelly 1993). University club members are subjected to the rigors of social hierarchy that are common in the working world of Japan, to the point that they are often sought out first in the job-hunting season of a student's third year (Kelly 1993, p. 182). As Cave (2004) writes:

> The vital contribution of *bukatsudō* to the creation of order comes about through combining an appeal to individual enthusiasm and agency, opportunities for intense relationships, and demands for disciplined commitment. Here also we find the continued development of a sense of self as forged in relationship with others, as well as through individual choice and sustained effort.
>
> (p. 384)

While Cave's research focused on secondary education, we suggest that club activities are equally as important, if not more so, at the university level. First-year Japanese students will join clubs in the first weeks of school as a way to make friends and adhere to a peer group. These social groups will hold functions and rent out bars to welcome new members, in what are sometimes alcohol-soaked events that serve, in part, to develop a camaraderie in drinking that will become valuable in later life (McDonald & Sylvester 2013; Partanen 2006). Students drinking alcohol socially is not unusual in Japan (Osaki et al. 2003, Suzuki et al. 2003), although the legal age of majority is 20. Alcoholic beverages such as beer and saké are available for purchase in some areas in vending machines, and checking identification in bars and clubs is virtually nonexistent.

For first-year students in the spring of 2020, the possibility of such social interactions vanished. As one second-year student wrote: "We cannot invite freshmen to our club this year because of the pandemic, so the number of the freshmen of my club is smaller than in usual years. . . . I want to go [out] with our club members and enjoy my university life when we can spend a normal life."

The lack of club and circle activities impacted third- and fourth-year students as well, as this was their time, as *senpai*, to lead. "I am the captain of the futsal club this term," wrote one student, "so it is very unfortunate that I cannot do club activities." Even when clubs did meet, they were altered to suit the requirements of maintaining social distance. "I'm a member of rugby club," wrote one athlete. "We started rugby practice July 16, but we must not tackle during practice. I can't say this is rugby. I'm looking forward to doing real rugby." This sentiment was echoed repeatedly in student writing. One volleyball circle member complained: "After the virus began to spread, we cannot use the gym and the government told us we shouldn't go to other prefectures. I can't not only play volleyball, but also, can't see my friends."

Other students were more sanguine about the sudden cessation of club meetings.

"Club activities are just a part of merely something to do. I found another exciting hobby, and I do not feel disappointment," wrote one. Another girl wrote of how her "travel circle" made the most of the online environment, organizing "virtual tours" whereby participants conducted online tours of other countries for two hours each week. Activities included virtual sightseeing, online meetings, virtual trips to cities and museums, online cooking, and even a virtual pub crawl. As one student buoyantly noted: "If you can't change your environment, [the] only thing you can do is change yourself."

Discussion: Shifting Fields, Insecure Capital, Altered Habitus

The COVID-19 pandemic markedly altered the field of Japanese university education. In Japan, as in many countries, the doxa persists that a university degree is an important cultural capital for "joining society," a term which in English may seem idiosyncratic but in Japan is called *shakai sanka* 社会参加, literally "social participation" (Clark 2017, p. 38).[4] This may seem unremarkable in the sense that students in higher education all over the world may imagine that a university degree may provide them entrée into certain employment that may otherwise be unattainable. In Japan, however, the academic side of university is almost peripheral to the institution's wider purpose, which involves not only acquisition of cultural capital in the form of a diploma but the move away from the strict confines of high school life and a freedom to develop personally. University is a time for students to internalize a way of interacting with the world, or a particular *habitus*. The relevant habitus in this case includes not simply language socialization but the proper disposition one must attain (subconsciously, via repeated interaction) to simply deal, seamlessly, *with other Japanese*, in the hierarchical manner that is so ingrained in the expected "next step" of life: the field of the business world of larger Japanese society, both professionally and socially (Cook 2018; Ishida 1993; Wetzel 2004). With online instruction and effective isolation from both other students and instructors, opportunities to internalize this habitus have altered considerably.

Tertiary education in Japan – or, more precisely, the experience of attending university in Japan – is also seen as a time of networking and socialization into the world of working with others and the development of social capital acquired through interactions with classmates (both *senpai* and *kōhai*), seminar professors, and participation in clubs and circles (Anderson 2019; Takada 2017). As Kelly (1993) has suggested: "Seminar students establish ties with their professors and form a kind of *habatsu* 派閥 [clique] which will later, upon graduation, provide them with personal introductions to employers" (p. 176). Our data suggest that the influence of COVID-19 has upset these processes in unprecedented ways, the ramifications of which are as yet unclear.

Student responses to the new environment were, not unexpectedly, varied. There was not a consistent, monolithic sensibility evident from the data. Nevertheless, certain themes became apparent. Positive responses included reflections that, with quarantine, came welcome changes in habitus such as more regular family time, eating meals together, and a more robust communication with parents and siblings that would otherwise be absent in the bustle of school. Students also claimed a freedom to pursue personal hobbies, and to manage their time in ways more convenient to their sensibilities (e.g., waking up later and doing schoolwork at their own pace).

Students did not shirk, however, from noting the considerable negative aspects of the pandemic. "I can't go to college to make friends" and "I feel alone when I take classes" were plaintive statements representative of a majority of the responses. Opportunities to accumulate the social capital typical of university were obstructed or delayed indefinitely. Fundamental activities as simple as enjoying a friendly conversation before class with a classmate simply evaporated. Students who normally might spend their days participating in *bukatsu* 部活 [extracurricular activities] found themselves instead playing guitar alone in their homes, or practicing yoga on their verandah. These activities, of course, may lead students down new pathways of personal development, and alone-time, as reflected in participant comments, were not always viewed as negative. Some new realities, however, resisted even the most optimistic outlook: First-year students who had imagined the first semester of college as a time to meet their future friends for life found themselves staring at a computer monitor of unfamiliar faces, faces which blipped in and just as quickly out, with whom the only interaction was what the teacher might have decided for the lesson.

Personal economic capital for students also in some cases dramatically decreased, especially for students working part-time jobs in restaurants and cafés, which, in the spring of 2020, either closed or drastically reduced hours – this in a country where university undergraduates have been reported to have more spending money than any other segment of the population (Kelly 1993). In April 2020, the Japanese government distributed to those who applied an "emergency supplemental income" (labeled, in English, by the Japanese public broadcaster NHK as a "100,000 yen handout") to all citizens (Yamamoto 2020), but even this was met with skepticism by some students: "Personally, I am happy because I can receive money from the government without working, (but) I think the government should pay out the money for persons who are really suffering from the bad situation." Students responded similarly to the government's distribution of two cloth masks per household, which were delivered over several months: "(the government) distributed meaningless mask and they are slow in judgement. And they do not take care of people who lost their jobs." Some students reflected that although they were not making as much money, so, too, were they not spending as much money, as they simply stayed home. One student wrote that because she so often stayed home that "I don't have to pay much attention to my clothes or makeup [anymore]." While some students expressed fear of going out among the public to work, others claimed contentedly that they would save all their money now for future travel, in the hope that, sooner rather than later, the world would again be open to them.

Conclusion

The forms of capital available from attending and graduating university continue to shift under the strain of the measures taken by higher education to stave off the COVID-19 pandemic, which, at the time of the writing of this chapter, has not abated. While many university administrators decided that schools would finish the 2020 academic year entirely online, other institutions adopted hybrid face-to-face/online lessons, with a percentage of students in classrooms, and others viewing lessons remotely. Other universities kept all instruction in an "on demand" basis, where students potentially never interacted directly with either their instructors or their classmates.

Meanwhile, in the wider field of Japanese society, businesses that had once inspired students to increase their foreign language ability, drastically reduced hiring – hospitality industries fell stagnant, companies temporarily furloughed large numbers of staff, and some airlines announced that they would halt all hiring for 2021, and reduce hiring by 90% for 2022 (Kyodo 2021). In January 2021, after one year and three waves of infection, Japan had a new prime minister, Yoshihide Suga, who declared a new *hijou jitai*. These dramatic, unexpected changes in the larger fields of Japan and Japanese society have altered nearly every aspect of life, from work, to socializing, to entertainment. So, too, the habitus of the "typical university student" in the field of the university has changed in similar ways, the effects of which are yet unknown.

Notes

1. See Qie et al. (2019) for a discussion of the *kōhai*/*senpai* relationship.
2. For a more complete discussion of coding types, see Saldaña (2009).
3. All university and program names are pseudonyms.
4. It is not our assertion that only those of university age who attend university must navigate the various cultural requirements for "joining society." For a discussion of *shakai sanka* among Japanese who do not enter higher education, see Roberson (1995).

References

Anderson, Fred E. 2019. Nails That Still Don't Stick Up: Revisiting the Enigma of the Japanese College Classroom. In Paul Wadden and Chris C. Hale (eds.), *Teaching English at Japanese Universities* (pp. 125–136). London: Routledge.

Blumer, Herbert. 1969. *Symbolic Interactionism: Perspective and Method*. Berkeley: University of California Press.

Bourdieu, Pierre. 1986. The Forms of Capital. In John Richardson (ed.), *Handbook of Theory and Research* (pp. 241–258). New York: Greenwood.

Bourdieu, Pierre. 1990. *The Logic of Practice*. Cambridge: Polity Press.

Bourdieu, Pierre. 1991. *Language and Symbolic Power*. Cambridge: Harvard University Press.

Bourdieu, Pierre, and Loïc Wacquant. 1992. *An Invitation to Reflexive Sociology*. Cambridge: Polity Press.

Cave, Peter. 2004. Bukatsudō: The Educational Role of Japanese Clubs. *The Journal of Japanese Studies* 30(2): 383–415.

Clark, Phillip M. 2017. The Place That Was Promised: Japanese Returnees at a Foreign Language University in Japan. Ed.D. Dissertation, Temple University Japan.

Cook, Haruko M. 2018. Socialization to Acting, Feeling, and Thinking as Shakaijin: New Employee Orientations in a Japanese Company. In Haruko Cook and Janet Shibamoto-Smith (eds.), *Japanese at Work: Communicating in Professions and Organizations* (pp. 37–64). London: Palgrave Macmillan.

Daigaku enkaku jugyō de toraburu [Trouble in University Classes' Distance Learning]. 2020. *Nihon Keizai Shimbun*, September 11. www.nikkei.com/article/DGKKZO6368 1870Q0A910C2KNTP00/.

Emerson, Robert M., Rachel I. Fretz, and Linda L. Shaw. 1995. *Writing Ethnographic Fieldnotes*. Chicago, IL: The University of Chicago Press.

Hatch, J. Amos. (2002). *Doing Qualitative Research in Education Settings*. Albany, NY: State University of New York Press.

Ishida, Hiroshi. 1993. *Social Mobility in Contemporary Japan*. London: Palgrave Macmillan.

Ishikawa, Mayumi. 2009. University Rankings, Global Models, and Emerging Hegemony: Critical Analysis from Japan. *Journal of Studies in International Education* 13(2): 159–173.

Kelly, Curtis. 1993. The Hidden Role of the University. In Paul Wadden (ed.), *A Handbook for Teaching English at Japanese Colleges and Universities* (pp. 172–192). Oxford: Oxford University Press.

Komeda Coffee. n.d. *Our Commitment to Your Relaxation*. Accessed March 28, 2021. www.komeda.co.jp

Kyodo News. 2021. *Japan Airlines to Slash 2022 Hiring of New Graduates by 90% Amid Pandemic*. February 25. Accessed March 1, 2021. https://english.kyodonews.net/news/2021/02/cdc154a627e3-jal-to-slash-hiring-of-new-graduates-by-90-in-2022-amid-pandemic.html

McDonald, Brent, and Kate Sylvester. 2013. Learning to Get Drunk: The Importance of Drinking Japanese University Sports Clubs. *International Review for the Sociology of Sport* 49(3/4): 331–345.

MEXT. 2020a. *Package of Emergency Economic Measures MEXT*. Accessed December 9, 2020. www.mext.go.jp/en/content/20200722_mxt_kanseisk01-000008961_1.pdf

MEXT. 2020b. *Education in Japan Beyond the Crisis of COVID-19: Leave No One Behind*. Accessed December 9, 2020. www.mext.go.jp/en/content/20200904_mxt_kouhou01-000008961_1.pdf

Nash, Roy. 1999. Bourdieu on Education and Social and Cultural Reproduction. *British Journal of Sociology* 11(4): 431–447.

Osaki, Yoneatsu, Masumi Minowa, Kenji Suzuki, and Kiyoshi Wada. 2003. Adolescent Alcohol Use in Japan, 1996. *Yonago Acta Medica* 46(2): 35–43.

Partanen, Juha. 2006. Spectacles of Sociability and Drunkenness: On Alcohol and Drinking in Japan. *Contemporary Drug Problems* 33: 177–204.

Qie, Nan, Pei-Luen Patrick Rau, Lin Wang, and Liang Ma. 2019. Is the Senpai-Kouhai Relationship Common Across China, Korea, and Japan? *Social Behavior and Personality* 47(1): 1–12. https://doi.org/10.2224/sbp.7404

Roberson, James E. 1995. Becoming Shakaijin: Working Class Reproduction in Japan. *Ethnology* 34(4): 293–313.

Saldaña, Johnny. (2009). *The Coding Manual for Qualitative Researchers*. London: Sage.

Suzuki, Kenji, Yoneatsu Osaki, Masumi Minowa, Kiyoshi Wada, Takashi Ohida, Yuriko Doi, and Takeo Tanihata. 2003. Japanese National Survey of Adolescent Drinking Behavior: Comparison between 1996 and 2000 Surveys. *Nihon Arukoru Yakubutsu Igakkai Zasshi [Japanese Journal of Alcohol Studies and Drug Dependence]* 38(5): 425–433.

Takada, Haruki. 2017. 大学生サークル集団への入団理由と 組織構造との関連 [Examining the Relation Between the Reasons Students Join University Clubs and the Organization Structure of Clubs]. *Rikkyo Psychological Research* 59: 25–46.

Wetzel, Patricia J. 2004. *Keigo in Modern Japan: Polite Language From Meiji to the Present*. Honolulu: University of Hawaii Press.

Yamamoto, Satoshi. 2020. Japan's Coronavirus Assistance Slow to Reach Those Most in Need. *NHK World*, June 15. Accessed March 29, 2021. www3.nhk.or.jp/nhkworld/en/news/backstories/1144/

7 The Classroom as a Space for Power and Healing

Examining the Case of New York City After Trump's Election

Salma Waly

Introduction

The election of Donald Trump in 2016 impacted the social and political climate of the United States in many ways. In particular, the divisive rhetoric used by the Trump administration and the postelection policies by right-wing politicians fueled negative sentiments toward people of color, immigrants, and refugees. Pollock (2017) explains that thousands of incidents of hate, harassment, violence, and bullying were reported as soon as Trump was elected to office. The impact of the election found its way to schools and other academic institutions. For instance, teachers reported a drastic increase in hate incidents, which severely affected the social and emotional well-being of many students. These included chants and vandalism in schools where the majority of the students came from traditionally marginalized backgrounds (Vara-Orta 2018). When the Southern Poverty Law Project surveyed 2,000 teachers nationwide to understand the impact of Trump's election on their students, teachers explained that the election created a sense of fear, insecurity, and severe anxiety (Kuek Ser 2016).

In response to this, researchers started investigating ways through which teachers can effectively handle complex emotions and low morale in their classrooms. For example, Garcia and Dutro (2018) discussed the importance of training teachers so that they are able to create inclusive learning spaces for all learners. Similarly, Schenck (2020) suggested that in the age of Trump, teachers should put aside the neutrality hat and create learning spaces that promote resistance and change. Researchers have also stressed how important it is for teachers to develop an intersectional mindset so that they are able to relate specifically to the experiences of traditionally marginalized students (Friedman, Hallaran, & Locke 2020).

This study focuses on the perceptions of teachers regarding how teaching has changed following the 2016 presidential election. Specifically, the study looks at how teachers transformed their classrooms to inclusive spaces where students are empowered and where negative emotions are rechanneled into a positive sense of belonging. The research question that guides this study is: In what ways have classroom practices been impacted by the 2016 presidential

DOI: 10.4324/9781003258223-9

election and the public policies associated with it? The goal of this research is to explore some trends in teaching and learning that emerged following the 2016 election so that one can understand the relationship that exists between sociopolitical tension and pedagogical practices in urban schools in New York City.

Review of Literature

The role played by teachers at times of sociopolitical tension cannot be overstated. A significant body of literature has been dedicated to examining the connections that exist between what teachers do in classrooms and what happens in the world outside (Godfrey & Grayman 2014; Rapa, Bolding, & Jamil 2020). In this section, I start with a presentation of research that examines the impact of social and political events on teaching and learning. I then shift attention to research findings on democratic practices that are typically used by educators to empower students at times of crisis and tension.

The Impact of Sociopolitical Events on Education

Researchers have long been interested in investigating the impact of sociopolitical events on education. For example, there is a significant body of research that focuses on the role of educators in the civil rights movement in the years between 1954 to 1964. In his work, Ling (2012) highlights the efforts played by African American educators in preparing a generation of leaders who later played pivotal roles in the civil rights movement. The African American community first established Myles Horton's Highlander Folk School's Citizenship Education Program (CEP), Tennessee. Through community literacy classes, the CEP gradually transformed into a model of social mobilization. When Highlander School later faced closure, it transferred the CEP to the Southern Christian Leadership Conference (SCLC). Civil rights activists then attended SCLC's teacher training programs, which in return impacted communities especially in regard to political education and human rights. Similarly, Baker (2011) studied the role played by African American teachers in the South in the years leading to the civil rights movement. He explains that the teachers created lessons and extracurricular activities that encouraged students to participate in strikes, boycotts, and demonstrations. These educators helped make the civil rights movement possible by preparing students who fully understood their rights as citizens and worked collectively to change inequality in all its forms.

The role of schools during the civil rights movement was not limited to classroom teachers. It extended to university personnel who acted in different capacities to meet the needs of students at such a critical time. Gaston-Gayles et al. (2005) studied the roles played by student affairs professionals in universities from the 1950s through the 1970s. The researchers concluded that student affairs professionals during the civil rights move-ment assumed roles such as educators, advocates, and change agents in order to resolve issues that occurred in campuses as a result of the civil rights era.

Another example of how sociopolitical events impact education is found in Eastern and Central Europe in the early 1990s. Countries such as Poland, Hungary, and Romania witnessed massive sociopolitical events demanding economic and political reform that greatly impacted youth activism in these countries. Van Hoorn et al. (2000) explain that youth understanding of abstract ideas, such as government and democracy, deepened in Hungary and Poland following these events. Similarly, Walker and Stephenson (2010) discuss how the events that took place outside the classroom increased the political maturity of students at that time. In particular, they enhanced stu-dents' knowledge and helped them realize the important role that they could play outside the classroom. Tereshchenko (2010) also discusses the impact of sociopolitical events in Eastern Europe on developing students' sense of love for and belonging to their countries by focusing on the idea of place-based pedagogy. According to Tereshchenko, place-based pedagogy is a form of critical pedagogy that raises the awareness of the youth of the social, political, and economic situation around them. She recommends this pedagogy as a tool to enhance social and political awareness and organize students for the purpose of making change.

Another geopolitical area that has seen sociopolitical unrest in the past decade is the Middle East. Since the beginning of the Arab Spring in 2011, researchers have been keen on learning about the impact of revolutions in places such as Egypt, Tunisia, Libya, and Yemen on classroom practices and youth activism. Sharobeem (2015), for instance, looked at the impact of the Egyptian revolution on the curriculum of a public university in the city of Alexandria. She explains that some of the effects of the revolution included the introduction of new courses, topics, and activities that aimed to develop students' awareness of the value of activism and the role they could play to develop their communities. Similarly, Waly (2013) examined the classroom practices that English as a Foreign Language teachers used with their students after the revolution in Egypt. She concludes that the teachers used a wide range of activities to instill notions of equality and common purpose and to inspire students to resume their roles as active citizens who can change the country so that everyone is treated with respect and dignity.

The examples in this section highlighting the role played by educators in times of instability or crisis provide a context to this study, which sheds light on the changes that Trump's election brought to classrooms in a diverse urban setting, in particular, New York City. By doing so, we see the impact of the Trump presidency on learning and the ways through which students can be further supported, academically and socio-emotionally, in urban class-rooms across the country.

Classroom Practices That Promote Inclusiveness and Agency

In recent decades, scholars have discussed a number of teaching pedagogies that empower students, educate them about issues taking place in their communities, and equip them with the skills needed to face social and political challenges (Campbell, Levinson, & Hess 2012; Kawashima-Ginsberg 2013). One practice that has been at the center of research is discussion. Campbell (2005) and Rodriguez and Huemmer (2019) identified classroom discussions as an essential tool for promoting inclusiveness and establishing a shared purpose. Discussions help students gain knowledge about their communities and allow them to critically analyze issues. They, moreover, help students develop good listening skills. Levine (2008) articulates the benefits of utilizing more discussions in the classroom. He argues that discussions not only enhance communication but also expand the knowledge of students in the areas of politics and social change. Similarly, Milner (2010) urges educators to use reflective dialogues to help students explore current issues, develop a deeper understanding of social and political dilemmas, and create solutions that aim to combat social problems of all kinds.

Another teaching strategy that teachers draw on is critical literacy. By discussing authentic texts, such as current news articles on social and political issues, teachers help their students develop a better understanding of the realities that exist outside of the classroom. Waly (2013) discusses the value of using readings about current sociopolitical issues in the classroom. Through her work with teachers during periods of political unrest, she explains that using readings about the current issues facing one's community not only helps students become more critical thinkers but also enhances their trust in their teachers and schools. In addition to using literacy resources to educate and empower learners, Garcia, Seglem, and Share (2013) promote the idea of critical media literacy in which learners are taught to be discerning media users so that media is used as a tool to understand power structures and dismantle underlying bias.

A third classroom practice that has been promoted for a long time by researchers worldwide is community-based learning. Dewey, in his 1923 writings, explains that community-based activities can enhance students' self-concept and self-efficacy. In recent years, researchers, such as Kirshner (2009), highlight the role that community projects can play in teaching civic skills that are essential for active civic participation outside the classroom. Khalifa (2020), on the other hand, urges educators to establish connections with local communities so that students can continuously interact with their members and work on projects and initiatives that give back to these communities.

The studies in this section highlight the value of deliberate efforts by teachers to use their classrooms as spaces where students are equipped with the skills needed to actively participate in their communities. The pedagogical choices that teachers make determine how students view their roles in ever-changing societies. They also provide students with the capacities that are needed in order to stand in the face of bias and discrimination and create more tolerant communities.

Theoretical Framework

The theoretical foundation on which this study is based is critical pedagogy. According to Aliakbari and Faraji (2011), critical pedagogy is an approach to teaching and learning in which students become active learners who question, analyze, and discuss critical issues in an attempt to find solutions for such issues. The purpose of using critical pedagogy according to Kincheloe (2005) is to transform oppressive power structures and empower learners so that they assume more active roles in developing their communities. Not only does critical pedagogy explain the value of linking classroom instruction to community development, but it also offers examples of what teachers can do to transform their classrooms into spaces of power and resistance (Saunders 2020).

The notion of critical pedagogy was first introduced in the early 1900s. The most influential work that formed the basis of critical pedagogy is Dewey's writings on community service learning. Besides the importance of linking knowledge to practical experience, Dewey (1923) discussed the value of engaging students in their communities so that they would gain a better understanding of public issues. Dewey's teachings, overall, require teachers to go beyond factual knowledge to a form of critical inquiry that allows students to research current issues and work collectively to improve living conditions for all members of the community. Similarly, Freire's work in the 1970s stressed the importance of critical consciousness as a tool to transform communities and create citizens that are oriented toward justice and public welfare.

In recent years, many researchers have continued to highlight the value of critical pedagogies. Giroux (2011), for instance, explains that learning should take place by examining power and dominant interests. In his view, students should be exposed to power structures, encouraged to be critical thinkers, and assisted in their pursuit of being active citizens of the society. In the period after the Trump election, many educators across the United States started utilizing critical pedagogies to create positive learning experiences for all students. For example, Rodriguez and Huemmer (2019) explain that the use of critical pedagogies creates a sense of purpose in the classroom and helps students view their roles in a clearer and more defined manner. McLaren (2020) explains that by empowering traditionally marginalized students and creating spaces for all learners to grow and thrive, freedom for all will be obtained. For that reason, teachers should be cognizant of the role that they play in the classroom and use practices that allow students to develop the skills needed to stand in the face of injustice, bias, and inequality.

Data Collection and Analysis

Considering this theoretical foundation, I conducted a small-scale exploratory study with three teachers to look at how the sociopolitical climate after Trump's election affected their instruction. Three teachers[1] were chosen from a pool of educators that I had previously worked with or supervised, based on several criteria: They represented a wide range of ethnicities, years of experience, and backgrounds and they had a considerable number of minoritized students as well as newcomer, refugee, and immigrant learners in their classrooms.

The participants included Lina, a white female with over ten years of experience. The second teacher is Younis, who comes from a West Indian background. He is the oldest and most experienced of the three teachers with over 20 years of experience. The third teacher is Kaleb, an African American male with slightly over five years of experience. The teachers work in urban schools in Brooklyn and Queens.

After providing written consent, the participants were interviewed to discuss their teaching practices and how their instruction was impacted after Trump's election. As a follow-up, I sent a number of open-ended prompts to the three teachers to freely write about their thoughts and beliefs specifically pertaining to the impact of the current events surrounding the election on self and on teaching and learning. The teachers each submitted around two pages of written responses. Both the interviews and narratives were completed in 2018 or about halfway through Trump's presidential period. The analysis process started with an inductive analysis of the interviews (Folkestad 2008). Interviews were read multiple times to highlight common themes that emerged from the responses of all participants. The goal, in particular, was to highlight the common trends that existed between the three teachers in the way they reacted to postelection events such as hate speech, violence, and white supremacy. The written narratives were then used to further support these trends.

Findings

In order to understand the factors that influenced their dispositions as educators, the teachers were asked to talk about their backgrounds and aspirations. They then spoke about the needs of their students, their teaching styles, and some of the practices they use to accommodate and empower all learners following the elections.

"I Dreamed of Being That Person": Teachers' Backgrounds and Aspirations

When asked about her teaching experience, Lina, a middle school teacher in a mostly immigrant neighborhood in Queens said:

I have been working at the same school for my entire career. My school is a middle school. It is predominantly Hispanic, but there is a growing Arabic speaking population and there has always been Eastern European populations. We have some Mandarin speakers. I think that is all the languages I have seen.

Kaleb, a first-grade teacher in a school in Queens, on the other hand, explained: "My kids come from different backgrounds. I have a lot of Latinx students. We just got a kid yesterday from Yemen. [It is] very diverse. I would say probably 90% are African American." Similar to Kaleb, Younis, a high school teacher in an African American neighborhood stated: "I teach biology and earth science in a high school in Brooklyn. My students are mostly Black. They come from low socio-economic backgrounds."

The student populations that the teachers worked with mostly belonged to low-income minoritized groups that have been directly affected by post-election policies. Many are Latinos and African Americans, which are two groups that had been stigmatized and negatively labeled by the administration (Zeiders et al. 2020; Clayton, Moore, & Jones-Eversley 2019). Many are also Muslim, which is a group that suffered as a result of the implications of the 2017 Travel Ban. Yemeni students, in particular, are believed to be a group that suffered tremendously as a result of the Travel Ban. School administrators in different parts of the country have described regular bouts of crying and confusion among their Yemeni students who believed that they might never see their close family members again (Desmond-Harris 2017).

Teachers were asked to discuss the reasons that motivated them to pursue a career in teaching and on the early experiences that prompted them to make such a decision. Two teachers discussed the influence of family in encouraging them to become teachers. Younis, for example, talked about the role of his mother. He said:

> My mom, first and foremost, [was the reason] because she felt it was a worthwhile profession and a life-long career. Also, my religious upbringings . . . the years of experience I acquired in institutions of learning, and the many years of experience in teaching all impacted me.

Lina explained that she went through a Catholic school system in which she felt lost because her teachers were untrained. This helped her realize the importance of being a good teacher and the impact this can have on children in need. She then compared that to the experience of her own father who came to the United States as an immigrant with very limited English proficiency. She explained:

> My father immigrated to this country at the age of 15. When he arrived, ESL was a new concept. My father did not receive the support he needed. However, he managed to excel by his own accord. He often

spoke about a teacher who took special interest in him and tutored him in the mornings. He believes that she is the reason why he was able to learn English, keep up with classes, and ultimately attend college. My family owes a lot to this woman, and I dreamed of being that person for today's newly arrived immigrants in need of language teaching.

The life experiences that the participants discussed in this section show the relationship between teachers' life histories and their teaching tendencies. Altan and Lane (2018) discuss the importance of teachers' significant life experiences in determining their dispositions. Many of the experiences that teachers go through in life dictate, in one way or another, the kind of educator that they want to be in their classrooms. In the case of the three teachers, being immigrants or people of color, themselves, inspired them to create more inclusive learning settings. Also, religious identity, as Nelson (2010) explains, can motivate teachers to create spaces where acceptance of everyone is key.

"Just Trying to Give Them Hope": Teacher Concerns and Practices

The teachers seemed to have a very similar understanding of the realities facing their students, and the practices that they should use to support learners of all backgrounds. Even though the teachers discussed a wide range of topics during the interviews, this section discusses the two most pressing issues that emerged during data analysis. These issues include attending to the emotional well-being of students and educating them about the events taking place outside the classroom so that they can have a more nuanced understanding of the potential roles they can play in their communities.

Social and Emotional Support

All the teachers in this study felt that Trump's election negatively affected the social and emotional well-being of their students. With the majority of the students being immigrants and/or students of color, the teachers explained that their students felt unwelcomed and stigmatized. The students also felt that they had to continuously try to dismantle misconceptions and stereotypes about their cultures. When asked to give a specific example, Lina spoke about the struggle of her Arab students with Islamophobia. She said:

> I think because of the political climate and how it has a racist tone and [that it] criminalizes other groups of people. I think because of that, we've seen a lot of people coming forward advocating for these groups. You know, our Arab population, there's Islamophobia and that stems from 9/11 and then now with our president, he's kind of increased that mindset.

Lina then highlighted the need for emotional support for all her students. She explained that she received mental health training in order to be able to best support her newcomer, immigrant, and minoritized learners who constantly need to defend themselves. Lina said:

> I think this population, especially in all schools, really needs more focus on emotional health and mental health. And we are just not there yet at all. We have three guidance counselors for 1,100 kids, and the guidance counselors have to see the kids with [severe problems] and then anyone else is kind of [not receiving the support needed]. So, I think the political climate is kind of increasing these mental health issues, and it is kind of this vicious cycle. I am currently in a program for mental health. So, I am taking what I learned in my studies of mental illness and psychology and bringing it into the classroom so I can see [each] student more like a whole person.

Kaleb, on the other hand, approached the topic of social and emotional support from a different angle. He highlighted the importance of "care" as a teaching pedagogy (Howard 2001) to help the students realize that there is more to them than being students. When asked to elaborate on that, Kaleb said:

> That was always lacking for me [growing up]. And I was like "I wish somebody would ask me how my day went." Not saying that I had a bad childhood but knowing that my teachers cared for me [would have] mattered a lot.

Asked to specifically explain why care is an important element of teaching in the Trump era, Kaleb said:

> [When Trump was elected to office], one of my kids actually was scared that her family might get sent back to Mexico. She was crying. What she should be thinking about [is] that I am at school, I am with my friends. Those are the hard conversations that I try to be open [about] and empathize and make sure that they are okay. Because they are in a learning environment, you have to be comfortable. I try my hardest to let them know that everything is going to be okay. I am just trying to give them hope and reassure them that everything is going to be fine.

A teacher's sense of care and support was also mentioned by Younis, the high school teacher. However, Younis discussed the role of his beliefs and religious background in choosing a pedagogy of care. He said: "My religion has taught me to approach tasks with patience, and to treat others, especially young people, with care and understanding, and these beliefs have helped shape my teaching style."

Choosing a pedagogy that supports students in a way that relates to their needs as learners from various backgrounds is one which Ware

(2006) has extensively written about and supported. In her work with African American students, the researcher explained the benefits of warm demeanor as a pedagogy that enhances the learning outcomes of minoritized students. She also described the connection between care pedagogy and creating culturally responsive learning environments for all learners. Similarly, Ennis and McCauley (2002) have discussed the role of establishing trust by listening to the concerns of all students. Both researchers explained that trust-based learning communities enhanced the outcomes of all students in the long run. As shown in this section, all three teachers played a nurturing role in the classroom where students felt cared for and trusted.

Helping Students Grow, Glow, and Transition

Teachers also discussed the idea of helping the students realize their strength and assume active roles within their communities. Despite these being good teaching practices in any era, the teachers in this study stressed that it was important to focus on the affective side of learning at such a critical time in the nation's history. When asked why he tries to create an inclusive learning space for all his students after Trump's election, Younis said: "because cultural and social norms are at stake, as well as religious beliefs and rights, based on which party or presidential candidate acquires the mantle of leadership." He added that he tried to help students understand that one should be whoever she/he wants regardless of the political climate in the country. Similarly, when asked about her main focus in class in light of the Trump election and its subsequent policies, Lina explained that her goal was "first and foremost to foster the idea of zero tolerance for bullying and zero tolerance for marginalizing certain groups for certain things." Lina further reflected on the needs of her students by saying:

> I think people forget the trials and tribulations the students had to go through to get here especially in light of the current events. We have newcomer students who have not been reunited with family members here [as their families were not able to enter the country after the election]. It is not only a new way of life, a new language, a new school, but also a new family structure.

I then asked the teachers to explain what they do in the classroom in order to create an inclusive space for students to grow, glow, and realize their roles as members of the society. They discussed the need for open discussions, presentations on current events, and readings on social and political issues to help students voice their opinions, discuss their concerns, and think critically about the here and now. The teachers were then asked to discuss examples of instructional changes that they adopted after the 2016 election. Lina explained that the first step of helping students adapt to the current events is selecting materials that show all narratives and present all points of view. She said:

> I started to include more articles [controversial topics]. It is okay to have an opinion on them. They should read multiple sides of the story. Especially for ELLs [English Language Learners], we have a lot of students from Venezuela, let us talk about what is happening there [referring to the protests in Venezuela since 2014 due to violence and economic disparity]. We want to hear what it is like over there, and we want to see both sides of the story. So as much as I can, I like to bring in what is going on in our world today.

Younis agreed with what Lina said and also added that since the Trump period had been marked with a charged and negative racial rhetoric, he constantly made sure that he highlighted the contributions of people of color in science and scientific research in his classroom. He said: "After we read [the information] in the textbooks, we try to have a broad perspective as to who are the people making contributions to science. I highlight the contribution of people who come from [diverse] backgrounds." This approach is particularly useful in times of sociopolitical tension because it shows that hate rhetoric that aims to demonize certain groups is not accurate. It confirms everyone's right to exist and succeed in the society.

Kaleb, whose students are mainly black, Asian or Latinx, also highlighted the need to shed light on the role of people of color in his classroom not only to diversify the narrative but to also empower students. He said:

> I have been reading a book called *Little Heroes*. I read [about] two African American women today. I read about a Latino woman. Tomorrow I am going to read [about] an Asian woman. I am trying to include the demographics that is in my classroom, so my students do not feel left out especially after the elections when students of color feel alienated.

Similar to Kaleb, Younis added that for the purpose of empowering his African American high school students, he regularly arranges visits to a big African American museum in Brooklyn. He said:

> Our school is in a predominantly Black neighborhood. There are a lot of connections with the community that the students are exposed to normally. There is an African Museum right in the community that was put together by some African American students and our parents. It is a walking distance, and it is showing Black cultural heritage.

The teachers also explained that one way of creating an inclusive classroom is by openly discussing the impact of politics on the student groups that they teach. Lina, for example, said: "If we don't discuss these issues, then the lines that separate us will continue to grow. Communication is key. Shying away from hot topics doesn't model good communication skills for our students." Social and political topics that the teachers discussed with their students included immigration, discrimination, and police brutality. The teachers found it necessary to include such issues so that they would establish their credibility in the classroom and assert that they really cared about all learners. Kaleb spoke to why he discusses issues related to policing more now than before. He said:

> I mentor a group of sixth grade boys and our conversations [revolve] around how to deal with police, how to deal with women that might look at you as a threat and how to [handle] personal appearance perceptions. I talk to them more about what you say and mannerisms and body language. Because as young black men, people do not necessarily wait until that moment to ask them a question. They already have their preconceived notions of who they are based on their appearance. I am trying to tell my young men [that] it is important to not lose yourself, but also be aware of how people perceive you. I find myself having those types of conversations with them more often now.

This section highlights how the teachers in this study modified their classroom instruction to respond to the election. Examining the role of educators after the Trump election, Pollock (2017) stresses the importance of teachers sharing and discussing facts with their students and making sure that all students have the opportunity to learn and thrive. The three teachers in this study attempted to do exactly that. They aimed to clarify that social division only brought chaos and that their students were able to change the narrative to one that promoted unity and harmony.

Discussion

When Trump was elected to office in 2016, many minoritized groups across the country were demonized and alienated (Edwards & Rushin 2018). The impact of the Trump presidency on education, as the findings of this study show, is mainly seen in how students felt about the political climate in the country and how teachers responded to these feelings. Fear, for instance, because of in-school bullying or out of school policies mainly pertaining to immigration was a feeling that the teachers in this study had to carefully handle and deal with. Rodriguez (2019) interviewed newcomer students after the election of Donald Trump and explained that fear was also a feeling that the students expressed. Fear, fueled by white supremacy, violence, deportation, and anti-immigrant policies in general also negatively impacted the students' sense of belonging to the country.

To counter the climate of anxiety and fear, the teachers in this study used care pedagogy to create inclusive classrooms where all students can grow and thrive (Watson, Sealey-Ruiz, & Jackson 2016). Care pedagogy is seen in how the teachers engaged in genuine conversations with students to reassure them they were safe. It was also evident in how teachers viewed their classrooms as safe spaces where bullying was not tolerated and where everyone, regardless of their culture or background, was valued and appreciated. Following the elections, researchers – such as Rossatto and Mansour (2020) – described care and compassion in the classroom as an ontological necessity especially in multicultural settings. They discussed the need for classrooms to be spaces where students feel safe and feel good about each other.

Through briefly discussing their life histories, one can see that the three teachers realized the crucial role they played as teachers. They also recognized that there is a connection between education and societal conditions and believed that education can be a tool for dismantling bias and misconceptions (Hytten & Bettez 2011). Besides creating an inclusive space where students can heal, the teachers also tried to empower students by engaging them in critical discussions, connecting them with community members, and openly talking about issues of race and politics. This is seen through Kaleb's discussion of police brutality with his students and Younis's continuous efforts to connect students with the communities in which they live. This is also seen in Lina's attempts to talk about issues that concerned her students the most such as immigration and identity. These teaching practices are widely supported by research findings in the Trump era. For example, Payne and Journell (2019) found that talking about politics even with elementary school students after the elections was necessary and beneficial. It helped students understand what the country was going through and created a sense of clarity for many students who were confused about the current events. Similarly, through their work with high school teachers, Anderson and Zyhowski (2018) concluded that talking about political events in the classroom can enhance students' future civic participation. Establishing partnerships with community members is another practice that Khalifa (2020) extensively writes about. It does not only humanize the experiences of students of color but also highlight ways through which students can give back to the communities in which they live.

Conclusion

Even though Trump is no longer in office, his presidency has empowered a large segment of the population who feel that they have a right to terrorize others. This is still evident in how part of the political rhetoric continues to demonize immigrants and people of color. With constant attacks on groups such as Asians and Muslim Americans, for example, educators need to continue using their classrooms as spaces of empowerment where all students feel valued, fully accepted, and appreciated (Ferrechio 2021; Abdelkader 2021)

This study showed that education, especially in a city as big and diverse as New York, was negatively affected by the divisive and racially charged rhetoric of the Trump administration. The teachers in this study began to re-evaluate their professional roles and navigated channels through which they could best support all their learners. With a focus on the child as a whole and on raising awareness and empowering all learners, the three teachers paid extra attention to the social and emotional development and the mental health of their newcomer, minoritized, immigrant and refugee students. They were able to create safe environments for their students to thrive and stand up for themselves. The teachers also selected a wide range of classroom practices that aimed to raise political awareness and enhance the skills necessary to survive and succeed in society at such a difficult time. Putting aside labels, stigma, and racial smears, the teachers focused on nurturing their students' love for learning and their aspiration to excel by focusing on their value and self-worth.

Even though the results of this study highlight the practices employed by some teachers in New York City schools, these practices are not necessarily playing out in all schools across the city. New York City is home to the biggest school district in the United States. With over 1,800 public schools in the city's five boroughs, there is a wide range of opinions, standpoints, and strategies that teachers use in order to either react to or ignore the effect of the sociopolitical climate on education. More research is needed in order to look more particularly at the impact of classroom practices after the Trump election on mobilizing students and helping them organize as active citizens in their communities. While research with a similar scope was conducted in various parts of Europe and the Middle East, youth activism following the Trump election in the United States is an area that is not yet fully explored.

Note

1. Pseudonyms are used for participants to ensure confidentiality.

References

Abdelkader, Engy. 2021. As Hate Crimes Grow More Violent, Here Are Some Policy Recommendations to Protect the communities they Impact. *ABA Journal*, March 8. www.abajournal.com/columns/article/as-hate-crimes-grow-more-violent-here-are-some-policy-recommendations-to-protect-the-communities-they-impact/

Aliakbari, Mohammad, and Elham Faraji. 2011. Basic Principles of Critical Pedagogy. (2nd International Conference on Humanities, Historical and Social Sciences.) *International Proceedings of Economics Development and Research (IPEDR)* 17: 77–85.

Altan, Servet, and Jennie Farber Lane. 2018. Teachers' Narratives: A Source for Exploring the Influences of Teachers' Significant Life Experiences on their Dispositions and Teaching Practices. *Teaching and Teacher Education* 74(1): 238–248.

Anderson, Derek L., and Joni Zyhowski. 2018. Teaching Trump: A Case Study of Two Teachers and the Election of 2016. *The Social Studies* 109(2): 101–111.

Baker, Scott. 2011. Pedagogies of Protest: African American Teachers and the History of the Civil Rights Movement, 1940–1963. *Teachers College Record* 113(12): 2777–2803.

Campbell, David E. 2005. Voice in the Classroom: How an Open Classroom Environment Facilitates Adolescents' Civic Development. CIRCLE Working Paper 28. Center for Information and Research on Civic Learning and Engagement (CIRCLE), University of Maryland.

Campbell, David E., Meira Levinson, and Frederick M. Hess (eds.). 2012. *Making Civics Count: Citizenship Education for a New Generation*. Cambridge, MA: Harvard Education Press.

Clayton, Dewey M., Sharon E. Moore, and Sharon D. Jones-Eversley. 2019. The Impact of Donald Trump's Presidency on the Well-Being of African Americans. *Journal of Black Studies* 50(8): 707–730.

Desmond-Harris, Jenée. 2017. "Crying Is an Everyday Thing": Life After Trump's "Muslim Ban" at a Majority-immigrant School. *Vox*, February 16. www.vox.com/identities/2017/2/16/14584228/muslim-ban-trump-immigration-ban-children-kids-schools-anxiety

Dewey, John. 1923. *Democracy and Education: An Introduction to the Philosophy of Education*. New York: Macmillan.

Edwards, Griffin Sims, and Stephen Rushin. 2018. The Effect of President Trump's Election on Hate Crimes. *SSRN*, January 18. http://dx.doi.org/10.2139/ssrn.3102652

Ennis, Catherine D., and M. Terri McCauley. 2002. Creating Urban Classroom Communities Worthy of Trust. *Journal of Curriculum Studies* 34(2): 149–172.

Ferrechio, Susan. 2021. Schumer: Trump Bears Blame for Rise in Hate Crimes Against Asian Americans. *Washington Examiner*, March 18. www.washingtonexaminer.com/news/congress/schumer-blames-trump-rise-hate-crimes-asian-americans

Folkestad, Bjarte. 2008. Analysing Interview Data Possibilities and Challenges. Eurosphere Working Paper Series (EWP), No. 13. Eurospheres Project.

Friedman, Tanya E., Armineh E. Hallaran, and Mallory A. Locke. 2020. Rubberbanding in a Liminal Space: Teachers Contemplate Intersections of Dis/ability and Race in Inclusive Classrooms. *Race Ethnicity and Education*. https://doi.org/10.1080/13613324.2020.1753677

Garcia, Antero, and Elizabeth Dutro. 2018. Electing to Heal: Trauma, Healing, and Politics in Classrooms. *English Education* 50(4): 375–383.

Garcia, Antero, Robyn Seglem, and Jeff Share. 2013. Transforming Teaching and Learning Through Critical Media Literacy Pedagogy. *Learning Landscapes* 6(2): 109–124.

Gaston-Gayles, Joy L., Lisa E. Wolf-Wendel, Kathryn N. Tuttle, Susan B. Twombly, and Kelly Ward. 2005. From Disciplinarian to Change Agent: How the Civil Rights Era Changed the Roles of Student Affairs Professionals. *NASPA Journal* 42(3): 263–282.

Giroux, Henry A. 2011. *Education and the Crisis of Public Values: Challenging the Assault on Teachers, Students, & Public Education*. New York: Peter Lang.

Godfrey, Erin B., and Justina Kamiel Grayman. 2014. Teaching Citizens: The Role of Open Classroom Climate in Fostering Critical Consciousness Among Youth. *Journal of Youth and Adolescence* 43(11): 1801–1817.

Howard, Tyrone C. 2001. Powerful Pedagogy for African American Students: A Case of Four Teachers. *Urban Education* 36(2): 179–202.

Hytten, Kathy, and Silvia C. Bettez. 2011. Understanding Education for Social Justice. *Educational Foundations* 25: 7–24.

Kawashima-Ginsberg, Kei. 2013. Do Discussion, Debate, and Simulations Boost NAEP Civics Performance. CIRCLE Fact Sheet, Tufts University. https://circle.tufts.edu/sites/default/files/2020-01/discussion_debate_naep_2013.pdf

Khalifa, Muhammad. 2020. *Culturally Responsive School Leadership*. Cambridge, MA: Harvard Education Press.

Kincheloe, Joe. 2005. Reinventing and Redefining Whiteness: Building a Critical Pedagogy for Insurgent Times. In Leeno Karumanchery (ed.), *Engaging Equity: New Perspectives on Anti-Racist Education* (pp. 149–162). Edmonton, Alberta: Brush Education.

Kirshner, Ben. 2009. "Power in Numbers": Youth Organizing as a Context for Exploring Civic Identity. *Journal of Research on Adolescence* 19(3): 414–440.

Kuek Ser, Kuang Keng. 2016. What's the "Trump Effect" in Schools? Here's How 2,000 Teachers Explain It. *The World*, April 20. www.pri.org/stories/2016-04-20/whats-trump-effect-schools-heres-how-2000-teachers-explain-it

Levine, Donald N. 2008. *Powers of the Mind*. Chicago: University of Chicago Press.

Ling, Peter J., and Johannah Duffy. 2012. Backing Dr King: The Financial Transformation of the Southern Christian Leadership Conference in 1963. *The Sixties* 5(2): 147–165.

McLaren, Peter. 2020. The Future of Critical Pedagogy. *Educational Philosophy and Theory* 52(12): 1243–1248.

Milner IV, H. Richard. 2010. What Does Teacher Education Have to Do With Teaching? Implications for Diversity Studies. *Journal of Teacher Education* 61(1–2): 118–131.

Nelson, Jason. 2010. Teacher Dispositions and Religious Identity in the Public School: Two Case Studies. *The Journal of Negro Education* 79(3): 335–353.

Payne, Katherina A., and Wayne Journell. 2019. "We Have Those Kinds of Conversations Here . . .": Addressing Contentious Politics with Elementary Students. *Teaching and Teacher Education* 79: 73–82.

Pollock, Mica. 2017. Three Challenges for Teachers in the Era of Trump. *Educational Studies: Journal of the American Educational Studies Association* 53(4): 426–427.

Rapa, Luke J., Candice W. Bolding, and Faiza M. Jamil. 2020. (Re)Examining the Effects of Open Classroom Climate on the Critical Consciousness of Preadolescent and Adolescent Youth. *Applied Developmental Science*. https://doi.org/10.1080/10888691.2020.1861946

Rodriguez, Lilian V. 2019. Navigating a Climate of Fear: Adolescent Arrivals and the Trump Era. Dissertation, UC Santa Barbara. https://escholarship.org/uc/item/6pt4w2np

Rodriguez, Nathian Shae, and Jennifer Huemmer. 2019. Pedagogy of the Depressed: An Examination of Critical Pedagogy in Higher Ed's Diversity-Centered Classrooms Post-Trump. *Pedagogy, Culture & Society* 27(1): 133–149.

Rossatto, César A., and Jennifer L. Mansour. 2020. Challenging Fear and Hate: Caring and Compassion as Essential Components of a Critical Pedagogy School Curriculum. In Jared Keengwe (ed.), *Handbook of Research on Diversity and Social Justice in Higher Education* (pp. 149–159). Hershey, PA: IGI Global.

Saunders, Laura, and Melissa A. Wong. 2020. *Instruction in Libraries and Information Centers: An Introduction*. Urbana-Champaign, IL: Windsor & Downs Press. https://doi.org/10.21900/wd.12

Schenck, Stephanie Madison. 2020. The Trump Effect and the Damage Done: A Mixed Methods Study Exploring Sociopolitical Hostility and Teacher Responses in Language Classrooms. Ph.D. Dissertation, Clemson University.

Sharobeem, Heba. 2015. The Impact of the Arab Spring at an Egyptian University: A Personal Experience. *Middle East-Topics & Arguments* 4: 110–121.

Tereshchenko, Antonina. 2010. Ukrainian Youth and Civic Engagement: Unconventional Participation in Local Spaces. *Journal of Youth Studies* 13(5): 597–613.

Van Hoorn, Judith L., Akos Komlosi, Elzbieta Suchar, and Doreen A. Samelson. 2000. *Adolescent Development and Rapid Social Change: Perspectives from Eastern Europe.* Albany, NY: SUNY Press.

Vara-Orta, Francisco. 2018. Hate in Schools. *Education Week*, July 29. www.edweek.org/leadership/hate-in-schools/2018/08

Walker, Charles, and Svetlana Stephenson. 2010. Youth and Social Change in Eastern Europe and the Former Soviet Union. *Journal of Youth Studies* 13(5): 521–532.

Waly, Salma Gehad. 2013. Reflections of EFL University Instructors on Teaching and Learning after the Revolution in Egypt. *Education, Business and Society: Contemporary Middle Eastern Issues* 6(1): 4–14.

Ware, Franita. 2006. Warm Demander Pedagogy: Culturally Responsive Teaching that Supports a Culture of Achievement for African American Students. *Urban Education* 41(4): 427–456.

Watson, Wanda, Yolanda Sealey-Ruiz, and Iesha Jackson. 2016. Daring to Care: The Role of Culturally Relevant Care in Mentoring Black and Latino Male High School Students. *Race Ethnicity and Education* 19(5): 980–1002.Zeiders, Katharine H., Rajni L. Nair, Lindsay T. Hoyt, Thaddeus W. W. Pace, and Angela Cruze. 2020. Latino Early Adolescents' Psychological and Physiological Responses During the 2016 US Presidential Election. *Cultural Diversity and Ethnic Minority Psychology* 26(2): 169–175.

8 Vignettes From the Underground

The Difficulty of Challenging Educational Spaces

Ann Frkovich & Tameka Carter-Richardson

Navigating Challenging Educational Spaces

Tameka, a Black educator, and Ann, a White educator – having taught in both predominantly Black schools in low-income communities and predominantly White, wealthy schools – know what it means to challenge and to be challenged as educators. Here, we understand the idea of challenging educational spaces as the contested space between educators and policies and institutions in practice. We explore the complications of contesting these spaces and the ways that race and class position us, and create specific insecurities for us, within these spaces. In fact, it was during a car ride home from an academic conference over a decade ago that we (Tameka and Ann) commiserated over the veracity with which educators are confronted with dangerous educational spaces related to race and social class and contribute to the precarity of composing a life dedicated to the profession of education. It is imperative that we are clear here that it is not the students that are demanding, or the communities from which they come, although they can be.

In 1963, James Baldwin, in his *A Talk to Teachers*, emphasizes that we are "living through a very dangerous time," a "revolutionary situation." He urges teachers who work to shape the "minds and hearts" of young people to be:

> prepared to "go for broke." Or to put it another way, you must understand that in an attempt to correct so many generations of bad faith and cruelty, when it is operating not only in the classroom but in society, you will meet the most fantastic, the most brutal, and the most determined resistance. There is no point in pretending this won't happen.
>
> (Baldwin 1998, p. 678)

Sixty years later, amidst our revolutionary situations related to both the global pandemic and the Black Lives Matter movement in the United States, this chapter focuses on the complications of "going for broke" that we continue to experience as educators amidst many generations of educational cruelty.

We experience destabilizing moments related to the intersection of our social class and racial identities, teaching in specific low-income and wealthy

DOI: 10.4324/9781003258223-10

spaces, often predominantly occupied by Black and Brown students, or predominately White students. At root here in our experience in both spaces is that educational goals are often fixated on the maintenance of standards for a school, for conduct, for professionalism, for what is to be taught and how, for the measurement of student growth. While standards seem like benign necessities in schools, they should be questioned and interrogated (Freire 1974; Illich 1983), as they often function to replicate culture (Porfilio & Carr 2010), which often maintains power for the powerful through reproducing inequitable social structures (Freire 1974; Giroux 2011). Often in the name of standardization, the teaching profession has narrowed, individualism has been constrained, and knowledge has been commodified along with the mass proliferation of competition and high-stakes testing (Giroux 2011). Neoliberal educational reforms exacerbate lasting social and racial inequity in the United States (Delpit 1995; Ladson-Billings 1994; Watkins 2001; Noguera 2003) and teachers are often forced into maintaining standards, to be complicit in reproducing inequality.

We "go for broke" here, confronting the various ways we are implicated in maintaining standards that contribute to lasting inequality. This chapter informs the role race and social class play in schools in the United States today and the many complications these structures pose for educators in these spaces. It is too often an unintended necessity for teachers that we keep quiet about inequality related to race (hooks 1994; Green 1995); teachers are demanded to collude in reproducing power dynamics in the spaces they inhabit. With this chapter, we push back; we chose to publish what we have been previously afraid to share. As if smuggled out to the reader, from an imaginary subversive press that is forced to run underground, here we offer vignettes from the underground that capture moments we were complicit in educational inequality so that we may better understand the complexities we experience related to education in these spaces and the larger systems that govern them.

Methods

Taking up the call to action for a new critical approach to research that works against oppression in a quest for solidarity and resistance in our contentious times (Fine 2018), we worked in the autoethnographic tradition (Ellis 2004), to reflexively study ourselves (Ellis & Bochner 2000). We examined our teaching lives at specific moments in our practice we viewed as critically related to our racial identity as educators, modeling our work here after the collaborations of Geneva Gay (2010) and Gloria Ladson-Billings (1994, 1995, 2006a, 2006b). We modeled their process of reflection related to their teaching and work with students. Like them, we recognize the challenges we face in widely diverse spaces, from low-income to wealthy schools. We considered how we might creatively represent in writing the pluralism of perspective in educational research today (Fine 2018).

Stories of classroom life help us understand school culture and address the need to create a bridge between aesthetics and empiricism in educational research (Lawrence-Lightfoot 1983). We can say that schools are poor or wealthy, or we can say that in one school students dine on (free and reduced-price[1]) shrink-wrapped, microwaved, smiley-faced chicken nuggets in an aluminum tray with a packet of ranch dressing and tater tots while the others dine on made-to-order sushi, fresh fruit dipped in chocolate fountains, and fare from artisan food trucks. While this example is not taken up in the vignettes, these extreme examples are our shared experience, and seeing and sharing these details are important to us – they inform the reality of the difficulties we face in these spaces. For this chapter, we took turns writing vignettes related to times that we felt most confronted as teachers in schools related to our racial and class identity. In writing them, we focused on pulling readers into the moment as we lived it.

Of each of the vignettes, we interrogate how we, as educators in these experiences, situate our own class and racial identity and the ways in which race and class dictate power dynamics in the schools where we teach. We consider what standards we are upholding in these situations and how they contribute to lasting educational inequity. We ask what is and is not possible for educators like us in these situations. Finally, we examine what makes these educational spaces trying, and difficult to navigate for us, relative to our own race and social class.

Vignettes From the Underground

The following six vignettes include three from educational spaces for low-income communities and three from educational spaces for wealthy communities. Three from Tameka (two from her work in wealthy schools for predominantly White students, one from her work with predominantly Black students in a low-income community), and three from Ann (one from her work in a wealthy school, two from her work with predominantly Black students from low-income communities).

I.   *Ann in a Low-Income School*

> After I was hired to help start a charter school,[2] I met with the author of the new school's curriculum model, a very tan, chain-smoking White man with a PhD and experience working in a think tank. He was the long-time chair of an English department at a predominantly White school in the suburbs. He was famous for drastic increases in student test performance. He was a legend – we heard again and again about how his model brought in Gates[3] money. From him, I learned straight away that my job is clear: learn about his curriculum and use it at a brand-new school on the south side with predominantly Black students. The curriculum model we inherited from the north side, the one I am expected to enact and enforce, at all costs, is simple. Students take the Pre-ACT[4] as freshmen and then spend the rest of their high school careers going to school to learn to take the ACT.

I befriend a teacher who understands the curriculum model very well, a math and science teacher who had taught at a school that used it. She assures me that this is what I have to do to not get fired: hang gigantic, color-coded posters of ACT skills correlated to ACT scores all over the hallways and classrooms; collect weekly practice tests, scan them, and spend all our time with teachers in professional development working out which questions students most frequently got wrong; itemize and create lessons and units around these exact ACT skills; teach teachers how to do the same; make new posters to replace the old posters, and drill it in, and in, and in. We march around the halls ensuring that this sort of teaching is happening in all classes, at all times. Our every focus is that a solid connection to the ACT is clear in every lesson-plan, and in every single student evaluation. If you want to keep your job, this is the job you did. Everything any teacher ever does needs to be connected to this, or they are deemed ineffective, and ineffective teachers, and their ineffective administrators, are fired.

Monthly, at least one other White woman drives down to the school to check on our progress relative to the ACT. This visit includes a "learning walk" where together we roam the halls, walk-in (unannounced) on teachers and students having class (who then have to pretend that business continues as usual), and observe how things were (or are not) connected to the ACT. During one of these monthly visits, we walk in on Ahmad, our Spanish teacher. Today Ahmad is clearly not teaching Spanish. His students, however, very much unlike all the other days we are busy teaching the ACT, sit enraptured. On the screen blazing before them is a documentary about the Black Panther Party. This becomes a moment in slow-motion. Ahmad starts to sway and visibly sweat. He turns off the TV and starts to stutter. He knows: this was not on the ACT. He throws me a piercing glance, lightning-quick, full of anger and contempt, a sort of "the man" is here and has silenced us, yet again, look. But he is instantly snapped back to his task at hand, as there we are, and there they are, 27 students no longer enraptured.

Opening this school, Ann, along with other White teachers and administrators, are put in a position to define what is and is not possible for Black students. She becomes the person in charge and assumes responsibility for the standardization of what knowledge and experiences are possible for the students (those on the test) and what knowledge and experiences are not possible (those not on the test). For these students and the teachers who teach them, everything becomes measured by the test, and all education is dictated by the content that is to be tested. The curriculum employed at the school narrows to the skills tested on the ACT. What becomes deeply troubling here is the insecurity teachers experience when curriculum is narrowed to test-prep and when teachers are forced to comply with systems of accountability related to this, tasked to maintain a profoundly narrow construction of learning.

In this example, Ann works to maintain success as defined by the language and ideas of the dominant culture of power (Levinson, Foley, & Holland 1996): accountable for teaching to the test, which is to be positioned to maintain and enforce racial and cultural dominance. Therefore, teaching in these spaces becomes incredibly difficult. As seen directly in this example, videos of the Black Panther Party in the late sixties in a test-dominated curriculum is an educational pariah – threatening the push for test-aligned standardization seen in low-income communities. It is demanded of Ann in these spaces to be complicit in this, despite what appears to be the total engagement of these students with the Black Panther Party documentary.

Ann normalizes the narrowing of learning to assessment: the only way these students matter is how they measure. In this vignette, we see how resistance to this or a teacher's ability to "go for broke" becomes futile when education is controlled by standardization and high-stakes testing and when all pedagogy is aligned and relative to this (Garrison 2009). Ahmad is aware of this – in fact, perhaps his teaching of this content in this space was a "going for broke" moment. Yet, this is a moment Ann is trusted to extinguish, despite whatever she feels about it, and despite the level of student engagement with it. We see how educators become enlisted to take part in and enforce educational inequity and how they are held accountable for this every day, in every class, in far too many educational spaces.

II.   *Tameka in a Low-Income School*

In my fourth-year teaching Spanish, at the start of the year, I found 10 Spanish dictionaries for each class. In total, I bought 60 gently used Vox Spanish to English dictionaries and told my students that I would sell the dictionaries for one dollar each. In my 3rd period class, some students ask why I wasn't giving them away for free, and I am ready to explain how I will be using the 60 dollars to buy other needed classroom supplies for us all. Before I can explain, Leo smacks his teeth and says to the class, "Man, why y'all always asking to get stuff for free." The class is completely quiet. "Ms. Carter, can I buy mine now?"

Awkwardly, I say, "Of course." Another student abruptly raises a dollar in the air without saying anything and so I grab two dictionaries from my grey locker sitting behind my desk in the back of the classroom. Feeling guilty, I look around the class while giving Leo his dictionary and say, "If you don't have a full dollar, then I will take coin donations. Maybe you have 50 or 70 cents?"

Leo looks at me with a frown, "Aw hell naw! If I am paying a dollar, everyone is paying a dollar. Y'all better give her your dollar if you want a dictionary. I'm not trying to fail this class just because I don't have a book."

Another student says, "Ms. Carter, give me one, please" and hands me a dollar.

As I go back and forth to the locker, I began to hear students bargaining with each other and splitting the cost of the dictionary. I overhear a student say, "Ay, I'll give you 50 cents to share your dictionary.

Another student asks Leo, "Break this for me."

Leo smiles at his peer and then snatches the 5-dollar bill from the student. He holds the 5-dollar bill to the ceiling, "I guess you good." We all laugh.

Leo Adams always did his homework and would scold others for not doing theirs. Leo Adams would even scold me when I taught lessons that he didn't understand and would make me reteach lessons. His favorite part of the class was learning vocabulary words. Leo had such a knack for memorizing words and prided himself on doing well on spelling tests. I imagined Leo Adams going to college, traveling the world, taking care of his kids beyond the hardships that he was experiencing. I saw Leo Adams being much more successful than me. Not only did I believe this, but I positioned myself to help Leo Adams in any way I could.

Later that year, we are using our dictionaries to make flashcards, and I am laughing about something that was said when security knocks on my door and two police officers walk into my classroom. They look at Leo Adams and gesture for him to stand up. Without expression, Leo turns around at his desk and puts his hands behind his back, and says, "Ms. Carter, can you keep my books for me." I didn't say anything. . . . I froze. Leo then said it louder, "Ms. Carter, keep my books for me, ok?"

I say, "ok." I walk after him and security reminds me to stay with the class. I walk back into the class, and all of the students are still working silently on their flashcards.

No one says anything during class. I just sit and the kids use their dictionaries to look up words to write on a stack of flashcards on their desk. When the bell rings, students file out of the classroom and one student remains. He looks at me and says, "Ms. Carter, don't worry, ok? Leo is straight. He gonna be ok."

Tameka comes to terms with teaching Black students in this low-income school and the responsibility she feels for them because of their shared Blackness, and their shared history: how together they understand the ways that race and social class construct everything. We see her working beyond the resources the school provides to secure Spanish language dictionaries, to repair and restore what is possible for these students (McKinney de Royston et al. 2021). But despite all this, as the police come for Leo Adams, she is told to manage her class. We see her positioned within a system that is broken for people that look like her and share her racial identity.

We see the hope Tameka manifests, how the classroom becomes a place of pragmatic disagreement and debate, of community. The challenge here is that the community Tameka creates is very quickly interrupted by a larger system that reminds her she is, in fact, powerless.

We see Tameka develop the idea of selling language dictionaries and how she works to subvert the system to sell the dictionaries and get student buy-in. We also see how she works this dynamic to her advantage, giving her students the power to control their environment, including Leo Adams, who works to assist his teacher in understanding and navigating power within the community of the class. She gets her students engaged, but she struggles with the recognition that the larger social system will not allow her to educate her students. We see that the dreams Tameka has for Leo Adams work in direct conflict with his reality. This vignette exemplifies the difficulties Black teachers face when caring about low-income students within a system that works to oppress them both (Lyiscott 2019). Black teachers, like Tameka, feel powerless to protect the children in their care, to change the circumstances that come with learning in a low-income community, and they are denied the ability – the needed resources and support – to make learning possible.

Tameka witnesses Leo led away in handcuffs in front of his friends and peers. She is then tasked with acting as if it were normal – and her students do the same as they return to flashcards. She maintains a standard of teaching professionalism in this low-income community, being a "good manager" of an intense situation. "Going for broke" here may include Tameka encouraging her students to talk about their feelings during this volatile moment in the classroom – voicing the authentic responses of seeing someone they care for being walked away from their class in handcuffs. Tameka ultimately could have taught ideas related to race, social class, and self-advocacy in the United States while working to help herself and her students process their trauma. Instead, Tameka is directly responsible for teaching how to stay on task and ignore trauma. This vignette shows how educators are forced to provide an education that is in no way reflective of the real lives that their students are presented with (Foster 1997; Ladson-Billings 1994; Love 2019; Lyiscott 2019).

III.   Ann in a Low-Income School

Hired as a literacy consultant to help turn-around a public school destined for closure given its low-test scores and poor attendance, I asked where the library is. The brand-new Dean of Academics, a woman with tremendous energy and a zeal for rooting out weakness, gets on her walkie talkie.

"Hello, this is LaFrench . . ." (She refers to herself by her own last name, and I assume it is because she always means business). "Where's the library?"

The walkie talkie kicks back some noise. Someone says, "Third floor, by the old gym." LaFrench and I keep steady pace to the old gym. She spots some double doors, then realizes she doesn't have the key.

"This is LaFrench again. I need someone to come up here with the key to the library." The walkie talkie spits out noise, then silence. Someone grumbles into it that they are on their way. LaFrench and I make small talk. "Did you check on Norton, kids got into a fight yesterday in her 9th grade, third period class. She has them again this morning . . ." The janitor arrives with the key, he lets us in. LaFrench walks in, looks around, the walkie talkie makes some noise, she is needed elsewhere, and she leaves.

The library, which is locked down, unavailable to teachers and students, and hard to find, has a long history, but most recently, it had bed bugs and because of this, nobody, ever, wanted to go there. They fumigated, but it didn't matter: students loathed it, and teachers knew to stay away. Over 100 years old, its vast collection of least a few thousand books, new and old, lay dusty on ornate antique wood shelves, none of them digitally categorized, the remnants of the Dewey Decimal System in the corner, old computers lay here and there, various systems of checking out books layered on top of each other over the decades, all with a panoramic view of the city and its surrounding neighborhoods. A diamond in the dirt.

The English department book room (where all the books used in English class were kept) is the same. The book room is also unused and locked down. In order to open it, you have to summon the one man with the key: the English department chair (a skinny White guy who was always running around in tennis shoes). The day I ask him to show me the book room he sprints down the hall, turns down an abandoned back corridor, stops, and then produces a gigantic assortment of keys from his pocket. He riffles through the keys, finally finds the right one, and opens the room with a flourish. And there it was: thousands and thousands of books, books on books on books on books, dumped in corners, stacked on monstrous shelves, towering and ready to bury you alive should they fall.

"Well, there it is," he says as I stand gawking. "Good luck" he deadpans, "take the key and give it back to me when you're done."
And with that, he ran down the hall.

While working toward the general goal of school improvement, Ann is granted access to the library and the book room, and to what is described as "over 100 years" of resources, by other White teachers with the same access. She focuses here on two projects connected to organizing the school's library, books, and reading-related resources, which are described as isolated, shunned, chaotic, plagued, and consequently, they become an overwhelming obstacle.

Ann's idea of secondary-level academics, an organized library and resource center for teachers and students, works against the reality of academics available to the Black students at the school.

Ann attempts to work past this – trying to create an academic community space for the students and their teachers. But for Ann to do so, it means subverting the very structure of the institution itself that normalizes that these students do not have a library or a resource center, as if they had no need for such things (Love 2019). Ann experiences how, in this school, there is no place for the students and teachers to be learners and thinkers or readers in a shared space.

For Ann, pursuing the organization and use of these resources, creating spaces for thinking and community, is an insurmountable, impossible task. To do so means she is acknowledging the project of cleaning-up decades of bad faith efforts and cruelty, the cavalier disregard for the education of the students at the school. Much like Tameka in the previous vignette, Ann realizes that the larger system of race and power is bigger than her and that she is powerless to affect it. We see a system of intellectual neglect and what may feel like the useless provocation of unlikely dreams, or a dreamless reality where education is not there to care for Black and Brown children (Cole 1997; Greene 1995; Ladson-Billings 1994; Love 2019; Noguera 2003). It is in this space, in the face of systemic powerlessness, that educators work to extend and expand the little power they have, finding ways to give access to the resources and the education that is historically, systematically, and institutionally denied Black students (hooks 1994; Ladson-Billings 2006b). In selling Spanish dictionaries, or organizing book rooms, they exert a new form of powerful powerlessness – wherein, aware of their own lack of power within a larger system that works to maintain injustice in low-income communities, they take the little power they have and wield it for justice. They cannot "go for broke" as this is not a poker game, where one can go "all in." What is at stake is the real lives of teachers and students, local actors, positioned within a Goliath of a social system they are kept from dismantling and tasked specifically with upholding.

IV.   *Tameka in a Wealthy School*

This is not my favorite class. It takes a lot of energy out of me to teach the students. The white walls blend with our conversations at times. It is bland. The truth is that I feel truly ineffective in the class, but I love the content. Many times, the students stare at me in silence like I have some type of third eye.

This school was different from my previous school downtown. I was used to managing spirited conversations in a classroom with 25 kids or more, where students and I often competed to speak. New to teaching in private schools, I noticed you rarely saw kids running to class and you definitely did not hear a chiming bell or all-school announcement telling us when to begin class instruction. Class at this school began at the time in our planners or when I, as the teacher, showed up.

With only nine students in this class, I didn't understand why our class discussions didn't have as much depth as I had previously experienced with other classes outside of this school setting. I had to work a little harder to get my students to speak confidently and critically about course topics. I was unsure; this class felt inauthentic.

I decided to give the students a survey in order to figure out what the students were thinking about the class. I added questions like, "what are some things you enjoyed learning" "what are some things that you didn't like." I told the students to "please" take 15 min to complete the survey and then I would allow them to leave class early and take advantage of our "open-campus" policies.

Students turn in their surveys and make sure it is ok to leave before the end of class time. Two girls walk up to my desk. One says, "Ms. Carter, can I tell you something?" I'm a bit excited, because I can't believe she actually wanted to talk to me. She smiles, with her shoulders pressed towards her ears, "You are the first Black teacher that I ever had, and I really like you as a teacher."

"Oh, that's good, right?"

They both nod their heads and the other says, "At first I was nervous, but you really are a good teacher." I am still sitting down and start to feel sweat coming down my cold armpit, and I am hoping that no one walks in the room. "You are so different from my other teachers. Are you ok?"

I repeat the question, "Am I ok?"

In unison, they reply, "Yes."

The shorter of the two continues, "It has to be difficult to be teaching here."

The room suddenly feels smaller, and I am ashamed knowing that they are checking on me.

In transitioning from a low-income to a wealthy school, Tameka is trying to understand her new school culture. She transitions from (at best) daily work at a form of powerful powerlessness – and a focus on learning how to develop and leverage specific individual relationships with students, in a new space that feels very different. She says it is not her favorite class, and it seems in this vignette that developing relationships with students does not come as easy. She reconciles all of this with trying to understand where she fits in and the ways she belongs. She wrestles with the notion of who she is and what her value is to this predominantly White, wealthy school.

Ultimately, she learns very clearly that her purpose is defined by the students and the school itself – to be a Black teacher. As Tameka is approached by two students who tell her she is the first Black teacher they have ever had, and they check in to see how she is doing, she is surprised they are even talking to her. But they do so in order to recognize what Tameka is to them – a Black teacher – further, they are ensuring that she is okay with this position in the power structure. We see Tameka embrace her new proximity to this power, but at the end of the lesson, she is tasked with representing Blackness – speaking for it, embodying it. Even the students in this example are aware of this, and want to know if she is okay with it.

The difficulty of "going for broke" for Tameka in these spaces is the weight of representation, and how aware she is that she is stuck in-between two worlds: the maintenance of power for the affluent and the reckoning of her Blackness. She had been engaged in subversive work for the betterment of her own culture and community, but her experience within this wealthy school feels different. She is clearly consigned to a purpose – to represent Blackness – as defined by the students and educators at the school, using their White lens. Tameka in these moments becomes aware of the ways that her Blackness has become commodified – that she is on display as a Black woman for the education of wealthy White students about Blackness. Being stuck between two worlds means having to make impossible choices related to race and identity (Bonner et al. 2014; Foster 1997); "going for broke" here in wealthy educational spaces is an oversimplification of complex dynamics. To be part of this space, Tameka must choose to maintain the standard they have set for her participation: that she is complicit and that she accommodates the power structures that are already existing and in place within the school. She must work to placate her own marginalization and positioning, fully aware that she is allowing others to define her by her race as who she is professionally.

V. Ann in a Wealthy School

> The 11th grade students are reading *The Great Gatsby*, F. Scott Fitzgerald's (2004) novel about the hollowness of the American Dream, set in New York in the roaring twenties; I want to get kids excited to read this book. My classroom is on the second floor of a 100-year-old palatial country estate, has a marble fireplace and double doors to a veranda that overlook a formal garden, designed

at the turn of the century to resemble the gardens of grand country estates in Europe, like Versailles. This is where the students now, in their free-time, play frisbee, sun themselves, and dine al fresco on snacks.

Jay Gatsby, the lead character of the book, famously holds raucous parties at his home, which helps the books' readers to understand the excess of the twenties and his personal wealth. I announce we will be having "Gatsby's Party" one evening after school. I describe the event as a chance to create fiction on fiction – students need to develop an original character that would have attended a party at the home of Jay Gatsby. They will dress as these characters and spend an hour in character attending Jay "Gatsby's Party" in the pristine, white-marbled garden room of the mansion.

The day of the event a tiered platter of cupcakes and punch arrive from the school's catering kitchen, along with tiny clear plastic cups, tiny napkins, doilies, white linen, a table, and a man from catering asking me where I want him to set everything up. The students themselves came in varying degrees of twenties costuming. Most tried as if their grades depend on it. They approach me with various worries: they were not in costume enough; they need to leave early because of sports commitments; they want to know how I am grading this; they want to know what to say, to do, and how to act to be perfect.

Ann, in a wealthy school, works to gain student buy-in for the study of a classic American novel about wealth, power, and social stratification. As she works to plan an event for these students, she becomes aware that these students have already "bought-in," have read the book, and are striving for perfection. There is no negotiation with them about why they should study this American portrayal of wealth and power and the effects of social class displayed in the book. Here, they are most concerned with maintaining their power within this space – they want to know exactly what to do here, what to think, and how to behave. They want to know how their understanding of the book will be measured and graded. They want to understand how in this moment, to have power, and they want to learn how to do the right things in the right ways that will allow them the ability to wield and extend that power. They are learning how to live well, in excess, not to push back, which would not be in their own self-interests.

Ann becomes complicit in normalizing the power of the powerful in wealthy educational spaces – it is taught as unapologetic, overt, and unquestioned. Teachers teach American novels written by American men involving White Americans and their historical quest for wealth and status, in English. We see a school with marble and gardens, aggrandizing excess wealth and luxury (Giroux & Penna 1979), providing the real-world trappings of an elite life as imagined in the novel itself. We see students in this space not needing buy-in to claim their power here. Rather, surrounded by wealth and power, they are happy to read about wealth and power. We see Ann experience a wealthy schooling system as a power mill for the powerful.

Naming and being conscious of the ways that we teach the powerful in affluent spaces about their power is difficult for educators in those spaces. As exemplified by this vignette, wealthy systems of education remind educators that their job is about maintaining standards related to the replication of power. Schooling becomes the development of skills needed for power. This is the secondary education of the future CEO, of the one percent, of future presidents, in short, the education of the elite. Students in this space learn about all the power they have in all they are tasked to do and in all the ways they are tasked to do it (Giroux & Penna 1979); teachers are expected to facilitate this experience. To educate in wealthy spaces means the acceptance and maintenance of the larger inequitable system, not the disruption of it.

To "go for broke" in these wealthy spaces suggests that teachers help students to learn how to resist their own power, how to share it, and how to give it away. But this sort of educative work means one teaches in a state of constant insecurity. It would mean not fitting in with a school culture that embraces wealth unproblematically, and the possibility of being perceived as a pariah, not a positive change agent.

VI.   *Tameka in a Wealthy School*

As I look through my inbox, I see an invitation to have a dialogue with the administration about the hiring and retention of diverse faculty. I think about how I love this school, and I happily start packing up my bag to get ready to go home.

I hear the beep of a keycard entry in my department's shared office, and I see my colleague walk towards the center of the office and place her keycard on the table in front of my desk.

"Hello" she says, with neither a smile nor frown as an expression.

"Hi. How are you?" I say this with intentional cheer, knowing that traffic would soon be at its worst if I did not leave within the next ten minutes.

"Oh, I'm fine", she replies. "Ready for the weekend. Do you have any big plans this weekend?" I was not used to sharing personal information with her. This was my first time speaking with her since my interview at the school.

"I'm excited about attending a dialogue with the administration."

She stands erect with her eyebrows lifted. "Oh! You were invited to that?" she says with a high pitch.

"I have never been to anything like this and it should be really interesting, no?" My pace quickens even more, and I mumble, "Yeah, you know, I don't know. I guess they think I have something to add." I laugh and roll my eyes to downplay myself. My experience with certain White people has taught me to always brace myself when the pitch and tone of their voice change.

"Oh yeah, so you are like the token. Yeah, I get that," she responds.

"Excuse me? What did you just say?" I stand erect, look at her with wide understanding eyes.

Her pitch becomes higher, "Oh yeah, I don't mean to offend you. Oh my gosh, I hope I didn't, but it's just I don't understand why they would invite you and you just started here. I mean, it's like you wouldn't have much to add, but they probably just invited you because you are the token Black, you know." She laughs and smiles at me.

Wait! What? Did this White woman just call me a token to my face? I try my hardest not to make my thoughts audible. It is hard to suppress what I really want to say, but I have been trained by some of the stealthiest Black women. I smile back at her, "I'm sure I'll have something to add."

"Oh, of course, yeah", she says, looking even more erect.

We look at each other in silence, I put my bag on my shoulder and say what I was taught to say whenever I want to end a destructive conversation. "Okay, well, I have to go. I hope you have a blessed day."

This dialogue reveals the way that Tameka feels understood in a wealthy, predominantly White educational space. She encounters a fellow teacher who questions her inclusion in an administrative-related work meeting. Throughout the conversation, we see the difficulty here is becoming tokenized in predominantly White, wealthy schools, and in this example Tameka is made aware of her colleagues' perceptions of her contributions directly. By the end, we see Tameka's growing awareness that if a seat at the table is offered, that seat is always perceived as a powerless show. We see her come to understand that in this space, she becomes a token, and consequently, her work will be devalued and diminished. We see her come to terms with her participation in a schooling system built for the powerful and with her own complicity in creating an illusion of diversity and shared power.

Often in low-income schooling, injustice becomes very visible for educators: poverty, literacy rates, attendance rates, student homelessness, the narrowing of curriculum, and the tightening of teacher accountability measures. But, in this example from a wealthy community surfaces the racism and difficulties inherent in teaching in predominantly White, affluent schools – that power given to Black teachers can become tokenized as an example of diversity (Bonner II et al. 2014). We see how those who maintain power destroy the confidence of those who bring different perspectives and values to systemic norms (Foster 1997; hooks 1994). For Tameka, we see she is excited to be invited to a place where decisions are being made and offered an opportunity to share her work. Yet, she is quickly reminded that she is powerless, reminded that her work, or rather her value to the school community is only a token to those in power used to make themselves feel good, as someone more progressive or benevolent, because they have now "achieved" diversity.

The difficulty in these spaces for teachers is in being aware of the racial dynamics that construct and retain power (Love 2019). As experienced by Tameka, there are people that maintain and enforce power, and she is tasked to either become complicit in this and create an identity within this, or work elsewhere.

Conclusion

In low-income spaces, Ann replicates and enforces narrowed educational standards. She is kept from resisting dominant power structures and from asking critical questions. Instead, it is a necessity of the job that she bears witness to systemic educational neglect. In these spaces, we see the personal and subversive ways Tameka works for hope within a larger racist system and the powerlessness she experiences working within a system that standardizes the oppression of people like her. Tameka and her students are forced to endure race-related trauma and to press on. These examples illustrate how in low-income spaces, educators experience schooling as an exercise in being forced to accept educational cruelty and neglect, while also being demanded to maintain it.

In wealthy spaces, Tameka becomes defined and given meaning by students and colleagues. The tokenization she experiences from both students and teachers impacts her identity as an educator and her perception of power. In these spaces, Ann becomes complicit in normalizing unquestioned wealth and privilege and in teaching children how to grab power that is unchecked and unquestioned. In service to the wealthy, Ann and Tameka experience tremendous difficulties in different ways, being Black and unseen and being White and unquestioned, destabilizing experiences in wealthy spaces we share with many teaching in the United States today.

In some ways, we experience complexities related to race and social class similarly. We are often rendered powerless and just part of a larger system of oppression we are actively kept from dismantling. We see how we both navigate our complicity in systems of educational inequality and inequity in both low-income and wealthy spaces. In both educational spaces, we maintain systems of oppression – work that is always unstable, unpredictable, and dangerous.

We can only imagine that, similar to ourselves, educators can identify the ways that they experience precarious educational spaces, and how their own identities are implicated in these dynamics. When educators share the stories they have of the difficulties, challenges, instability, unpredictability, and danger they face, they begin to create bridges of communication across the lines of race and social class – like we did here. They allow for conversation as resistance to oppression – glimmers of opportunity to extend the little power they have. In this space, educators may finally find a place to "go for broke" (Baldwin 1998) and dismantle decades of bad faith and cruelty that have persisted within the educational system and society more broadly. While these discourses may run underground, those who engage in them fight back. And they lay the groundwork for action and transformative change.

Notes

1. The number of students qualifying for "free and reduced-price" lunch at public schools in the United States is often how schools report the income status of parents (Ladson-Billings 1994, 1995; Noguera 2003; Gay 2010). Using this proxy for socioeconomic

status, schools often report on the number of low-income families they service (Harwell & LeBeau 2010).
2. Charter schools are publicly funded schools that are often managed by private companies or nonprofit organizations. The "charter" is an agreement with the school district that exempts the school from some of the district processes, replacing them with an agreed-upon alternative approach.
3. "Gates" money refers to money donated by the Bill and Melinda Gates Foundation. The philanthropic efforts of tech entrepreneurs and their foundations, such as this one, often direct and set educational policy for poor children (Giroux 2011).
4. The Pre-ACT refers to the standardized test given to grade 10 students that is intended to predict their success on the ACT (American College Test), which is a standardized test commonly taken by some American high school students in grade 11 to assess university readiness for college. In the above example, 9th graders (freshmen) were preparing for a test taken in the 10th grade to predict success on the ACT taken in the 11th grade.

References

Baldwin, James. 1998. *Collected Essays*. New York: Library of America.

Bonner II, Fred, Arethea F. Marbley, Frank Tuitt, Petra Robinson, Rosa Banda, and Robin Hughes (eds.). 2014. *Black Faculty in the Academy: Narratives for Negotiating Identity and Achieving Career Success*. London: Taylor & Francis.

Cole, Johnetta B. 1997. *Dream the Boldest Dreams: And Other Lessons of Life*. Atlanta: Longstreet Press.

Delpit, Lisa. 1995. *Other People's Children: Cultural Conflict in the Classroom*. New York: The New Press.

Ellis, Carolyn. 2004. *The Ethnographic I: A Methodological Novel About Autoethnography*. Walnut Creek, CA: AltaMira.

Ellis, Carolyn, and Arthur P. Bochner (eds.). 2000. Autoethnography, Personal Narrative, Reflexivity. In Norman Denzin and Yvonna Lincoln (eds.), *Handbook of Qualitative Research*, 2nd edition (pp. 733–768). Thousand Oaks, CA: Sage.

Fine, Michelle. 2018. *Just Research in Contentious Times: Widening the Methodological Lens*. New York: Teacher College Press.

Fitzgerald, F. Scott. 2004. *The Great Gatsby*. New York: Scribner.

Foster, Michele. 1997. *Black Teachers on Teaching*. New York: The New Press.

Freire, Paolo. 1974. *Pedagogy of the Oppressed*. New York: The Seabury Press.

Garrison, Mark. 2009. *A Measure of Failure: The Political Origins of Standardized Testing*. Albany, NY: SUNY Press.

Gay, Geneva. 2010. *Culturally Responsive Teaching: Theory, Research, and Practice*. New York: Teachers College Press.

Giroux, Henry. 2011. *Education and the Crisis of Public Values: Challenging the Assault on Teachers, Students, and Public Education*. New York: Peter Lang.

Giroux, Henry, and Anthony Penna. 1979. Social Education in the Classroom: The Dynamics of the Hidden Curriculum. *Theory & Research in Social Education* 7(1): 21–42.

Greene, Maxine. 1995. *Releasing the Imagination: Essay on Education, the Arts and Social Change*. San Francisco: Jossey-Bass Publishers.

Harwell, Michael, and Brandon LeBeau. 2010. Student Eligibility for a Free Lunch as an SES Measure in Education Research. *Educational Researcher* 39(2): 120–131. www.jstor.org/stable/27764564

hooks, bell. 1994. *Teaching to Transgress*. New York: Routledge.

Illich, Ivan. 1983. *Deschooling Society*. New York: Harper Colophon.

Ladson-Billings, Gloria. 1994. *The Dreamkeepers: Successful Teachers of Black Children*. San Francisco: Jossey-Bass.

Ladson-Billings, Gloria. 1995. Toward a Theory of Culturally Relevant Pedagogy. *American Educational Research Journal* 32(3): 465–491.

Ladson-Billings, Gloria. 2006a. From the Achievement Gap to the Education Debt: Understanding Achievement in U.S. Schools. *Educational Researcher* 35(7): 3–12.

Ladson-Billings, Gloria. 2006b. "Yes, But How Do We Do It?" Practicing Culturally Relevant Pedagogy. In Julie Landsman and Chance W. Lewis (eds.), *White Teachers/Diverse Classrooms* (pp. 162–177). Sterling, VA: Stylus Publishers.

Lawrence-Lightfoot, Sarah. 1983. *The Good High School: Portraits of Character and Culture*. New York: Basic Books.

Levinson, Bradley, Douglas Foley, and Dorothy Holland (eds.). 1996. *The Cultural Production of the Educated Person: Critical Ethnographies of Schooling and Local Practice*. Albany, NY: SUNY Press.

Love, Bettina. 2019. *We Want to Do More Than Survive: Abolitionist Teaching and Pursuit of Educational Freedom*. Boston: Beacon Press.

Lyiscott, Jamila. 2019. *Black Appetite, White Food: Issues of Race, Voice, and Justice Within and Beyond the Classroom*. New York: Routledge.

McKinney de Royston, Maxine, Tia C. Madkins, Jarvis R. Givens, and Na'ilah Suad Nasir. 2021. "I'm a Teacher, I'm Gonna Always Protect You": Understanding Black Educators' Protection of Black Children. *American Educational Research Journal* 58(1): 68–106.

Noguera, Pedro. 2003. *City Schools and the American Dream: Fulfilling the Promise of Public Education*. New York: Teachers College Press.

Porfilio, Brad J., and Paul R. Carr (eds.). 2010. *Youth Culture, Education and Resistance: Subverting the Commercial Ordering of Life*. Rotterdam: Sense Publishers.

Watkins, William. 2001. *The White Architects of Black Education: Ideology and Power in America, 1865–1954*. New York: Teachers College Press.

9 Fleeing Home, Finding Home, and Chasing Dreams

Refugee Journeys to New Spaces for Belonging

Yacoub Aljaffery

Introduction

Nearly 54,000 refugees resettled in the United States in 2017 and about 45,000 in 2018, mostly from Iraq, Syria, Democratic Republic of Congo, Somalia, and Burma (Fratzke 2019; Zong & Batalova 2017). Refugees cannot return to their countries – to qualify as a refugee one must have a well-founded fear of persecution or death (UNHCR 2018). Before resettling in new home countries, refugees pass through several phases of migration, and they may spend years in refugee camps or other interim locations before they are either approved or rejected by a host country. This chapter examines the experiences of ten refugees from a variety of countries, with a focus on how education has played a role in their transitions from their homelands to settling in the United States. All participants arrived in the United States during their high school years.

   The impetus for this study with refugee students grew out of my own experience as a teenage refugee who came to the United States as a high school student, pursued a career in teaching English as a Second Language (ESL), and taught refugee students. While many existing studies focus on immigrant students, few have examined refugee students' academic and social experience in US public schools. This study chronicles their journeys to the United States and experiences of finding a sense of home in their new schools and communities, as a basis from which to chase their dreams.

Literature Review

Journeys from homelands through temporary places provide a necessary context for understanding experiences related to settling in a new land and becoming integrated into a new society. Educational experiences are shaped by those histories.

Refugee Life and Migration Experience

Refugees migrate, but not all immigrants are refugees. Refugees are those who flee their home country to escape death or persecution, seeking a safer

DOI: 10.4324/9781003258223-11

place in another country. They have to meet certain criteria to be considered refugees before qualifying for resettlement.[1] Migration studies scholarship makes it clear there are various phases in the migration process. For refugees it is similar, although the experiences in those phases can be quite different due to the conditions that forced their migration journeys. Most scholars identify three phases to migration. The first relates to how families make decisions and prepare to migrate, the second is the actual journey, and the third is the often much longer settlement phase of becoming integrated into the new land (Chavez 2013; Massey et al. 1987). In Anderson et al.'s (2004) work with refugees, they call these phases pre-migration, transmigration, and post-migration.[2]

The pre-migration phase refers to the experiences and context prior to migrating. For refugees, this usually includes the conditions in their countries they experience related to persecution and genocide, human rights violations, or warfare, which qualify them to be considered refugees. During this period, many refugee children either witness or directly experience the murder of family members, sometimes forcing them to flee without any accompanying adults (Anderson et al. 2004).

The transmigration phase is the period when they are moving to safety, sometimes on foot, and often to a temporary location such as a refugee camp. During this phase, food, water, and shelter are often in short supply, and the journeys can last weeks or months before some semblance of safety and stability is reached (Anderson et al. 2004). In addition, access to education is often limited if it even exists, and schools are short on supplies and teachers. Therefore, many refugees arrive in their country of resettlement with limited literacy skills and often with large gaps in their formal educational experience (Dryden-Peterson 2016).

The third phase of post-migration starts after refugees arrive in their final country of resettlement. In this phase, refugee students and their families face a mixed set of positive and negative experiences. They adapt to new cultures and forms of social participation, and learn about new education systems. The formal refugee resettlement process involves short-term support to meet sponsors, to find housing and work for adults, and to enroll in school for children and youths. This social integration and cultural adaptation process is long and often difficult, although it can be made easier by informed teachers. School experience is the main institutional space where newcomers learn about their new society's ways of living and learning.

Schooling Experience

Refugee students face both negative and positive experiences throughout their migration journeys before and after their formal resettlement in their new country. Some of these experiences include interrupted schooling, bullying, and discrimination. Students' experience is influenced by how they feel they are understood by teachers.

Student Educational Experience

Interrupted education and questionable quality of schools are two issues refugee students experience prior to their arrival in their country of final resettlement. In their countries of origin, formal schooling is often interrupted during times of war and strife. Enroute, schooling can be further interrupted. In 2014, only 50% of refugee children received formal education (UNHCR 2016), either because some countries do not allow refugee children to enter their schools. The UN Refugee Agency (UNHCR) is not permitted to build schools for refugees in some locations (Dryden-Peterson 2016) or because the routes to schools are too dangerous. Some students face legal restrictions entering schools in countries of asylum. For example, the Rohingya refugees are considered to be undocumented immigrants in Malaysia and so their children are not allowed to enter schools (Dryden-Peterson 2016). Those with access to schools in their host countries or refugee camps often face poor school quality. Some experience a lack of textbooks and materials, and others might not have the chance to be taught by a professional teacher.

Bullying and discrimination are other issues researchers shed light on. Refugee children can face discrimination in the country of their first asylum (Dryden-Peterson 2016) and also in the schools of their host country (Ennab 2017). Discrimination can be based on their accent, nationality, and migration status (Mthethwa-Sommers & Kisiara 2015).

Although some refugee adolescents might be marginalized in US high schools, many turn their negative experiences into empowering ones (Ryu & Tuvilla 2018). Ryu and Tuvilla (2018) found that students valued their lives in the United States and saw them as opportunities for a better future, despite the challenges. Refugee students tend to be ambitious and goal driven.

Teaching Refugee Students

For students who have experienced trauma, it is important for teachers to help them adapt by providing extra time to listen and converse so students feel safe and appreciated (Abud 2017). Due to their interrupted education, some refugee students might need extra academic and emotional support from teachers (Mendenhall, Bartlett, & Ghaffar-Kucher 2017). Empathetic teachers can be a positive addition to refugee students' academic progress. According to Ryu and Tuvilla (2018), teachers who encourage their refugee students to speak up in class and talk about their experiences have had positive influence on their students. Furthermore, schools and teachers play an important role in creating a more inclusive learning environment for refugee students through activities and approaches that foster meaningful relationships, including interacting with parents and community members (Block et al. 2014).

Teachers who also have experienced migration or refugee life may have an advantage: "Due to their shared experiences with marginalization and discrimination, teachers of diverse linguistic and cultural backgrounds are well-positioned to develop positive relationships with their students" (Faez 2012, p. 68). Meaningful relationships create a basis for learning, and learning needs to be broad and varied for refugee (and immigrant) students, i.e., they need to learn more than just the English language.

Methodology

To understand the experiences of refugee students in US public schools and how, from the students' perspectives, their teachers engage with them and account for their precarious past, I drew on narrative inquiry as a research methodology (Clandinin & Connelly 2000). Using narrative inquiry allows participants to narrate their own stories. These stories reveal how they make meaning of their experiences.

Participants were recruited based on refugee status, having arrived in the United States during high school, and currently attending college. Their narratives focused on educational and life histories prior to arrival and their experiences in secondary school. The ten participants were each interviewed twice for a total of two to three hours. All interviews were conducted in English because I did not share language with some of them and because those with whom I shared language, when given a choice of the language they wanted to use, chose English.

Introducing the Participants

All ten participants arrived in the United States during their high school years. When interviewed in 2019, all were in two-year community colleges or four-year colleges; their ages ranged from 18 to 26 years. They had been successful enough in their schooling in the United States to matriculate into college. Since the participants were in college, they had had time to reflect on their migration and US high school experiences.

Out of the ten participants, five are from Burma (Myanmar[3]); two from Syria; and one each from Iraq, Somalia, and Ethiopia. Six are men and four are women. (See Table 9.1.)

Table 9.1 Participants

Pseudonym	Gender	Age	Country of Origin	Ethnic, Cultural, or Religious Affiliation
Htoo	Male	22	Burma	Karen
Moses	Male	18	Burma	Karen
Napoleon	Male	19	Burma	Karen
Lah	Female	25	Burma	Korani/Karen
Kwa Lar	Male	20	Burma	
Eynas	Female	19	Syria	
Mohammad	Male	21	Syria	
Ghassan	Male	26	Iraq	Christian
Naema	Female	19	Somalia	
Fatima	Female	23	Ethiopia	

All participants in this study came to the United States via refugee camps or countries neighboring their home countries due to war, violence, and persecution. Their journeys varied in length and trajectory, as will be presented in the next section.

Findings: Fleeing Home – Finding Home

The interviews with these refugee students reveal a mixture of feelings, including sad and happy stories, challenges, and also experiences of support. Their narrations include rich detail about their migration journeys before resettling in the United States and how their high school experiences then facilitated a new sense of belonging.

Journeys From Home to the United States

Migration is not a short or predictable path for most refugees, without a clear distinction between pre-migration and migration. All participants came to the United States with refugee status. When families arrive in refugee camps, they apply for refugee status with the UNHCR. The wait time varies. Some spend many years or maybe decades waiting to be deemed a refugee. Some refugees end up in refugee camps, which are usually governed by the UNHCR, and some find their way to cities in neighboring countries. Those in refugee camps are often not allowed to leave their camps and find work outside, and those who flee to cities in neighboring countries are often not allowed to work or even rent a place (Obi 2021). Many of the participants lived in refugee camps, some in multiple camps or locations. Their journeys took from 3 to 17 years between leaving their home countries and resettling in the United States. They all talked about the rough and sometimes deadly journey they had to take to escape their countries seeking a safer place to live.

Htoo's village was attacked by the Burmese army.[4] At age three, Htoo was too young to remember the details, but his parents told him repeatedly about the raping and murdering that took place in their village. Htoo's family is from the Karen ethnic group, which has been in conflict with the Burmese majority for decades. In 2000, Htoo's parents fled Burma to a refugee camp in Thailand,[5] where they thought it would be safer for the family. Htoo and his family crossed the mountains, walking for several days to get to Thailand.

Moses and Napoleon, also ethnically Karen, witnessed murder and rape by the Burmese soldiers in their villages, and they both talked about a tough path to the refugee camps. Napoleon was born in a refugee camp in Thailand and lived in two more camps before being granted refugee status. Napoleon said:

> The refugee camp [is] similar to jail. You cannot go out or communicate with Thai people or any people outside the Karen people. I mean, when they put you in place and you cannot move anywhere.

Lah also fled Burma and lived in Thai refugee camps from age three to 19. Kwa Lar was born in a Thai refugee camp. After losing their home and farm in Burma, Kwa Lar's family fled to a refugee camp in Thailand through the jungles. His family told him many stories about the killing and raping that happened in their village. Kwa Lar's father was the leader of their refugee camp. Napoleon said they moved from camp to camp because their camps were flooded and their houses, made of bamboo trees, were destroyed. Then, they had to walk for six to seven days to reach the other, safer refugee camp. Moses shared his experience:

> There were so much problems. I saw children get killed and women get raped. . . . You wake up and you hear guns and women and children cry. My parents decided to leave to Thailand to a refugee camp. . . . They carried me and we walked for several days and at nights in the dark, you cannot even have light because it is too dangerous. They maybe shoot you. We had little bit for rice to have for food. But after we finished our rice, we eat everything we find in the forest. Then we had to cross the river to Thailand. It was dangerous.

Many of the participants experienced wars and described this as very scary. Eynas and her family fled Syria to the border with Iraq after war broke out in their city, Aleppo – she was ten years old. Eynas experienced the beginning of the war between the government army and the people who demonstrated for freedom. Then, religious militias took over the city, and the government started bombing their city. After living in the camp in Iraq for two years, her family went to another refugee camp in Turkey, where they stayed for three years until coming to the United States.

Ghassan fled Iraq at age 10 and lived in Jordan for five years. When the United States invaded Iraq in 2003, a civil war among different ethnic groups broke out. Ghassan is Christian, and his people were attacked by other religious militias that belonged to Al-Qaeda. After failing to arrive to Europe through a smuggler, Ghassan's father got stuck in Nepal, leaving Ghassan to be the person responsible for the household. He worked as a mechanic at a shop to support his family.

Similarly, Mohammad, Fatima, and Naema also talked about their memories of wars they experienced before fleeing to refugee camps. When Naema was seven years old, a civil war broke out in her small town in Somalia. Tribes were killing each other; attacking houses; and killing men, women, and children. Naema lost some of her relatives in the war. She described the war and the sounds of bombs as the worst experience of her life. At age seven, Naema, her mother, and six of her siblings – including twin infant brothers – escaped from Somalia to Ethiopia. They took a bus to the Somali-Ethiopian border. The bus took three days to reach the border because it took different routes to avoid the rebellion; if caught, they would have been killed. She arrived in the United States at age 17. Fatima's family fled Ethiopia in 2008 to Kenya because of the civil war between the Amharic and Oromo, and two years later arrived in the United States. Fatima has not reunited with her family yet. She came with her father, but her mother is still in Ethiopia because she could not leave the country. Mohammad left Syria for Lebanon after a civil war broke out in Syria, and both of his uncles were arrested. They have not heard anything about the uncles to this day.

The difficulties these students faced did not end in the refugee camp or in their home countries, although all would say that life in the United States is safer. These students' lives after resettling in the United States were also a mixture of happy and sad stories.

Education Before and During Migration

Schooling experiences in their homelands varied, as did their educational experiences enroute between fleeing home and arriving in the United States (see Table 9.2). Their educational histories ranged from having no formal education prior to arrival in the United States (Fatima) to having finished secondary school prior to migrating (Lah). Most had some schooling either in their home country or in refugee camps, and some repeated grades. Htoo and Moses experienced only a few years of schooling prior to arriving in the United States. Schooling occurred primarily in refugee camps for those from Burma. Refugee schools are usually not the same as going to formal, established schools. Teachers can be volunteers, some without any training. Usually in refugee camps, teachers are from the same refugee camp and are the same age as their students. Moreover, schools in refugee camps lack basic resources, such as textbooks, supplies, and electricity (Ramírez Carpeño & Feldman 2015).

Table 9.2 Participants' Educational Histories

Pseudonym	Education Prior to Arrival in the United States	Grades Attended in US High Schools	Current Year in College[6]
Htoo	Kindergarten in refugee camp	9th to 12th grades, repeated 12th grade twice	2nd year
Moses	Kindergarten multiple years, in refugee camp	9th to 12th grades	1st year
Napoleon	In the refugee camps in Thailand: Karen school to grade 5, then Burmese school to grade 7, then Karen school	9th to 12th grades (age 14). 10th grade twice	1st year
Lah	Finished high school in refugee camp (no diploma); speaks three languages; taught children there	9th, 11th, switched back and forth; finished before age 21	Community college, 2nd year

Pseudonym	Education Prior to Arrival in the United States	Grades Attended in US High Schools	Current Year in College
Kwa Lar	10th grade in refugee camp	9th to 12th grades	Community college, 1st year
Eynas	Partial 6th grade in Syria	11th to 12th grades	1st year
Mohammad	Until 6th grade in Syria	9th grade, then got cancer, went back and finished high school	3rd year
Ghassan	Iraq, until 4th grade Jordan – gap, then school until 6th grade	10th to 12th grades	4th year
Naema	1st to 10th in refugee camp in Ethiopia	10th to 12th grades	1st year
Fatima	No formal education, knew how to read and write	9th to 12th grades, repeated 12th' three-year gap before college	2nd year

Eynas, Mohammad, and Ghassan had some formal education before fleeing their home countries, but others – especially those who were born in refugee camps – did not attend any formal schooling, although they did learn basic reading, writing, and math. Despite limited schooling, these students are linguistically talented. Some of them speak two or three languages; for example, Lah speaks Karen, Koran, and Thai and Naema speaks Somali and Amharic.

Journeys Through US High Schools

Adjustment processes varied, after arrival in the United States, with teachers seen as integral to the students' settlement experiences, which enabled to chase their dreams.

Adjusting to US Schools

Schools are social spaces that can be both supportive and challenging for all students, but for newcomers, adjusting to a new school as well as a new country can be difficult. The students in this study experienced academic, cultural, and social struggles in their high schools. Several explained that their lack of language skills caused many problems, especially during their first year of high school. Moses and Napoleon said their poor language and thick accents impeded their interactions in and outside class. Class discussions were also a challenge. A number of participants said they had no background about the topics discussed in class and felt completely lost. For example, Eynas said that at home, they only watched Arabic television, and when the class discussed an issue on US news or a recent movie, she could not understand the topic and was unable to take part in the conversation. When the class discussed something related to American culture, she became anxious and hoped her teacher would not call on her because she would not know what to say.

Mental health challenges, such as depression, also affected students' academic performance. Some of them talked about depression and anxiety as it is related to their experience in refugee camps and settling in a new culture. Several talked about having no desire to do homework or attend school. Lah was more articulate about her mental health, and she spoke about it in more detail, explaining that she missed many school days because she did not want to leave the house and because the smell of the air made her feel uncomfortable. Often, she fainted in class because she felt dizzy due to her depression and anxiety and did not want to be around people.

Some teachers knew little about them, their circumstances, or about the parts of the world from which they came. Most teachers never asked – they taught the students as if they had no history or life before high school in the United States. For example, Ghassan said his math teacher did not allow him to ask questions and she told him to seek help from his parents if he needed extra help, which he found difficult since his parents did not have enough education to teach him. This same math teacher also claimed she was busy whenever he went to her office, which upset Ghassan. Eynas told of how her history teacher did not want to learn about her history and when she gave a presentation about her country for a class assignment, the teacher thanked her and asked her to have a seat, without asking or allowing for any questions, as was done for other students.

Unfortunately, refugee students often face obstacles, not only language barriers and the unfamiliar school system but also poverty, posttraumatic stress, and insecure housing (Block et al. 2014). Despite having to flee home and violence, often witnessing murder, living in limbo for years with inconsistent formal schooling, and facing new cultural norms, all the students have persevered, successfully completing high school, and now in college. They attribute much of their success to their high school English teachers who showed interest in them.

Finding Home at School

The participants appreciate the support they received from many of their ESL high school teachers. Several noted the encouragement they received, as they motivated them to have goals. Naema described a paper she had to write for her ESL writing class and her uncertainty about a topic. Because she is from Somalia, the teacher showed her a video of Ilhan Omar.[7] This helped to connect the writing class to something meaningful in her life and was motivating.

Teachers used many practices that were motivational. Prayer was a practice that most students mentioned. Some said that every morning their ESL teacher would allow five to ten minutes for students to pray or meditate, depending on their religious practice. When Naema's ESL teacher did so, Naema recited verses of the Quran, which helped to relax her. Htoo and Napoleon said they sat in a circle and prayed every morning and that enabled them to focus and relax.

Sharing stories in class was also an important practice that the students mentioned. They liked the activities their ESL teachers used to help them share their stories. For example, Htoo was proud when his teacher asked him to tell his story in class, and students asked him questions afterward, showing interest.

In addition to teaching practices, the students valued how close they felt to some of their teachers. Similar to Naema, Kwa Lar believed that he had a good relationship with his ESL teacher because the teacher understood him due to having been a volunteer teacher in Thai refugee camps. He believed that, because she had seen what refugees in Thailand experience, she understood his needs and knew how to make him feel welcomed. Napoleon also felt his teachers had more relevant experience because they had taught many refugees. Eynas and Moses's ESL teachers were former refugees themselves, so had similar experiences. Moses described his relationship with his teacher: "you know, my ESL teacher teach in same refugee camp I live before. She know everything. . . . She always teach me about other subjects in free time." Eynas also saw her ESL teacher, who came from Bosnia as a refugee, as a role model. These participants felt closer to their teachers who shared similar life experiences. They felt like their histories and current experiences were understood, and felt seen, accepted, and welcomed in their ESL classes.

Many participants talked about how they felt comfortable with some school practices. For example, Naema felt that her ESL teachers made school a second home. Her school had all religious and cultural celebrations – Eid, Diwali, and Christmas – which all ESL students attended. Naema said these celebrations made her and her friends feel that their religious and cultural practices were important. In talking about her teachers, she notes:

> When came like a celebration day. They celebrate with us. They wear the Hijab even if they are not Muslims, so she can show us like how [to] respect our culture or what we believe. . . . I feel like so happy. I'm like, wow, we have someone loves my culture and someone who respect me. I was crying. . . . Yeah. So I actually feel like I belong to this school, and I feel like this school is my home and teachers [are] like my family.

For Eynas, school activities also made her feel that she belonged. Her ESL teacher took students to "game day" at the gym where they played different games. In addition, Eynas' teacher took the class to the Festival of Nations[8] every year, and those excursions gave her a sense of comfort, especially when her country was presented at the festival. Similarly, Moses felt that being part of the school's sports team was an important influence on his school adaptation and success, which was also motivational:

> Like, when I was freshmen, my ESL teacher tell me about join the sport team because she know I like wrestling. . . . I like it so much. I feel very comfortable, the team, the coach, they were all good. I feel school is more fun, and also if you play sports, it can improve your grades in science too, so I was improving my grades.

In conclusion, refugee students certainly appreciated support from their teachers, which helped them remain positive and motivated. Learning opportunities where students share their stories and write about former refugees has a positive impact on them. The support and care teachers have shown with these students helped them feel a sense of home in their high schools.

From Precarious Histories to Chasing New Dreams

All participants talked about their dreams for the future. Their dreams are not limited only to continuing their education but also finding well-paying jobs and, for some of them, owning a house for the first time in their lives. This orientation arose out of noticing precarious condition of the past and appreciating new opportunities in the United States, and from family and teacher support.

All participants wanted to make their parents proud, a goal that kept them on the right academic track. Napoleon, for example, believed that he needed to pay back his parents because they went through a hard life to get to a better place and better future. Similarly, Moses said his parents always reminded him about their past and the lack of educational opportunities, which was one reason they came to the United States. For Moses, these reminders were a huge motivator that compelled him to chase his dreams.

Moreover, parental support was important. Their parents had little or no education, and could not help with their homework. However, their parents pushed them to study and learn, and some said their parents prayed for them to be successful, as Naema observed: "My mom didn't, she never went to school. She never went to school. So, like I want be, but she want us to be educated people too . . . she would push us. Like go to school and learning."

Witnessing their parents' struggles, their own challenging lives in the refugee camps, and their parents' encouragement to succeed made these students stronger. Their parents brought their children to the United States for a better life, as Ghassan shares:

> I think for me, I tried to push myself harder and challenge myself, thinking about my parents and how much they did for us to provide the life we have today. So, I cannot take that for granted. So, I think the biggest motivation, you know, all the hard work that family provided for us.

Education is understood as the main source of a better life in the United States. They wanted to show that they were not simply refugees, but they were educated refugees and able to contribute to society. Htoo said, "education is very important to me. It's gonna have your future. In my culture, if you have education, if you know that thing [have knowledge], people gonna respect you. They gonna put you on top." Similarly, Moses tried to connect his refugee camp experience with his new life in the United States to help him continue chasing his dreams, remarking:

> In refugee camp we think of living, food, and water but don't think about education because, you know, we don't have opportunity. In America there is more hope and more education. So, I want [to] complete my education, so my parents become proud of me and happy because they don't go to school in our home country.

In addition to education, several students, especially those from the refugee camps in Thailand, said they were grateful to have legal documents for the first time in their lives. Moses explains:

> When we come here we come with no documents. We don't have ID card or anything, but we come with blue bag from the IOM [International Organization for Migration], from UNHCR, and this is like our passport. They open it, and they give us I-94 card.⁹ It was my first document in my life.

Several students remarked how much it meant to them to be able to practice their religion and freedom of speech without fear. For example, Napoleon said that he was happy to be here practicing his religion and culture and speaking his own language, because in Burma, if one tries to write in the Karen language, the government would cut off one's fingers.

The United States has given them many opportunities including education, medical care, jobs, and the opportunity to own property. Moses appreciates the financial assistance he received until he was settled and found a job. Kwa Lar values the financial aid for his college education – in contrast to education in his refugee camp, which was not free. Napoleon acknowledges that his family was able to buy a house for the first time. Several participants also identified a hopefulness in envisioning a better future, and chasing dreams that were not possible previously. For example, Naema said:

> So when I was in Ethiopia I never dream of anything, like my dream was just how to live and how to survive every day, and maybe sometimes I dream of education, but because we are in camp. . . . But when I came here in America, I get like a lot of opportunity.

Replacing precarious histories with a greater sense of stability enables a vision for a better future for themselves and their families as they chase their dreams. Developing a sense of belonging is integral to moving into a future over which they can exert their own agency and have greater control.

Discussion: The Critical Role of Belonging

The participants in this study have clearly emerged from challenging histories of violence and oppression, forced displacement, and unpredictability to ultimately pursue their dreams. Necessary to that transition is the development of a sense of belonging, not only in but also beyond school.

Scholarship on belonging focuses on the relationships between people and spaces – individuals seek to belong in particular contexts, be they physical spaces or communities of people. Belonging is recognized in how we feel; it is "an emotional . . . attachment, about feeling 'at home'" (Yuval-Davis 2011, p. 10), which is shaped in part by outside forces, which Yuval-Davis (2011) calls the politics of belonging. Examples of these forces in this chapter include hiring teachers with knowledge of refugee life experience and interest in refugee students, along with teachers offering opportunities that are culturally relevant, inclusive, and center refugee students' voices (Ladson–Billings 2021; Jones & Sheffield 2018; Ryu & Tuvilla 2018; Faez 2012; Noddings 1992). The nature of parent encouragement also functioned as a politic of belonging that in turn shaped their sense of belonging.

A sense of belonging is constructed through narrating our identities. Identity narratives are a necessary basis for the development of agency, and agency is how we shape our own destinies. The participants in this study have done that – their narratives reveal a forward-looking sense of belonging in their future lives built on their experience of belonging in their school environments. Several of the participants expressed this as finding a sense of home in school. Their sense of belonging in school was conditioned by their teachers, their parents, and by other external forces – elements of the politics[10] of belonging – along with their own agency.

Conclusion

Precarious histories that create challenges can be, with a lot of work, transformed into positive visions of the future (Casas-Cortés 2021). Refugee stories about fleeing their home, witnessing violence, and experiencing years of living in a state of uncertainty now coincide with stories of positive experiences in safer and more comfortable spaces. Experiencing a sense of belonging doesn't come from nowhere. Contextual structures and processes – the examples of the politics of belonging named above that stretch across family, school, community, and society – are integral in shaping the experience of belonging. Having a space to belong not only provides an antidote to experiences of precarity but is also vital to chasing their dreams.

Notes

1. Asylum seekers are also fleeing dangerous conditions and have to meet similar qualifications, which they apply for on arrival to another country. Refugees apply prior to arrival.
2. Anderson et al.'s (2004) terminology is similar to that in migration studies more generally. (See Brettell & Hollifield 2015; Chavez 2013; Massey et al. 1987.)
3. The country's name changed from Burma to Myanmar in 1989, although the US government continues to use the name Burma. The participants also referred to the country as Burma for political reasons, so this name is used in this chapter.
4. Burma has about 135 different ethnic groups. Most are Burmese who make up to 66% of the country, and the remainder are from different minority groups including the Karen group, to which most of the participants in this study who are from Burma belong. In the civil war, the Burmese army attacked the Karen people using all sorts of violence – including killing and raping (Falcone 2016).
5. According to the Burma Link (2015) website, most of the refugees in Thai camps, about 79%, are Karen and 10% are Karenni, from eastern Burma. These refugees escaped the horrendous persecution by the Burmese military. Thousands of villages were burned, including houses, farms, schools, and religious places. Most fled through the jungle to refugee camps in Thailand. Refugee camps were set up in Thailand in the mid-1980s and are said to house 200,000 people; refugees began being resettled in the mid-2000s. The clashes between the Burmese and the Karen people began in 1949, shortly after Burmese independence from the British; it continues to today.
6. Four-year colleges, unless stated otherwise.
7. Ilhan Omar is a former Somali refugee and a current representative in the US House.
8. The Festival of Nations is an annual cultural festival that takes place in the city where these refugee students live.
9. An I-94 card is for non-US citizens and those without permanent residency. It indicates lawful entry into the country. IOM is the UN's migration agency.
10. Politics, in this sense, refers to relations of power and its negotiations – a much broader concept than governmental action. Choices were made by people in positions that mattered to these students – their teachers and parents, for example. People in relative positions of power were able to act in ways that created a space for students to belong. Offering ESL courses and hiring teachers with refugee backgrounds are examples of a politics of belonging.

References

Abud Jr., Gary G. 2017. Student Trauma Is Real. But Connection Can Heal. *Education Week*, July 12. www.edweek.org/leadership/opinion-student-trauma-is-real-but-connection-can-heal/2017/07

Anderson, Angelika, Richard Hamilton, Dennis Moore, Shawn Loewen, and Kaaren Frater-Mathieson. 2004. Education of Refugee Children: Theoretical Perspectives and Best Practice. In Richard Hamilton and Dennis Moore (eds.), *Educational Interventions for Refugee Children: Theoretical Perspectives and Implementing Best Practices* (pp. 1–11). London: Routledge.

Block, Karen, Suzanne Cross, Elisha Riggs, and Lisa Gibbs. 2014. Supporting Schools to Create an Inclusive Environment for Refugee Students. *International Journal of Inclusive Education* 18(12): 1337–1355. https://doi.org/10.1080/13603116.2014.899636

Brettell, Caroline B., and James F. Hollifield (eds.). 2015. *Migration Theory: Talking Across Disciplines*, 3rd edition. New York: Routledge.

Burma Link. 2015. Refugee Camps. *Burma Link Website*. www.burmalink.org/background/thailand-burma-border/displaced-in-thailand/refugee-camps

Casas-Cortés, Maribel. 2021. Precarious Writings Reckoning the Absences and Reclaiming the Legacies in the Current Poetics/Politics of Precarity. *Current Anthropology* 62(5). DOI: 10.1086/716721

Chavez, Leo R. (2013). *Shadowed Lives: Undocumented Immigrants in American Society*, 3rd edition. Belmont, CA: Wadsworth.

Clandinin, D. Jean, and F. Michael Connelly. 2000. *Narrative Inquiry: Experience and Story in Qualitative Research*. San Francisco, CA: Jossey-Bass.

Dryden-Peterson, Sarah. 2016. Refugee Education in Countries of First Asylum: Breaking Open the Black Box of Pre-Resettlement Experiences. *Theory and Research in Education* 14(2): 131–148.

Ennab, Fadi. 2017. *Being Involved in Uninvolved Context: Refugee Parent Involvement in Children's Education*. Winnipeg: Canadian Centre for Policy Alternatives Manitoba.

Faez, Farahnaz. 2012. Diverse Teachers for Diverse Students: Internationally Educated and Canadian-born Teachers' Preparedness to Teach English Language Learners. *Canadian Journal of Education* 35(3): 64–84.

Falcone, Daniel. 2016. Myanmar and the Karen Conflict: The Longest Civil War You Have Never Heard of. *REIFF Center Blog*, January 18. http://reiffcenterblog.cnu.edu/2016/01/myanmar-and-the-karen-conflict-the-longest-civil-war-you-have-never-heard-of/

Fratzke, Susan. 2019. In Wake of Cuts to U.S. Refugee Program, Global Resettlement Falls Short. [online] *migrationpolicy.org*, December 13. Accessed July 14, 2021. www.migrationpolicy.org/article/top-10-2017-issue-6-wake-cuts-us-refugee-program-global-resettlement-falls-short

Jones, Steven P., and Eric C. Sheffield (eds.). 2018. *Why Kids Love (and Hate) School: Reflections on Difference*. Gorham, ME: Myers Education Press.

Ladson-Billings, Gloria. 2021. *Culturally Relevant Pedagogy: Asking a Different Question*. New York: Teachers College Press.

Massey, Douglas S., Rafael Alarcón, Jorge Durand, and Humberto González. 1987. *Return to Aztlan: The Social Process of International Migration From Western Mexico*. Berkeley: University of California Press.

Mendenhall, Mary, Lesley Bartlett, and Ameena Ghaffar-Kucher. 2017. "If You Need Help, They Are Always There for Us": Education for Refugees in an International High School in NYC. *The Urban Review* 49(1): 1–25.

Mthethwa-Sommers, Shirley, and Otieno Kisiara. 2015. Listening to Students From Refugee Backgrounds: Lessons for Education Professionals. *Penn GSE Perspectives on Urban Education* 12(1). https://files.eric.ed.gov/fulltext/EJ1056671.pdf

Noddings, Nell. 1992. *The Challenge to Care in Schools: An Alternative Approach to Education*. New York: Teachers College Press.

Obi, Chinedu Temple. 2021. How Refugees' Decision to Live in or Outside a Camp Affects Their Quality of Life. *World Bank Blog Development for Peace*, March 2. https://blogs.worldbank.org/dev4peace/how-refugees-decision-live-or-outside-camp-affects-their-quality-life

Ramírez Carpeño, Eva, and Hannah Isabelle Feldman. 2015. Childhood and Education in Thailand-Burma/Myanmar Border Refugees Camps. *Global Studies of Childhood* 5(4): 414–424.

Ryu, Minjung, and Mavreen Rose S. Tuvilla. 2018. Resettled Refugee Youths' Stories of Migration, Schooling, and Future: Challenging Dominant Narratives about Refugees. *The Urban Review* 50: 539–558.

UNHCR. 2016. UNHCR Reports Crisis in Refugee Education. [online] *UNHCR*. Accessed July 14, 2021. www.unhcr.org/news/press/2016/9/57d7d6f34/unhcr-reports-crisis-refugee-education.html

UNHCR. 2018. What Is a Refugee? [online] *UNHCR*. Accessed July 14, 2021. www.unhcr.org/what-is-a-refugee.html

Yuval-Davis, Nira. 2011. *The Politics of Belonging: Intersectional Contestations*. Los Angeles: Sage.

Zong, Jie, and Jeanne Batalova. 2017. Refugees and Asylees in the United States. [online] *migrationpolicy.org*. Accessed July 14, 2021. www.migrationpolicy.org/article/refugees-and-asylees-united-states-2015

Part III

Pushing Back Against Precarity

10 From Embodied to Spectral

Teaching Transnational Feminisms in Times of Protest and Pandemic[1]

Sabrina González & Cara K. Snyder

During the COVID-19 pandemic, educators around the world were forced to transition from physical to digital classrooms. As we, the authors of this chapter, converted a study abroad in Argentina to a co-taught online course about feminist protest in Latin American and the Caribbean, activists across the Americas used the streets and social media to denounce racialized and gendered violence. This context, we suggest, calls for a transnational feminist pedagogy that links activism to the classroom and connects US students with Latin American and Caribbean histories of organizing against neoliberal,[2] sexist, misogynist, and racist regimes (Harvey 2005). The transnational feminist pedagogy that we practice opens the classroom to the world, teaches students to contemplate scales from the intimate to the global, exposes asymmetrical flows of power across borders, challenges the fixedness of the nation-state as a category, and builds transnational solidarities to take action both online and off-line. While the online classroom presents its possibilities to connect across borders and build transnational solidarity, online teaching presents serious limitations when compared with in-person instruction, especially for classes teaching about social movements and protest.

Inspired by feminist movements in Argentina, the class "Online and in the Streets: Women's Struggles for Justice in Latin America" was originally planned as a course taught on-site in Buenos Aires. We developed the course as a three-week study abroad program offered through a US university, between June 1 and 19, 2020. A main objective of the program we created was to build transnational solidarities between US and Latin American students, scholars, and activists as US-based students engaged with changemakers in and around Buenos Aires working to combat gendered violence. At the time of the program's inception, few students at our institution had experienced a massive grassroots movement. The study abroad program aimed to introduce a group of young people living and studying in the United States to the energy of a popular uprising. Ultimately, the goal of this immersive course was for students to feel and to witness a feminist revolution as they learned from and collaborated with feminists in Argentina.

When the COVID-19 pandemic forced us to reconfigure our pedagogical space, we converted our study abroad program to an online class while

DOI: 10.4324/9781003258223-13

asking ourselves what would be lost as the course moved from engaging Latin American activism in the streets of Buenos Aires to learning through the digital spaces of the classroom, social media, and art. Then, in June, during the first week of classes, uprisings against police brutality surged across the United States. It turned out that the students did not have to be in Argentina to experience a massive protest.

We found ourselves teaching activism online at a time when changemakers throughout the world were fighting for justice in both physical and digital spaces. These include the mounting protests in Hong Kong, Ecuador, and Chile, all of which borrowed tactics from each other. In Latin America, feminists marked the fifth anniversary of the first massive protest against misogynist violence organized by #NUM, which took place on June 3, 2015. According to Ni Una Menos, the campaign began as a "collective scream against machista violence" (2017), especially feminicide (Fregoso & Bejarano 2010). In the United States, uprisings for racial justice swelled under the banner of BLM, amidst the outbreak of COVID-19 and after the police killings of George Floyd, Breonna Taylor, and other precious Black lives. #BLM is a transnational campaign that began in 2013, and whose stated mission is "to eradicate white supremacy and build local power to intervene in violence inflicted on Black communities by the state and vigilantes" (BLM 2021, para. 1). Both uprisings localized issues of state violence for US-based students. Although our course focused on struggles for justice in Latin America, when the BLM protests started in May, students made organic connections between our course material and the protests happening in their local contexts. Because students were going to local protests, and our class emphasized relationships between theory and praxis, and between universities and social movements, they were able to make transnational connections between struggles in the United States and Latin America. Through virtual spaces, students could observe and connect with local movements throughout the Americas.

"Online and in the Streets" is a microcosm of larger-scale educational changes that are underway in K-12 school systems and universities. Educators are compelled to reinterpret the relationship between online teaching and activism. The novel coronavirus has forced activists and educators for social justice to rethink the ways to protest, demand, and teach social change. The need for protest remains urgent, as governments force poor people to make impossible decisions about whether to stay safe or to work so they can eat, as abusers terrorize femmes and children confined in unsafe homes, and as police continue to kill Black and brown people with impunity. Debates about the transition to online education have also exposed issues of access and especially the lack of digital infrastructure in the Global South and US-Third World (Sandoval 2000), one aspect of the digital divide. While educators have considered the possibilities of transformative pedagogy online, instructors must now reimagine what teaching for justice means in a world of social distance and physical isolation (Drabinski, Clark, & Roberts 2011; Larreamendy-Joerns & Leinhardt 2006).

What are the possibilities for transformative teaching in this educational context?

Based on our experiences teaching our advanced undergraduate seminar, we explore approaches to online instruction that honor feminist commitments to

1.   embodied knowledge;
2.   transnational solidarity and collaboration; and
3.   education for liberation.

We explore these approaches through course material; interviews with feminist artists, activists, and scholars; and major course projects we refer to as "experience sets" that asked students to synthesize course material, discussions, and experiences outside the classroom. The following section summarizes the structure of this course. Then, the chapter investigates the successes and challenges we faced as we enacted each of the aforementioned commitments – embodied knowledge, transnational solidarity and collaboration, and education for liberation – and taught toward a pedagogy of transnational feminism.

Situating the Class

As co-teachers, the content and method of our class were informed by our experiences and identities. Sabrina González is a feminist historian from Buenos Aires, a non-native English speaker, and a first-generation student from a working-class family. Her experience as an activist in community centers, student and teachers unions, alternative media, and nontraditional schools for adults shaped her research on the history of education and her approaches to popular and feminist pedagogies. Cara K. Snyder (she/they), a white, US-born professor of Women's, Gender, and Sexuality Studies, has lived and taught in Guatemala, Argentina, and Brazil. Their research and organizing with women and LGBT+ athlete-activists, and their two decades of experience teaching in a variety of settings, including multiple study abroad programs, inform Snyder's queer, feminist, anti-racist, anti-imperialist pedagogies.

The students' positionalities influenced how they approached the class material and the type of final projects that they developed. For example, the students who identified as Latinx (four) were able to further research their parents' home countries and the transnational connections between the United States and the region. Other students – three identified as white, US-born, and one student identified her own journey as part of the African diaspora in the United States – connected to the theory and praxis of Latin American feminisms via protests and street politics in the United States. The students ranged in age from 18 to 22 years, which meant that few had lived through a popular uprising. All but one identified as women, several identified as queer, and the majority of the class related intimately to gender-based violence. Some were first-generation students who worked and took care of their families at the time of the class, and these obligations made it difficult to keep up with the speed of a three-week course.

The content of a 15-week semester was covered at the equivalent of one week per day of class. Inspired by the digital pedagogy of Alexis Lothian (2021), each week comprised a unit, and an experience set that culminated with a weekly project: a feminist vlog (video blog), an oral history interview, and a creative response, in that order. Beyond the weekly project, students completed daily discussion posts and quizzes to ensure their comprehension of course materials. They were required to attend at least one of the three Zoom sessions offered weekly. A small class of eight students and shared teaching responsibilities allowed for weekly 1:1 meetings with students, something that would have been prohibitive with a larger class size. The co-teaching model allowed us to work collectively on discussion plans, the design of weekly projects, and the mentorship of students. It also allowed us to divide labor when we considered that our expertise could better contribute to the success of the class. For example, Snyder, PhD in Women's, Gender and Sexuality Studies, was responsible for the week 1 theme of "Feminist Foundations" – assigning reading materials, creating quizzes and discussion questions, and grading – while González, PhD candidate in History, led week 2, "A Long History of Women's Activism."

The three-week duration of the class meant tough decisions about what to include and necessarily limited class goals. Week 1 equipped students with "Feminist Foundations." In this interdisciplinary course, cross-listed in three units (Women's Studies, Latin American Studies, and History), the material for this week – which included readings, films, artworks, interviews, and digital explorations – established a shared language for students from different majors to discuss gender, sexuality, social movements, and racial formations in a Latin American context. The second week focused on women's histories of oppression and collective organization from the early twentieth century through the 1990s. The week's materials introduced the arc of women's movements during this time period. We studied interventions into the welfare state in the early 1900s, struggles for political and economic rights in the 1950s, and the resistance to the neoliberal dictatorships in the 1970s in the Southern Cone (the region today known as Argentina, Chile, Uruguay, and Brazil). Here, the class's short duration meant that we decided to focus on one geographical region, since one week would not be enough time to comprehensively address complexities across Latin America and the Caribbean. The third week focused on contemporary movements building toward feminist futures. Students learned about contemporary feminist tactics to denounce femicides and advocate for reproductive rights. We focused on #NiUnaMenos, #MeToo, and #AbortoLegalYa (#LegalAbortionNow), the campaign for the legalization of abortion in Argentina.

Embodied Knowledge

When we envisioned the class as an on-site course in Argentina, set to take place during the fifth anniversary of #NiUnaMenos, we imagined students would be fully immersed: participating in marches and trainings, dialoguing with local leaders, and working on projects alongside Argentine student activists. Along with feminist activists, students would have to *poner sus cuerpos* (putting their bodies on the line) by documenting the anniversary of #NUM, by dancing queer tango, by organizing a cultural activity with a local social movement, and by participating in *futbol feminino* (women's soccer). While this experience would be impossible to reproduce in an online course, we asked ourselves how the online class could translate such embodied elements. Incorporating physicality mattered both pedagogically – in terms of active learning – and also topically, because of the centrality of the body in Latin American feminisms.

In Latin America and the Caribbean, *"poner el cuerpo/a"* is a metaphor that feminists have used for decades to signal the embodied character of activism: perform a song, march in the streets, and sometimes put your body at risk in front of the police. According to an activist from the Argentine Movimiento de Trabajadores Desocupados (MTE – Movement of Unemployed Workers), "to question inequality is not exclusively a 'mental' activity. In order to make our voices heard, we have to feel [our demands], and have them come out of your whole body" (Colectiva Mala Junta 2019, p. 53). Since the 1980s, Latin American and Caribbean *encuentros* (meetings) have provided physical spaces for thousands of women and dissidents to discuss gender inequality; build collective power; and strategize local, national, and transnational feminist agendas. Beyond the *encuentros*, feminists have participated in local organizations and intervened in everyday life "putting their bodies" into transforming popular neighborhoods, cultural centers, schools, unions, universities, and the workplace (Gago 2019; Colectiva Mala Junta 2019; Mason 2007; Flores 2019).

Teaching transnational feminism in a digital environment devoid of personal contact and collective action with activists from the Global South presented serious limitations. However, the uprising in the United States transformed how the students experienced our course: For many, participating in local actions gave new meaning to Latin American and Caribbean mobilizing. For the group of young learners in our class, it was the first time they were witnessing a popular movement in the streets, observing police interact with activists, and debating with friends and family about racism and white privilege. Many of them were experiencing the tiredness of their bodies after a protest, the smell of tear gas, and the anger of racial inequality. For instance, one student, Thais[3] (who identified as white Latinx), encountered police violence for the first time when she was tear gassed by the cops while peacefully protesting. Thais shared that she was surprised to discover the violence at protests was coming from the police, while the mainstream media consumed by her parents portrayed a false narrative of violence as instigated by activists. The firsthand experience with police violence radicalized this student to join anti-policing ACAB actions and to share her perspectives online via Instagram and Twitter. Not all of our students participated in physical demonstrations, but even the students who were not in the streets (for a variety of reasons) gained new perspectives about policing and violence by listening to the stories of their friends and classmates like Thais and by seeing media depictions of protests, especially live streams. More research needs to be done in order to understand the multiple connections between the online classroom and the streets as well as the relationship between off-line and online activism. Yet, we believe that the protests happening at the local level and the active participation of our students in them gave practical meaning to the class material so the students could reflect about activist tactics, empathize with social justice causes, and ultimately connect state violence and protests in the Americas.

The conceptualization of digital spaces as valuable sites for social change helped students to make sense of their online practices and to consider themselves as producers of discourses, and collaborators in translocal movements for justice. *Performance Constellations: Networks of Protest and Activism in Latin America*, by Marcela A. Fuentes (2019b), looks at how bodily performances in the streets (from Ciudad Juarez to Buenos Aires) and social media campaigns work together to create "insurgent collective actions" (2) that denounce state violence, patriarchal power, and neoliberal policies, which disproportionately affect women, travestis, trans, and nonbinary persons. Fuentes's (2019a, 2019b) texts gave students the conceptual tools to understand digital and physical spaces as part of "co-created" activist networks where people are watching, commentating, joining, sharing, attending, documenting, replicating, recycling (p. 3). In our course, *Online and in the Streets*, students were engaging in social media, reading stories from alternative news sources, and looking at personal narratives expressed in words, songs, and images. In the class discussion board, students remarked on their ability to participate in movements even when they cannot leave their homes by "sharing poems, music, speeches, etc" (Piepzna-Samarasinha 2018). Students like Catherine noted they were using social media not only to organize "but also to educate people on white privilege, racism and institutional discrimination." Another student, Florencia, noted that trans-lation functions built into social media platforms like Instagram – which can be configured to automatically translate posts in any language into English – have made it easy for them to participate in campaigns across the world, like those in Hong Kong. Every response on the discussion board about Fuentes's text linked #NiUnaMenos with #BLM, evincing the transnational connec-tions that *Performance Constellations* elucidated. Some of the similarities students noted were practices of mourning, *denuncia* or public denouncements, overlap in slogans that call out the state for its role in enacting violence (and negating protections) on vulnerable people, and demanding the right to exist and be visible in public spaces, both digital and physical.

While recognizing the networked protests that bridged local actions in Argentina and the United States, online forms of engagement in both protest and pedagogy nevertheless remain, to an extent, disembodied. In our class, we created rituals that brought students back into their bodies such as meditation and free-writing activities. We started every synchronous meeting with a free-writing activity that allowed the students to connect class materials with their experiential knowledge and to process these through their bodies. For example, one activity asked students to reflect on: "what does your body need, what does your mind need, what does your spirit need." In their own words, students considered this activity "healing," and an "opportunity to keep your mind at peace" in a moment when they felt exhausted, frustrated, and alone.

These activities, along with the class materials, exposed students to feminist epistemologies that recognize women's experiences as legitimate sources of knowledge and as motors for political transformation. For example, Merle Collins's (2010) film *Saracca and Nation: African Memory and ReCreacion in Grenada and Carriacou* traces the African genealogies of *saracca* on the island of Carriacou where members of Collins's family are from. Collins links the intimate and the global, connecting her personal journey of self-discovery with the African diaspora in the Americas. The filmmaker documents the song, food, and dance of *saracca* to map exchanges between the Caribbean and Africa. At one point, Collins asks a village elder to identify her nation, and she responds with a song that the filmmaker traces to a tribe from the northwestern coast of Africa. One student noted that "instead of engaging with history passively, [the film examines] cultural traditions *to embody a history* that is told through language, song, dance and festival" (emphasis ours).

Indeed, if *saracca* illustrates how history exists in our bodies, Collins's own embodied experiences of anti-Blackness were part of her motivation for making the film. During an interview with Snyder, Collins modeled a process of self-reflection, and how personal experiences can become sites of knowledge. The filmmaker shared that reclaiming and celebrating African heritage challenge the veneration of all things European that she learned in school. Drawing inspiration from how Collins's life influenced her approach to knowledge making, and from her self-reflexivity about her journey, students created a feminist vlog. In the vlogs, the students were asked to connect their own corporeal and situated understandings of feminism with debates in Latin American feminisms they were encountering in the class.

In the online classroom, we could not give the students the opportunities for embodied knowledge that they would have enjoyed in Buenos Aires. Yet, a feminist pedagogy that centers the body made it possible for the students to connect the class material with their personal experiences, to understand that the personal is political, and furthermore to grasp that the meaning of personal and political must always be situated within a historical context that is also geographic – situated in physical and virtual space. Moreover, a feminist pedagogy that pays attention to students' experiences must also open the classroom to the world – making reading materials, assignments, and discussions relevant and meaningful by allowing the students to talk, discuss, and learn how and about what their bodies experience. In a context of uprising in the United States, the protests localized transnational debates about police brutality, oppression, and state violence against women and Black people.

Transnational Solidarity and Collaboration

We conceived of the on-site class in Buenos Aires as a way to create long-lasting relationships and exchanges between students, activists, artists, and scholars in Argentina and the United States. Transnational collaborations in this context signified a two-way flow, from the United States to Argentina and vice versa. Through a process of negotiation with local actors, the study abroad would have paid women leaders for their time and expertise and allocated material and human resources to organizations and public institutions for their time and space. Moreover, the collaborations between US institutions and local entities – like the *Red Interdisciplinaria de Género* (Interdisciplinary Network of Gender Studies) at the Universidad Tres de Febrero and the *Prosecretaria de Géneros y Políticas Feministas* (the Office of Gender and Feminist Politics) at the School of Humanities and Education Science in the Universidad Nacional de La Plata – would lend clout to local feminists building gender studies in the Argentine academy as well as visibilize their intellectual and organizational work. Conversely, as the first on-site course at our (US-based) university that centered feminist movements in Latin America, it would have presented an institutional paradigm where academia and activism exist in closer proximity (Ortiz-Riaga & Morales-Rubiano 2011; Cedeño Ferrín & Machado Ramírez 2012). The course aimed to introduce this paradigm to a US institution that aspires (but often fails) to serve the community where it resides.

Indeed, the fact that the on-site course was so popular (with over 30 applications submitted in the first year it was offered) put it on the radar for other professors and administrators; the course was mentioned in a college-wide email celebrating successful study abroad and we received messages of congratulations from the study abroad office and from colleagues. In their applications to the study abroad program, students indicated their interest in enacting transnational collaborations. One student shared they were "interested to see how sexism manifests itself differently in the US and in Argentina, and how class affects the goals and organization of women's movements." Another indicated that "working with organizations such as LatFem, who will likely be actively involved in the protests and advocacy, will be a great opportunity to watch social change as it happens from the perspective of those fighting at the front lines. To be in Buenos Aires at this time and in the context of women's justice movements will allow me to gain unique insight into the processes of social change." The course made feminist movements a legitimate study abroad course at our university, with social organizers as producers of knowledge.

Online and In the Streets did not allow for the type of lasting, meaningful, and reciprocal collaborations that we envisioned in the study abroad in Buenos Aires. Nonetheless, the online class was able to incorporate transnational approaches. We did this via course materials that highlighted (dis)connections across borders; analyzed asymmetrical flows of power; traced movements of goods, people, and ideas; examined questions of scale; and fostered thinking that challenges and goes beyond the nation. Moreover, we used oral history methodologies that asked students to connect global issues to their intimate lives and personal genealogies. Finally, students took part in transnational conversations with invited speakers: feminist scholars, activists, and artists working on and from Latin America and the Caribbean.

Through course materials, students understood the (dis)connections across borders (e.g. Falcón 2015; Cowan 2017; Santana 2019; Moraga & Anzaldúa 2015). For example, so that students could link the BLM movements happening in their streets with those in Brazil, we included material about Marielle Franco, "a black queer woman, mother, sociologist, socialist, human rights defender, councilwoman from the favela of Maré," (Caldwell et al. 2018, para 1) who was assassinated on March 14, 2018. The murder of councilwoman Franco took place amidst the rise of the Right in Brazil and in many countries around the world, fueling the need for activists and scholars to look beyond the narrow confines of their own national borders. Following her assassination, the hashtags #MariellePresente (#MariellePresent) and #QuemMatouMarielleFranco (#WhoKilledMarielleFranco) have kept her alive, mobilizing protests and demanding accountability for her murder. Through their introduction to Franco, students were able to compare and contrast movements for economic, racial, and gender justice throughout the Americas, challenging their US-centric view of the world. In addition to the collective statement of solidarity written by a group of US Black Feminist scholars, Brazilian Director Fabio Erdos's (2018) documentary *Marielle and Monica* helped students identify transnational trends in state violence, such as the increasing militarization of the police and their targeting of Black activists. At the same time, students situated Franco's murder within a long history of Latin American military dictators who "disappeared" political dissidents.

Another way students learned transnational methods was through oral history projects. (Portelli 1998; Leavy 2007; Borland 1991 Townsend 2019; James 1996). The second experience set asked students to explore feminist approaches to oral history in order to connect personal stories with global processes of migration, labor, and motherhood. In the context of a three-week class during a pandemic, most students conducted interviews with family members since it was more accessible. Many students, first- or second-generation immigrants, took the interview as an opportunity to get to know their families' stories of migration. These students wanted to understand how their *madres* (mothers) and *abuelas* (grandmothers) experienced gendered norms in their home countries and how migration to the United States affected their choices. Oral history methodologies functioned as a tool to engage questions of scale by drawing connections between the self, the community, the nation, and beyond: in this case, a knowledge about what is proximate opened into knowing of others' experiences.

Although family histories were not part of our original expectations for the interviews, we realized that each student had personal histories that they wanted to unpack. In the process, students were tracing a genealogy that Mexican anthropologist Marcela Lagarde (2018) conceptualized in her book *Claves feministas para mis socias de la vida* (*Feminist Keys for My Partners in Life*). Lagarde (2018) suggests that in order to build feminist leadership, we must understand where we come from; we must know the women who came before us, identify the conflicts they faced, and recognize how they navigated them. Even within the limited time of our accelerated course, the discussions that arose from the second project led some students to proudly claim their genealogies and to acknowledge women's roles as transnational actors, workers, migrants, professionals, educators, and mothers. Oral history proved to be a powerful feminist method to foster dialogues between grandmothers, mothers, and daughters. It helped students to humanize and empathize with older generations, rather than judge them. Moreover, they learned how to situate contemporary feminist agendas while acknowledging past struggles.

In addition to course materials and oral history projects, our class enacted transnational collaborations through recorded interviews with instructors and Latin American and Caribbean thinkers. Despite physical distance, digital technologies facilitated collaborations with scholars who work in Latin America or who are Latin Americanists. Invited speakers included Marcela Fuentes (Argentina–USA), Associate Professor of Performance Studies at Northwestern University, USA; Carolina Flores (Bolivia–Argentina), an activist and instructor at the Universidad Nacional Tres de Febrero, Argentina; Brandi Townsend (USA–Chile), a professor of History at the Universidad Catolica in Santiago, Chile; Josefina Vallejos (Argentina), a feminist activist, and Merle Collins (Grenada and Carriacou–Jamaica–Mexico–UK–USA), artist, activist, Professor and Director of Latin American and Caribbean Studies at the University of Maryland. Interviews were an alternative to the lecture, a genre that privileges the professor's point of view. They were made possible, in part, due to the labor of translation (Spanish to English) from instructors as well as the diverse networks of women the co-instructors brought into conversation. Yet, language was a factor that alienated many possible participants, especially activists from the working class. By and large, working-class people in Latin America do not have access to private instruction in English and do not have exposure to the language through international travel. Again, given the short duration of the class and limited resources, we were able to translate two interviews for our non-Spanish-speaking students; but the simultaneous translation was labor intensive and doubled the interview time. Still, as a tactic for transnational teaching, the interviews functioned as opportunities to conceptualize *with* and not only *about* Latin American actors.

The interviews facilitated dialogues and promoted connections across nations but ultimately transnational feminist collaboration requires resources, long-term projects, and more horizontal exchanges between university and social movements. In the online course, the transnational collaborations we aspired to were more ephemeral, lacking the teaching and learning alliances that in-person interchanges would have made possible. Transnational feminist scholars Ashwini Tambe and Millie Thayer (2021) have conceptualized these shifts as a movement from *embodied* to *spectral transnationalism*, in their book *Transnational Feminist Itineraries*. The authors describe how transnational feminist activism is increasingly forced to move online in light of neoliberal policies that defund social movements and prevent activists from physically gathering in order to make long-term alliances. In the 2000s, transnational feminism shifted into spectral forms, as "traveling feminists" returned home to confront right-wing surges and diminished funding, forcing feminist organizations to either close or transition to cheaper, online forms of activism (Tambe & Thayer 2021, p. 19). Youth movements emerged in ephemeral surges as activists debated how to sustain such movements in order to confront enduring forms of domination. In this context, Tambe and Thayer assert, "transnationalism persists but becomes spectral, still present but in out-of-body form," cross border campaigns meet in person less and less, and local politics take center stage (2021, p. 19). With a project that aimed to build connections between the United States and Latin America, the limits that we found in the transition online is constitutive of the shifts happening in transnational feminist activism, writ large. We suggest that spectral forms of transnational feminism are also present in pedagogy, as evidenced in our experiences with *Online and In the Streets*.

Education for Liberation

Just as we struggled to convert a class that emphasized embodied knowledge and facilitated transnational solidarity and collaboration, we were also presented with the limits and possibilities of online spaces for teaching that is liberatory. In moving from an on-site to an online setting, what elements of transformative pedagogy remain relevant? Latin America has a long tradition of liberatory education popularized by Paulo Freire's (2013[1968]) *Pedagogy of the Oppressed*. Freire, who developed his method in face-to-face settings in the Brazilian *Nordeste* (North East), advocated forms of teaching that value students' experiences and make student-teacher relations inside the classroom more horizontal. As feminine-presenting women, one of whom is a non-native English speaker from the Global South, we appreciate feminist critiques of horizontality that acknowledge the challenges women face in being recognized as authorities and knowledge producers. Furthermore, formal educational structures such as grading limit possibilities for democratizing the classroom. Within the multiple structural limitations of teaching at neo-liberal institutions, in general, and teaching online, in particular, what might constitute a transformative digital education?

"Online and in the Streets" aspired to liberatory methods through assignment structure, self-assessment, and collective input on the syllabus. First, we designed our class around three experience sets – a feminist vlog, an oral history project, and a creative response – that recognized students' experiences as sites of knowledge. This structure required students to draw critically from events outside the classroom and connect these to course materials and discussions. The experience sets also allowed students freedom and creativity since the direction of the assignments were largely self-determined. When students struggled with what to focus on, we asked them to prioritize projects that sparked their curiosity and that gave them pleasure. Second, self-assessments (students grading their own assignments) made students experts on their personal growth. Self-assessment de-escalated the pressure to produce work deemed worthy by professors and kept the emphasis on the joy of learning. This proved particularly important during the third experience set that asked students to either create or analyze a work of art, which was a vulnerable process for many of our non-artist-identified students. Because the set emphasized the process rather than the outcome, students found the exercise of making art liberatory. Third, a mid-course survey asked students to reflect on their process of learning and provide formative feedback including suggestions for topics they wished to incorporate during the third week. The practice of asking students about their interests gave them ownership over the syllabus and challenged a one-way flow of knowledge from teachers to students.

Students also felt ownership over creative assignments that drew from what we were learning in class about #NiUnaMenos and what they were learning in the streets from #BlackLivesMatter. Examples of student works making such connections included a zine on Black lesbian love, a drawing about indigenous women confronting gender stereotypes, and a digital storytelling of racialized beauty standards in Latin America. As a part of our concluding reflections, students collectively composed a poem, inspired by movements for justice across the Americas. According to students, in a feminist utopia:

> *bonds are formed through communities of care*
> *the idea of family is far beyond the constraints of blood relation*
> *child care is a community activity*
> *children and girls are allowed to live*
>
> *we look at one another*
> *there is no discrimination*
> *nobody is afraid to be who they are*
>
> *there is peace and acceptance of all people*
> *there is no fear of being who you are destined to be,*
> *everyone can be who they are*

we engage with love freely and vastly
consent is constantly practiced

women are at the same level as men
women can go outside without being targeted
women are intellectually strong to combat and change the system

those who identify as women:
can love who they want,
are not afraid to be by themselves at night,
are the sole decision makers of their own bodies,
their lands are protected,
their Human Rights are recognized

there is freedom
there is no war
people learn history properly in order to not repeat mistakes

we move from a space of social isolation to a space of togetherness[4]

Feminist, antiracist, and queer pedagogies insist that the classroom's transformations of ways of thinking – through critical processes of knowledge
production and exchange – can and should open onto larger transformations in the social and political world. Digital environments shift what such
transformations might look like. For instance, a physical class might require
an activist assignment where students work together to stage an intervention
on campus. The students' interventions in this course were smaller in scale,
aimed at self-reflexivity and mediations between intimate circles of family
and friends. In small ways, through the content and structure of our course,
we aspired to transformative teaching as a cornerstone of transnational feminist pedagogy.

Conclusions

This moment calls for a transnational feminist pedagogy that incorporates
embodied knowledge, transnational collaborations, and liberatory learning
practices for students. We are operating in a context in which neoliberal
policies reduce the budget for education at the same time that conservative governments in the Americas focus on profit over life, evinced in the
ongoing exploitation of human and natural resources. The danger of the
commodification of education via online teaching is present. Furthermore,
while schools struggle and while universities hunker down in anticipation of
deeper budget cuts, apparently there is always money for the police. While
writing this article, the police continued killing Black people in the United
States. In Argentina, the police disappeared Facundo Astudillo Castro, a
young, working-class activist from Buenos Aires. Activists throughout the
Americas continue to make state violence visible in its multiple forms: femi-
nicides, deforestation, police brutality, etc. Radical educators, teaching in

such precarious times, must similarly make visible these forms of oppression, exacerbated by the pandemic.

As aspiring transnational feminist pedagogues, and in the long tradition of marginalized people struggling for justice, we sought to meet the moment with the available resources. Precarity, in our class context, operated on multiple levels. First, in the unexpected changes from a study abroad to an online class. Second, in course content that focused on social stratifications laid bare by the pandemic. Third, in the lives of our students, who were affected by these multiple forces. Our pedagogy required that we understand our students (many of whom are queer, first-generation college students, and/or people of color) as part of those populations historically marginalized by an increasingly privatized higher education. While acknowledging these limitations, we also celebrate what we were able to accomplish, thanks to networks of support within our intellectual and activist communities throughout the Americas. The course was also the result of a long-term partnership between the authors that enacts transnational collaborations across the Americas. According to students including John, Maria, Christine, and Naminata, the class was successful because it gave them the opportunity to engage ideas and to encounter authors from Latin America and the Caribbean, to know their family histories of migration and labor, and to value their creative process. At the end of the course, some students, including Thais and Magdalena, even mentioned that they started thinking about themselves as activists.

Inspired by Fuentes' work we wanted to reconsider the possibilities of online teaching and activism as important in challenging the status quo in a digitally connected world. Throughout the sections of this chapter, we have shown that we do not have to lose our pedagogical principles because our medium changes. Online teaching can be a tool that facilitates transnational dialogues and honors students' different abilities and desires in learning. Because our students were mostly digital natives, they were open to this environment, perhaps more so than their instructors.

However, each section showed that online teaching, as part of *spectral transnationalism*, presents serious limitations when compared with in-person instruction, especially for classes teaching about social movements and protest. Regarding embodied knowledge, Latin American and Caribbean activists teach us that social change and structural transformations in the law, family, school, and media occur primarily through collective action, through *poner los/las/lxs cuerpos/cuerpas/cuerpxs* in the streets and local communities. The internet offers new possibilities for reverberations, echoes, and enunciations that amplify what happens in the streets, but it can never replace it. The course gestured toward a transnational feminist pedagogy by centering materials and scholars from the Global South. Through assignments like the oral history interview, we also encouraged students to reflect on and strengthen their own transnational connections. Yet, the inadequate amount of resources and planning time that went into this three-week class limited our ability to realize meaningful, lasting transnational exchanges: namely, we were unable to redistribute resources, pay for translation, and discuss with our collaborators in Latin America about shared goals and outcomes. Liberation is also a collective process, and digital spaces pale in comparison to the sense of community that often happens in the space of a physical classroom. Student experiences confirmed this claim; in their final evaluations, many expressed that the online setting impacted their interactions with peers and professors, and ability to stay focused and motivated.[5]

In an online environment, teachers face serious challenges to make their classrooms radical spaces for transnational activism. What would it look like, for instance, to work in solidarity with teachers in Latin America who are organizing campaigns to collect cell phones since online instruction remains impossible for poor students with limited access to the internet and digital devices? What might happen if teachers in the United States – facing budget cuts and *poniendo sus cuerpos* (putting their bodies) on the front lines of unsafe classrooms – understand our struggles for justice are inextricably linked? This article describes how educators might incorporate Latin American and Caribbean practices of resistance to neoliberal policies in the classroom in order to open the class to local protests happening in the streets, to give students the possibilities to reflect about social change, and to recognize embodied knowledge as legitimate sources of personal and collective liberation. We would like to suggest that a transnational feminist pedagogy – one that is adequately resourced and therefore able to build transnational networks of scholars, activists, artists, and students – is a pedagogy with the potential to enact change.

Notes

1. This chapter is a revised version of "Towards A Pedagogy of Transnational Feminism when Teaching and Activism Go Online," published in *The Radical Teacher*, forthcoming, vol. 121, and reprinted here with their permission.
2. We use the term neoliberal throughout the essay to refer to policies aimed at promoting free market capitalism and reducing government involvement and spending in areas including education and healthcare. According to political theorist David Harvey (2005):

   Neoliberalism is in the first instance a theory of political economic practices that proposes that human well-being can best be advanced by liberating individual entrepreneurial freedoms and skills within an institutional framework characterized by strong property rights, free markets, and free trade. The role of the state is to create and preserve an institutional framework appropriate to such practices. The state has to guarantee, for example, the quality and integrity of money. It must also set up those military, defense, police, and legal structures and functions required to secure private property rights and to guarantee, by force if need be, the proper functioning of markets. Furthermore, if markets do not exist (in areas such as land, water, education, health care, social security, or environmental pollution) then they must be created, by state action if necessary. But beyond these tasks the state should not venture. State interventions in markets (once created) must be kept to a bare minimum because, according to the theory, the state cannot possibly possess enough information to second-guess market signals (prices) and because powerful interest groups will inevitably distort and bias state interventions (particularly in democracies) for their own benefit (p. 2).

3. All names used to identify students are pseudonyms, to maintain students' privacy.
4. This poem is a compilation of student responses, inspired by a teaching and writing activity elaborated by feminist educator Jessica Ann Vooris (2019).
5. In an iteration of this class during Winter 2021, one student, Christopher, asserted: "the digital classroom can never really replace the physical one in the sense of communication and effectiveness." Madelyn commented: "It has been harder to create relationships with classmates and with the professors." Cayla said: "It is really hard for me to stay focused when I am learning in my house. I also miss the active discussions in the classroom, some teachers don't even bother with interacting with students and just put lecture videos up with no synchronous meetings." Charlotte recognized her privilege at having the resources at home to successfully study from home but still she agreed with Cayla: "I do miss in-person classes because I felt more motivated and could focus better when I was going to the class."

References

Black Lives Matter. 2021. Black Lives Matter, About. https://blacklivesmatter.com/about/

Borland, Katherine. 1991. "That's Not What I Said": Interpretive Conflict in Oral Narrative Research. In Sherna Berger Gluck and Daphne Patai (eds.), *Women's Words: The Feminist Practice of Oral History* (pp. 63–75). London and New York: Routledge.

Caldwell, Kia L., Wendi Muse, Tianna S. Paschel, Keisha-Khan Y. Perry, Christen A. Smith, and Erica L. Williams. 2018. On the Imperative of Transnational Solidarity: A U.S. Black Feminist Statement on the Assassination of Marielle Franco. *The Black Scholar*, March 23. www.theblackscholar.org/on-the-imperative-of-transnational-solidarity-a-u-s-black-feminist-statement-on-the-assassination-of-marielle-franco/

Cedeño Ferrín, Julio, and Evelio Felipe Machado Ramírez. 2012. Papel de la Extensión Universitaria en la Transformación Local y el Desarrollo Social. *Humanidades Médicas* 12(3): 371–390. http://scielo.sld.cu/scielo.php?script=sci_arttext&pid=S1727-81202012000300002

Colectiva Mala Junta. 2019. *Territorios Feministas. Experiencias, Diálogos y Debates desde el Feminismo Popular.* Buenos Aires: Batalla de Ideas Ediciones.

Collins, Merle. 2010. Saracca and Nation: African Memory and Re-Creation in Granada and Cariacou. Film. Maryland Institute for Technology in the Humanities.

Cowan, Benjamin Arthur. 2017. How Machismo Got Its Spurs–in English: Social Science, Cold War Imperialism, and the Ethnicization of Hypermasculinity. *Latin American Research Review* 52(4): 606–622.

Drabinski, Emily, J. Elizabeth Clark, and Sarah T. Roberts. 2011. Introduction: Shaped or Shaping? The Role for Radical Teachers in Teaching With Technology. *Radical Teacher* 90: 3–8. https://doi.org/10.5406/radicalteacher.90.0003

Erdos, Fabio. 2018. Marielle and Monica. *The Guardian*, December 28. Film www.theguardian.com/world/ng-interactive/2018/dec/28/marielle-and-monica-the-lgbt-activists-resisting-bolsonaros-brazil

Falcón, Sylvanna M. 2015. The Globalization of Ferguson: Pedagogical Matters about Racial Violence. *Feminist Studies* 41(1): 218–221.

Flores, Carolina. 2019. De Mujeres Piqueteras a Feministas Populares: Militancia, Vida Cotidiana, y Transformaciones Políticas. Master's Thesis in Social Sciences, Universidad General Sarmiento.

Fregoso, Rosa-Linda, and Cynthia Bejarano. 2010. *Introduction: A Cartography of Feminicide in the Américas. Terrorizing Women: Feminicide in the Américas.* Durham, NC: Duke University Press.

Freire, Paulo. 2013 [1968]. *Pedagogia Do Oprimido*, 54A edição edition. São Paulo: Paz e Terra.

Fuentes, Marcela A. 2019a. #NiUnaMenos (#NotOneWomanLess): Hashtag Performativity, Memory, and Direct Action Against Gender Violence in Argentina. In Gul Ayse Altinay, María José Contreras, Marianne Hirsch, Jean Howard, Banu Karaca, and Alisa Solomon (eds.), *Women Mobilizing Memory* (pp. 172–192). New York: Columbia University Press.

Fuentes, Marcela A. 2019b. *Performance Constellations: Networks of Protest and Activism in Latin America*. Ann Arbor: University of Michigan Press.

Gago, Veronica. 2019. *La Potencia Feminista o el Deseo de Cambiarlo Todo*. Madrid: Traficante de Sueños.

Harvey, David. 2005. *A Brief History of Neoliberalism*. Oxford: Oxford University Press.

James, Daniel. 1996. *Doña Maria's Story: Life History, Memory, and Political Identity*. Durham: Duke University Press.

Lagarde, Marcela. 2018. *Claves Feministas para Mis Socias de la Vida*. Buenos Aires: Batalla de Ideas.

Larreamendy-Joerns, Jorge, and Gaea Leinhardt. 2006. Going the Distance With Online Education. *Review of Educational Research* 76(4): 567–605.

Leavy, Patricia Lina. 2007. The Practice of Feminist Oral History and Focus Group Interviews. In Patricia Lina Leavy and Sharlene Nagy Hesse-Biber (eds.), *Feminist Research Practice: A Primer*. London and New York: Sage Publications.

Lothian, Alexis. 2021. *Queer Geek Theory, Classes*. www.queergeektheory.org/classes/

Mason, Laura. 2007. *Feministas en Todas Partes. Una Etnografía de Espacios y Narrativas Feministas en Argentina*. Buenos Aires: Prometeo.

Moraga, Cherríe, and Gloria Anzaldúa (eds.). 2015. *This Bridge Called My Back: Writings by Radical Women of Color*, 4th edition. Albany, NY: SUNY Press.

Ni Una Menos. 2017. Quienes Somos. Carta Orgánica. *Ni Una Menos*. Accessed August 7, 2021. http://niunamenos.org.ar/quienes-somos/carta-organica/

Ortiz-Riaga, María Carolina, and María Eugenia Morales-Rubiano. 2011. La Extensión Universitaria en América Latina: Concepciones y Tendencias. *Educación y Educadores* 14(2): 349–366.

Piepzna-Samarasinha, Leah Lakshmi. 2018. Preface: Writing (With) a Movement from Bed. In Leah Lakshmi Piepzna-Samarasinha (ed.), *Care Work: Dreaming Disability Justice* (pp. 15–29). Vancouver: Arsenal Pulp Press.

Portelli, Alessandro. 1998. Oral History as Genre. In Mary Chamberlain and Paul Thompson (eds.), *Narrative and Genre*. New York: Routledge.

Sandoval, Chela. 2000. *Methodology of the Oppressed*. Minneapolis: University of Minnesota Press.

Santana, Dora Silva. 2019. Mais Viva!: Reassembling Transness, Blackness, and Feminism. *TSQ: Transgender Studies Quarterly* 6(2): 210–222.

Tambe, Ashwini, and Millie Thayer. 2021. The Many Destinations of Transnational Feminism. In Ashwini Tambe and Millie Thayer (eds.), *Transnational Feminist Itineraries: Situating Theory and Activist Practice* (pp. 13–36). Durham, NC: Duke University Press.

Townsend, Brandi. 2019. The Body and State Violence, from the Harrowing to the Mundane: Chilean Women's Oral Histories of the Augusto Pinochet Dictatorship (1973–1990). *Journal of Women's History* 31(2): 33–56.

Vooris, Jessica Ann. 2019. Poetry If I Were Not Afraid and It Was Snowing: A Choral Birth Poem. *Radical Teacher* 113: 111–117. https://doi.org/10.5195/rt.2019.484

11 Activists' Use of Trauma-Informed Frameworks

Insights From Popular Education Spaces in Buenos Aires, Argentina

Jennifer Lee O'Donnell, Rebecca John &
Guadalupe Valdivia

Introduction

Neoliberal economic policies in Argentina have negatively impacted poor and working-class communities in recent years (O'Donnell 2018). Consequently, women and girls have been made vulnerable to human traffickers, rampant femicides, domestic violence, and the difficult circumstances of earning a living wage in *villas*, or shantytown communities that, in the past 30 years, have spread throughout the city of Buenos Aires (Grinberg 2010). In response, Argentinean activists have found mechanisms to fight for improved living conditions within these neighborhoods through social movement organizing and popular education projects that foster leadership and camaraderie building, along with opportunities for personal and communal growth for residents.

In this chapter, we highlight the work of one such group of activists in The Union of Popular Organizations[1] (UP), particularly the work of their Gender Commission, that organized a series of gender-based popular education workshops to build community resiliency through trauma-informed teaching. Giving access to knowledge, resources, and support systems to disadvantaged community members with chronic stressors, like those who frequently participated in these workshops, served to heal those impacted by some of the detrimental blows to themselves and their communities brought on by neoliberalism. We discuss how UP activists generated pedagogy that addressed girls' and women's experiences through curriculum rooted in trauma-informed pedagogy and "difficult knowledge" (Britzman 2000), demonstrating the repercussions of this pedagogy on women who were then able to manifest personal and community change from places of pain and precarity.

To understand the significance and background of organizations like UP, it is important to know the history and context in Argentina that gave rise to neoliberal social policy as well as social movements like theirs.

DOI: 10.4324/9781003258223-14

Neoliberalism in Argentina

Throughout the 1960s and 1970s, Argentina underwent a political revolution led by trade unionists, journalists, artists, university students, and professors. The president at the time, Isabel Perón (1974–1976), gave military orders to exterminate radical groups to rid the state of their "seditious" behavior. Her governance led to her enforced removal from office by a military coup that would continue state-sponsored violence, kidnapping, torture, and death of Argentinean citizens. This era became known as the Dirty War (Lewis 2002).

This history is significant because, at the fall of the military dictatorship in 1983, democratization and the rebuilding of Argentina were done through negotiations with the International Monetary Fund and other global financial forces that promoted neoliberal economic policies that called for austerity measures and the defunding of the welfare state (Vanden 2007). The years that followed were plagued by unemployment, a valueless peso, and reduced social expenditures. With a lack of affordable housing and access to public resources for the poor and working class, many of the country's vulnerable citizens – immigrants from countries throughout Latin America, Mapuche and Guaraní farmers from the interior of the country, and the working class – had no choice but to occupy lands and build homes on grounds with no formal organization, paved streets, or running water. These communities, known as villas, are often built in unsafe health-threatening locations, over toxic dumps, polluted rivers, or flood zones. Residents who make their homes here are allowed to stay only because such sites are, for the time being, worthless to the city (Davis 2006).

In addition to hits on housing and personal savings, neoliberal economic policies have been disastrous for the country's public education system. Its business-focused logic decentralized the country's schools without considering the resources available to those in poor communities. Laws have reduced teachers' salaries, cut classroom supplies, and have eliminated services geared toward supporting disadvantaged social classes (Schugurensky 2003). As a result, the country has seen an increase in school dropout rates (Toubes & Santos 2006), with teachers reporting that many of their students are at "educational risk" (Sirvent & Llosa 1998). State-sponsored programs like Adultos 2000 [Adults 2000], Programa Deserción Cero [Zero Desertion Plan], and Progresar [Progress] have been developed by the Ministry of Education to change these conditions; however, many educators have found that these are not enough to address the breadth of inequality throughout the country.

What would come to be known as *la crisis* [the crisis], Argentina's economic collapse in the early 2000s has brought hundreds of thousands of citizens to the streets in protest of the detrimental conditions that they've experienced under neoliberalism. Coordinated efforts by those in social movements have taken action in villa communities through efforts in housing, education, environmental initiatives, and other socially minded endeavors to improve their living conditions. Through partnership formation, activists working within social movements have been instrumental in redefining the way Argentina's vulnerable citizens survive under the weight of historical, social, and economic violence done to their communities.

In this chapter, we show UP activists addressing trauma at the individual and community level at a celebration that took place to honor participants' completion of a series of gender-based training workshops. Through popular education and trauma-informed frameworks, these activists created opportunities for women in precarious circumstances to come together, learn from one another, and ultimately magnify their ability to make personal and community change possible. In the sections that follow, we present background literature on trauma-informed pedagogy and teaching with difficult knowledge. Following this, we describe the context of the present study and present findings on activists utilizing a trauma-informed approach with women living in villa communities. Finally, we conclude with a discussion on how the present study reflects and adds to the literature on trauma-informed pedagogy and engaging students in social movements to address personal and community hardships that serve to mobilize and transform communities plagued with precarity.

Trauma-Informed Frameworks

To paint a clear picture of the kinds of curriculum practiced at the UP workshops, this section reviews key literature on trauma-informed pedagogies in classrooms and communities. Trauma-informed approaches in educational contexts have been adopted from medical, psychological, and judicial frameworks to take into account trauma and its effects throughout the life span – some of which we will highlight here. Educators who practice trauma-informed pedagogy operate from the perspective that for learning to take place, teachers must not only address the cognitive needs of students, but also have a thorough understanding of trauma and other harmful effects on students' development and well-being (Carello & Butler 2014). Trauma-informed educators can identify if students' basic needs – be it psychological, physical, or emotional – are or are not being met, and are prepared to know how to respond, provide resources, or meet the pedagogical needs of trauma-survivors to minimize retraumatization (Carello & Butler 2014). These educators embrace values of safety, trustworthiness, student choice, collaboration, and empowerment at the heart of their curriculum, with the mindset of promoting students' abilities to self-monitor and maintain positive learning experiences (Fallot & Harris 2009).

Clinicians and clinical educators support the integration of trauma in traditional school curriculums to educate students on how to listen and react to difficult circumstances (Newman 2011). They have found that toxic stressors can be felt at one or more systemic levels (Ungar 2015). When they are extreme, environmental factors become a significant resource for a person's resiliency when compared to individual characteristics or cognitions (Ungar 2014). As we will demonstrate, with political and economic precarity throughout the country, Argentinean girls and women in this study experienced multiple levels of chronic stress caused by personal, familial, and community factors that made overcoming obstacles they and other women faced a challenge.

Public health researchers have confirmed that adverse *childhood* experiences (personal and familial) and adverse *community* environments (systemic and environmental) – hereafter, referred together as ACEs – when endured simultaneously and over the course of several years, exacerbate declines in mental and physical health throughout adolescence and on into adulthood (Burke et al. 2011). For a better understanding, Ellis (2020) depicts ACEs like a tree, with branches extended upward representing childhood experiences and roots growing downward representing community experience (Figure 11.1). At the level of the individual, these experiences include exposure to physical abuse, verbal abuse, sexual abuse, and physical and emotional neglect (Felitti et al. 1998). At the family level, it includes "witnessed experiences" like substance use, domestic violence, incarceration, mental illness, parental divorce, death, and abandonment (Felitti et al. 1998). Adversities at the community level can include persistent exposure to poverty and violence, which may be related to poor housing quality and environmental pollutants (Ellis & Dietz 2017). Other community-level experiences include discrimination and community disruption related to a lack of work and resource opportunities, economic mobility, and social capital (Ellis & Dietz 2017).

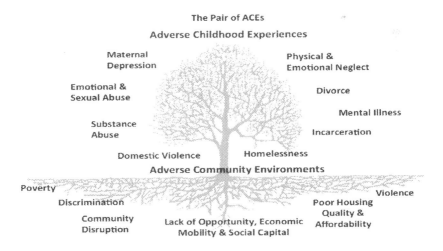

Figure 11.1 Adverse Childhood and Community Experiences.

Source: Ellis, Wendy R. 2020. Tools and Resources: The Building Community Resilience Approach. The Center for Community Resilience. Retrieved from: https://ccr.publichealth.gwu.edu/tools-resources/the-BCR-approach. Used with permission.

Studies have shown that Argentinian girls and women living in villa communities experience stressors at both the personal and community levels (Grinberg 2010; O'Donnell 2020, 2021). Their exposure to adversity at multiple levels, including continuous toxic stressors linked to environmental factors, may prevent them from building resiliency when experiencing trauma or violence (Ellis & Dietz 2017). As such, they are more likely to have behavioral disorders (e.g., substance abuse), emotional disorders (e.g., depression and posttraumatic stress disorder), and develop chronic disease (e.g., heart disease, asthma, cancer, and diabetes) in adulthood (Anda et al. 2006; Felitti et al. 1998). Trauma-informed therapists have cited that traumatic adaption in people who have experienced chronic adversity and stress could form a protective mechanism that can result in destructive, disrespectful, and resistant behaviors (Himelstein 2019) that delay healing and building resiliency.

How Community Activists Are Changing the Perspective

In response to the growing need to address not only individual trauma in adverse childhood experiences but also systemic adverse community environments, Ellis and Dietz (2017) developed the *Building Community Resilience* framework to provide a plan for school personnel to address adversity in childhood and community (Figure 11.2). There are four key components

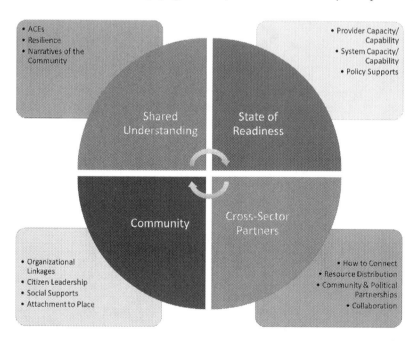

Figure 11.2 The Building Community Resilience Model.

Source: Ellis, Wendy R., and William H. Dietz. 2017. A New Framework for Addressing Adverse Childhood and Community Experiences: The Building Community Resilience Model. *Academic Pediatrics* 17: 86–93; p. 88. Used with permission.

of the framework: (1) developing a *shared understanding* among community stakeholders regarding toxic stress, adversity, and resilience – this includes a focus on shared narratives like the retelling of stories of trauma and adversity; (2) focusing on the *state of readiness* for building capacity and strengthening resiliency in communities, which requires building a willingness in community stakeholders to respond to adversity in ways that promote public health and healing; (3) building *cross-sector partners* to ensure that there is true collaboration between stakeholders, community members, and social and healthcare workers; and (4) *engaging the community* to enact change. This framework presents new ways of collaborating among professionals in the field of child health, public health, community agencies, and cross-sector partners to better understand the cause of toxic stress and adversity and provide new pathways to foster individual and community resiliency.

To address the root cause of toxic stressors and adversity experienced by women and girls in Buenos Aires' villa communities, social movement activists have taken a similar approach to the Building Community Resilience framework to initiate conditions where those most likely to suffer from personal and community traumas can heal and become agents for change. The efforts of UP's Gender Commission, for example, were conducted through multilevel systems using individual counseling, as well as in community workshops applying the popular education framework developed by Paulo Freire[2] (2000). UP activists adapted to and adopted community knowledge to provide opportunities for women to talk about conditions in their neighborhoods, mirroring the Building Community Resilience framework component that focuses on developing a shared understanding. Other elements of the workshop practiced or developed states of readiness for change, utilized the expertise of cross-sector partners, and engaged community members in confronting and combating the social ills that placed some members in vulnerable positions. Women participating in UP's gender-based workshops were able to grieve through therapeutic discussions that allowed them to change the narrative of their personal and community experiences and gave them opportunities to be agents of change in the villas where they lived. The popular educators utilized partners across multiple sectors to support these women in their individual healing, growth, and transformation. In other words, joining Freire's popular education with the Building Community Resilience framework allowed activists to attend to the needs of individuals and communities ignored by the social system. This, we will show, brought about leadership and change for many women who attended the workshops.

Teaching Trauma in Learning Communities

Integrating trauma into traditional or nontraditional education curriculum may be challenging, because pain, grief, or anger represented in instructional materials or classroom discourses may be deeply felt by those in the classroom. Britzman's (2000; Pitt & Britzman 2003) work, moreover, urges educators to look for areas in which difficult knowledge can be integrated into curriculum not only to provide reflections on societal wounds but also to offer optimism and reparation in a pedagogical context. This involves monitoring content and discussions for triggering subject matter, balancing the intensity of material with the emotional capabilities of students, and recommending self-care within the pedagogical and curriculum practices undertaken (Zurbriggen 2011).

Zembylas (2014) believes in the potential of trauma-informed pedagogy to interrupt antagonisms that develop in social circumstances where trauma has been present, because it sheds light on how we are all linked to others emotionally through common difficult knowledge. Teaching from challenging knowledge in classroom spaces highlights social trauma in the curriculum, as well as student ambivalence and distress in school and their everyday lives (Pitt & Britzman 2003). Educators should therefore strive to develop culturally competent approaches to teach trauma that are relevant to the social worlds and lived experiences of students, particularly minority students and students of color (Ladson-Billings 1992; Mattar 2011). These pedagogies emphasize the connectedness students have within their own circles of kinship and those of the world at large.

Some trauma-informed educators, such as Johnston (2014), make use of novels and stories of community or individual trauma to open opportunities for individuals to discuss traumatic experiences in ways that do not require them to make themselves vulnerable. Others like Pantas, Miller, and Kulkarni (2017) show how pedagogy can be used to open discourses on trauma, through their work with survivors of sexual violence on college campuses, by showing survivors and the community processing and healing through self-reflection, testimony, and "public grieving" (Butler 2004).

Alexander et al. (2004) explains problematic events do not necessarily become traumatic when a society experiences a massive disruption. Instead, for trauma to develop at the level of the community, members of the collective must "feel they have been subjected to a horrendous event that leaves indelible marks upon their group consciousness, marking their memories forever and changing their future identity in fundamental and irrevocable ways" (p. 1). He explained that trauma is the product of extreme pain "entering into the core of the collectivity's sense of its own identity" (p. 10). Often, there is a sense of threat to who they are, their historical background or future direction, and certain actors in the community, who Weber (1968) called "carriers," recognize and represent this social pain. These are the experts, thought leaders, authorities, and influencers (Alexander et al. 2004). As these carrier groups develop and circulate their personal narratives or "speech acts" across multiple domains, meaning-making occurs. This process provides an understanding of how social groups interact with emotions to create new social narratives, which create new and binding understandings of "social responsibility and political action" (Alexander et al. 2004, p. 1), helping communities move from trauma and pain, to healing, to social transformation.

Such work, consistent with the Building Community Resilience framework principles of developing a shared understanding and community involvement, promotes a growth mindset, encourages healing through shared experiences and dialogue, creates communal change agents, and tackles trauma as a social reality.

Activists in this study sought to engage poor and working-class women in discourses and practices that moved beyond the victimization they experienced living in villa communities, toward becoming social agents who could enact change in their community. These activist educators built pedagogical moments from historical tragedies that then manifest forms of solidarity among participants through feelings of anger, sadness, and inspiration for retribution. Women in the workshops were able to speak back to the tragedies they and their communities endured through storytelling, public performance, testimony, and group introspection that manifest into forms of resistance. In the following section, we discuss the context of this study where trauma-informed pedagogy was present and provide background on focal participants and sites of this study.

Methodology

In Buenos Aires, villas are made up of poor or working-class people. UP's Gender Commission project performed many social programs to assist these communities including tutoring for children, recreational activities, housing support, and aid in developing micro-businesses, and they ran popular education workshops that focused on the historical, social, economic, political, and cultural influences that contributed to gender oppression in their communities. Activists hosting the workshops we studied were composed mostly of women and some men from diverse fields – including psychology, law, social work, reproductive health, and education – who organized to combat violence faced by women and children, human trafficking, stigmas toward sexual diversity, and restrictive reproductive health policy. Likewise, they provided emotional, social, and joint support with social organizations and neighborhood institutions, as well as information on how women could get access to temporary housing, work, support groups, and other advocates committed to these issues.

Signs of their strength and impact in women's spaces could be seen throughout Buenos Aires – in food carts and diners where women were small business owners or employed, in cultural centers where they met to learn new skills, or in the streets where UP activists and members of communities they served marched to vindicate the rights of women. At the pedagogical level, UP's fight against gender inequalities could also be seen in community centers where the commission brought awareness, training, and education to girls and women through workshops geared toward unweaving sexist behavior from men and women, to transform communities into places without humiliation, violence, or exploitation. UP workshops assisted participants in becoming local leaders by providing them an opportunity to learn about social mobilizing and combating gender oppression. Here, they covered topics like violence against women, the legal rights of women, sexual and reproductive health, self-esteem building, gender myths, sexual diversity, as well as self-care, respect, and pleasure.

Data Collection and Analysis

In this chapter, we focus on data collected at a celebration that took place in Villa Beltra for women who completed UP's series of gender-based train-ing workshops.[3] Through participant observation and field note writing, interviews with women participating in the Gender Commission workshops, and audiotaping of large and small groups, we learned of the atrocities per-petrated by the state and other sectors against girls and women, particularly girls and women of color. We were told of human traffickers who plundered poor communities. We were informed of the history of state terrorism and the murder of *villeros*. Through this, we recount the difficult circumstances of living in the villas and the pedagogies used to make sense and make change from these experiences. In the section that follows, we discuss the data in the context of trauma-informed pedagogies, difficult knowledge, and communal grieving and healing practices.

Trauma-Informed Pedagogies in Popular Education Workshops

> We see violence when women are insulted or being beaten or harmed in some way. But it is also exercised in private institutions and at the level of the state, for example, when there are no jobs for women, no decent healthcare for women, when women are unable to go to school. Violence against women and girls occurs in different ways – physical, psychological, economic, political, cultural, through communication, sexual. As a team we understand that we cannot solve every problem, but we have found alternatives to help us resolve some issues and immediate problems . . . but political and social solutions still remain long term.
>
> (Elena, Interview)

In the above quote, Elena, a UP activist, notes that violence, for many of the women in villa communities, manifests in multiple facets of their lives. It is in their homes, at their jobs, in the air they breathe, and on the streets they walk. In alignment with the principles of trauma-informed pedagogy, the Gender Commission sought to disrupt the precarity women faced in villa communities through the popular education practices aligned with the Building Community Resilience framework. In this section, we discuss events that occurred during UP's Gender Commission's end-of-the-year celebration, during which we learn of just *how* these activists were able to encounter students' past traumas through practices that created opportunities for personal and communal healing.

We show how UP activists encountered traumas on two levels – the personal and the communal. Through the encouragement of connectedness and insiderness, inspirational speeches, and community events with food, music and games, workshop leaders taught from places of trauma and difficult knowledge to develop a shared narrative and instill feelings of belonging in their students. In doing so, they not only recovered students' confidence in themselves, but also encouraged pride in the spaces where they lived. Activists believed such pedagogy enabled many of their female students to confront unjust situations they encountered in their daily lives in order to manifest personal change. UP activists likewise engaged women in pedagogies linked with social justice (Alexander et al. 2004; Johnston 2014) in order for them to identify areas in their communities that needed change. This work was interdisciplinary and required a comprehensive wraparound approach from various experts to assist as they supported each woman to reassemble or improve her life. As one activist noted: "Each educator in our interdisciplinary team has different knowledge, experiences, and skills that they can bring to the table to share" (Elena, Interview).

The Gender Commission placed importance on developing a shared understanding of the traumas in their community and the changes necessary to address these injustices. They galvanized women to take action in their personal lives and to also ensure that judges, doctors, police, and employers complied with the laws and rights that have been fought for, and put in place, to protect women.

Making Trauma Pedagogical for Women

Lee O'Donnell, first author of this chapter, was invited by an UP activist educator, Marina, to attend an end-of-the-year celebration that the commission was holding to honor students who had completed a series of gender-based workshops in the neighborhood of Villa Beltran. Here, through stories, shared food, song, and dance, she documented some of the ways solidarity was being built among women, and how this solidarity was motivating others to stand up for their rights within a patriarchal society.

Lee arrived at Buenos Aires' train station in Constitución at 2:15 pm and to Villa Beltran about 30 minutes later. Two UP activists came to meet her at the train station to walk the three blocks to the Pampero Cultural Center where the commission's party was in motion. This particular community center was quite large, offering transitional housing, a free milk and bread program, clothing, and community garden space. Within it, artists, teachers, and activists offered free workshops such as dance, music, percussion, and sports. They also had a community radio and TV station, and published neighborhood newsletters.

The park located by the cultural center had beautiful palm trees and provided a nice shade for the event. A large, hand-painted sign read *Esta fiesta la hicimos entre todos* or "This party was made by all of us." There were about

100 or more men, women, and children in attendance. All were wearing free, militant green T-shirts with the UP insignia screened on the front. A table of party favors included mate cups, group photos, books, and handmade Che Guevara paperweights.

The setup and execution of the celebration illustrated how the educators worked to create intimacy in the crowd. Food was served – renaissance fair-sized chicken legs, Russian salad, ice cream, and tiny cakes you could eat without utensils. There was soda and pan de campo, decorations, tables, chairs, a sound system, and a music circle. Singing, chanting, and dancing ensued while men and women moved their bodies to the live drum rhythms. Typed handouts of pro-women chants were given to each guest, but everyone seemed to know the words already.

> Women will not be defeated
> by beatings, by kidnappings.
> Today we are still fighting
> with the strength of the oppressed.
> We can be found on any continent,
> fighting for a different world.
> If misery, poverty, and exploitation
> still reign across America
> then this we scream –
> Equal rights for women!
> Power to the people!
> Anti-imperialism!
> Countries without borders!
> For socialism!

Popular educators and the organizers of the celebration utilized joyful affects such as food, fun, drinks, and games to unify the community in the midst of discussions of cultural and community trauma. They built solidarity and social bonds with members by creating an environment of trust, celebration, and community. We mention this here because in spite of what we had come to learn of the shared difficult knowledge and stories of trauma in the community, the hopefulness and joy in the context of the celebration strengthened the unity of their social movement. As evidenced by the coming quotes, the teachers extended their bonds beyond that of teacher-student to one of friend, neighbor, and comrade. This illustrates aspects of trauma-informed pedagogy in the need for students to engage with empathy and take action to address social justice issues. Additionally, in an attempt to bring the community into action that seeks to improve the lives of individuals and the community environment as a whole, they utilized aspects of the Building Community Resilience framework such as engaging the community and coming to a state of readiness within that community.

Building solidarity among women in precarious circumstances was also evident in a speech Marina gave honoring the important *compañeras*[4] who helped organize the Gender Commission.

> When there are problems, when there is adversity, when one compañera has a problem in her home, luckily we have delegates who work hard, who are full of integrity, who care about what happens to each of our compañeras, who are attentive, who are interested in politics, human rights, who are honest, who help build our reputation, and fight for what we believe in and how we want to build this country. To change this country we have to learn to be caring, selfless, dedicated to the cause.
>
> (Marina, Party in Villa Beltran)

Here, though Marina referenced the trauma, it was also through her mention of "care" that solidifies its importance in the change she and others in the commission sought to bring to the lives of women and girls. Marina felt her role in the Gender Commission was encouraging women on an emotional level and galvanizing them to advocate for themselves. Her perspective mirrors other trauma-informed pedagogies dealing with difficult knowledge that emphasize the importance of optimism and opportunities for hope (Pitt & Britzman 2003) as well as the Building Community Resilience framework's emphasis on community engagement. As illustrated in the following quote, central to her pedagogy was speaking back to the discrimination her students received and explicitly teaching them to do the same in their community.

> We believe that there cannot be pedagogical silence against discrimination, against disrespect, against abuse – and so we teach our students about militancy, social rank, state agencies, unions, and how if we organize in solidarity, then cultural change is inevitable. But many of our students dream of things as simple and fundamental as being able to go to school. So we stress every day that they have the same rights to an identity, to an education, to a lifestyle of their choosing as anyone.
>
> (Marina, Interview)

Marina's interactions with women highlighted the centrality of hopefulness to speak out and speak back against discrimination. In the vignette that follows, she speaks of a workshop participant, Veka, who had come to her about halfway through the workshop feeling depressed and ready to quit school. Because of her past history with sex work, she felt she did not have a future.

> And I had to say to her over and over, "Veka, there are many possible futures." We must teach these women not to settle. We must teach them that though there are many things to be transformed in our society, we must not cling to what others have designed for us.
>
> (Marina, Interview)

The affect of "hope" was central to Marina's pedagogy and everyday interactions with the women in the community. This idea was also demonstrated in her use of "hope" for a better future as a rhetorical device throughout her speech during the celebration. Here, Marina mentioned the hope she had for the future of UP.

> I wanted to mention all of the progress that our organization has made, and in some way share this hope that sometimes the state, the government, the politicians take away. This hope to build a new world, we cannot let them take this hope away! Without hope we have nothing.
>
> (Marina, Party in Villa Beltran)

Here, trauma-informed pedagogy is not only about reliving trauma but also about the possibilities of change. The workshops and celebration, though joyful, were not an effort to romanticize the pain away but to intermingle students in communities while addressing anger against injustice and sadness over shared trauma. Both of these had a unifying effect on the community as they stood and spoke out against specific instances of violence against women. This was demonstrated in many of the speeches throughout the event as both activists and workshop participants referenced community violence and human trafficking. This kind of sharing reflects a key aspect of trauma-informed pedagogy, in which space is made for the discussion of trauma in a way that allows for community members to come to a shared understanding of trauma and its effects as well as an opportunity for individual and communal healing.

At the time of the celebration, Argentina had been in an uproar over what many citizens believed to be corruption permeating the state and judicial system. One cause that the community had organized around was injustice in a national case concerning Marita Veron, a young woman who, ten years prior, had been kidnapped from her home in the northwest state of Tucuman and sold into prostitution (Morcillo & Varela 2017). Marita's mother had been searching for years to find her and to bring those who took her to justice. Her search found and helped more than 20 women who were victims of human trafficking, but she had yet to find her daughter. Earlier that month, those who had been accused of kidnapping Marita Verón and selling her to traffickers who forced her into prostitution went on trial in a court in Tucumán. In spite of 130 witness testimonies saying otherwise, all were found innocent on all charges of human trafficking due to an alleged lack of evidence. Similar to how Johnston (2014) engaged students with stories of trauma of colonization in New Zealand, Marita Veron's case had been taken up as a story of the cultural trauma experienced by so many in the community, and used by the popular educators as a way to provide both opportunity to discuss and grieve over trauma, and to mobilize students and the community at large to engage in action for social justice.

Marina revealed in an interview that there had been an incident between Villa Beltran and the state department's Secretary of Security over the apparent corruption in the case. Since then, community members had been targeted by those in power to shut down their activism and mobilization, and that repercussions manifested in arrests, harsh words spoken to the press, and other measures designed to break their morale. These experiences of community trauma, while mourned, had a unifying effect on those present at the workshops, particularly those engaged in UP activism. Popular educators used community members' anger and trauma to bring them together to fight and speak out against the corrupt authorities and injustice at both the national and local levels. Marina spoke of this as particularly important because these corrupt actions of the state directly impacted the communities of women gathered at the event. As she stated in her speech:

> We stand together today against human trafficking, against the unjust ruling of three bastard judges who only make verdicts with their wallets. Against the politicians who acquitted thirteen suspects accused of kidnapping Marita Verón and forcing her into prostitution. Marita's mother crossed heaven and earth to find her daughter, and it makes me furious, furious at the justice system that is unfair to those on the bottom rung of society, justice is only for those on top in this country.
>
> (Marina, Party in Villa Beltran)

It was clear in her speech that the efforts of women teaching in the popular education sector were not solely restricted to the classroom – they extended further into the communities and the problems they faced for being people of color, for being poor, for being women. This illustrates the importance of recognizing the everyday lived experiences of students both in and out of the classroom and how trauma-informed pedagogies extend beyond the classroom into the community to allow for spaces of healing and authentic learning (Pantas, Miller, & Kulkarni 2017). The speeches at the event drew on the community's collective memory of difficult knowledge and stories that highlighted traumatic atrocities of the state and other sectors.

> We must keep fighting against violence against women, against human trafficking. We must remain aware that they are kidnapping poor girls, girls in the north, from the villas. They are kidnapped and sold for prostitution, negotiated by mafias who would not exist if they weren't supported by those with political power and the police. We all know that drug trafficking, prostitution, slave labor, the terror and misery that exists in our country exists with state complicity. Many of the girls who have reported being abducted said they did not dare go to court because the judges were also the ones abusing them. Injustice can only be defeated with popular organizing. So compañeras, will you continue to fight with us?
>
> (Marina, Party in Villa Beltran)

Marina's speech reminded the community of the difficulties they encountered every day. She used these affects of grief and trauma to organize them around the cause, closing with the final question "will you continue to fight with us?" After Marina's speech, many women in the group went to the microphones to show their solidarity. Some were receiving certificates for completing the workshops while others were educators and activists in the community. Those on the mic back up Butler's (2004) claim that trauma, loss, and grief are not necessarily privatizing, solitary conditions, but that such affective states can enhance our connections with others – in shared vulnerability, sadness, and anger that equally hold transformative possibilities in their grasp. The women's speeches echoed the themes of unity under the shared experiences of trauma and fighting against injustice.

> I got so excited during a recent march for Marita when we were sharing the sun that burned us, the rain that drenched us, and I saw so many of my compañeras join the fight. We are as tough as they say, we will continue to be united, and we will continue to fight and defend our lives.
>
> (Donna, Party in Villa Beltran)

> We have shared many moments together, compañeras. Everywhere you look, you can see that we are forming together as a unit. We are forming together on the train each day to work, we have shared responsibilities that now seem beyond what's humanly possible. Thanks for everything and we will continue to fight.
>
> (Estefania, Party in Villa Beltran)

> All of us have formed a family, a family fighting for the same things – for justice, education, work, homes. It is unfortunate that the state wants to prosecute the militants in the social struggle. But if they touch one of us it touches us all.
>
> (Carla, Party in Villa Beltran)

Donna, Estefania, and Carla each reiterated both the unity and the strength of the community. Donna refers to the community as "tough" and Estefania points out that together they are "beyond what's humanly possible." These speeches served to encourage the women in the community to not give up and continue fighting. Phrases like "forming together as a unit" and "sharing the sun" emphasize the aspects of unity necessary in this social movement. Carla refers to the community as a "family fighting for the same things," again, reiterating the unity and commitment in the community as though related by blood in their fight against injustices and for achieving the life they hope for.

UP activists in the Gender Commission were not only helping villa women recover from trauma and loss, but actively assisting them in becoming activist-leaders to improve their community. Their experiences with discussing difficult knowledge in the workshops spilled out into the public spaces of Villa Beltran. They not only took an active role in confronting injustice but also used those common experiences of difficult knowledge to unify the community and in turn activate social movement among the women.

Final Thoughts

Trauma intertwines with intimate stories of teachers, students, and communities. Pedagogically exploring this nexus opens space to discover the promises and challenges of trauma-informed pedagogy within schools and public spaces and provides a deeper sense of the ethical responsibility that mankind holds for each other. This chapter has shown how UP's Gender Commission negotiated workshop participants' and communities' difficult knowledge in pedagogical spaces and urban environments. We have outlined ways in which activists confronted this difficult knowledge and attended to the needs of their communities through curriculum and practices that addressed ongoing injustices and systemic oppression to advocate for social change. They did this through trauma-informed pedagogy and difficult knowledge, as well as tenants similar to those in the Building Community Resilience framework including building a shared understanding of trauma and its effects, cross-sector partnerships, and engaging the whole community in social activism.

We analyzed data collected during a celebration by UP's Gender Commission in Argentina. By highlighting the unity and strength of the community and the hopeful aspects of believing that another future is possible, educators urged the community to continue in solidarity and resistance. Educators confronted the traumatic atrocities of the state and other sectors through relating stories regarding the vulnerability of girls and women at the hands of human traffickers plundering their communities, the history of terrorism and murder in the villas, and the difficult circumstances of the villas themselves. Through public testimony, orators acknowledged the vast improvements made in the lives of women living in communities made possible through social movement organizing and community solidarity and inspired those present to continue to fight for change within their neighborhoods.

Through educators', activists', and students' words, you hear the ways in which difficult knowledge, knowledge of girls and the struggles many women face, was able to inspire others to continue the fight the Gender Commission proposed. Even though such knowledge may be too difficult or uncomfortable to be taken up easily in the classroom, as public-school curriculum is often preferred to be predictable and comforting (Pitt & Britzman 2003), pedagogy needs engagement with difficult knowledge by way of collective memory, justice, trauma, genocide, oppression, and survival. The challenge for teachers then is in understanding how difficult knowledge is both cognitive and affective, and how trauma can bring about calls for social action.

We are not your cooks,
We are not your laundresses,
or your babysitter.
We are militants!
We raise our fists in struggle (repeat).
We do not want violence,
we do not want machismo,
we want to say goodbye to patriarchy
so we raise our fists in struggle (repeat)!
On March 8 we do not want
flowers, we do not want chocolates.
This is a day of struggle.
It is a day of women fighting
and not returning to the doghouse.
So we raise our fists in struggle!
We raise our fists in struggle!

Notes

1. Names were changed to protect the identity of the social movement and all participants in the study.
2. Rather than using what Freire calls "banking methods," where teachers deposit information into empty student bodies, activists invested in the popular education framework promote problem-posing methods to students and foster dialogic and cooperative relationships in the classroom and community (Mayo 1999).
3. Data derived from a larger, four-year ethnographic study (2011–2015) exploring difficult knowledge and trauma-informed teachings in the popular education sector in Buenos Aires, Argentina (O'Donnell 2017). Original data analysis was conducted using Emerson, Fretz, and Shaw's (1995) open coding technique work detailing research procedures for ethnographic inquiry.
4. Spanish for comrade or fellow activist. Because of the "a" at the end (compañera vs. compañero), Marina is specifically speaking of and to the women present at the gathering.

References

Alexander, Jeffrey C., Ron Eyerman, Bernard Giesen, Neil J. Smelser, and Piotr Sztompka. 2004. *Cultural Trauma and Collective Identity*. Berkeley: University of California Press.

Anda, Robert F., Vincent J. Felitti, J. Douglas Bremner, John D. Walker, Charles Whitfield, Bruce D. Perry, Shanta R. Dube, and Wayne H. Giles. 2006. The Enduring Effects of Abuse and Related Adverse Experiences in Childhood: A Convergence of Evidence From Neurobiology and Epidemiology. *European Archives of Psychiatry and Clinical Neuroscience* 256(3): 174.

Britzman, Deborah P. 2000. If the Story Cannot End: Deferred Action, Ambivalence, and Difficult Knowledge. In Sharon Rosenberg, Roger I. Simon, and Claudia Eppert (eds.), *Between Hope and Despair: The Pedagogical Encounter of Historical Remembrance* (pp. 27–57). Lanham: Rowman and Littlefield.

Burke, Nadine, Julia Hellman, Brandon Scott, Carl Weems, and Victor Carrion. 2011. The Impact of Adverse Childhood Experiences on an Urban Pediatric Population. *Child Abuse and Neglect* 35(6): 408–413.

Butler, Judith. 2004. *Precarious Life: The Powers of Mourning and Violence*. London: Verso.

Carello, Janice, and Lisa D. Butler. 2014. Potentially Perilous Pedagogies: Teaching Trauma Is Not the Same as Trauma-Informed Teaching. *Journal of Trauma and Dissociation: The Official Journal of the International Society for the Study of Dissociation* 15(2): 153–168.

Davis, Mike. 2006. *Planet of Slums*. London: Verso.

Ellis, Wendy R. 2020. Tools and Resources: The Building Community Resilience (BCR) Approach. *The Center for Community Resilience*. https://ccr.publichealth.gwu.edu/tools-resources/the-BCR-approach

Ellis, Wendy R., and William H. Dietz. 2017. A New Framework for Addressing Adverse Childhood and Community Experiences: The Building Community Resilience Model. *Academic Pediatrics* 17: 86–93.

Emerson, Robert M., Rachel I. Fretz, and Linda L. Shaw. 1995. *Writing Ethnographic Fieldnotes*. Chicago: The University of Chicago Press.

Fallot, Roger D., and Maxine Harris. 2009. Creating Cultures of Trauma-Informed Care: A Self Assessment and Planning Protocol. Community Connections/Version 2.1, The Anna Institute. www.theannainstitute.org/CCTICSELFASSPP.pdf

Felitti, Vincent J., Robert F. Anda, Dale Nordenberg, David F. Williamson, Alison M. Spitz, Valerie Edwards, and James S. Marks. 1998. Relationship of Childhood Abuse and Household Dysfunction to Many of the Leading Causes of Death in Adults: The Adverse Childhood Experiences Study. *American Journal of Preventive Medicine* 14(4): 245–258.

Freire, Paulo. 2000. *Pedagogy of the Oppressed*, 30th Anniversary edition. New York: Continuum Press.

Grinberg, Silvia. 2010. Everyday Banality in a Documentary by Teenage Women: Between the Trivial and the Extreme. Schooling and Desiring in Contexts of Extreme Urban Poverty. *Gender and Education* 22(6): 663–677.

Himelstein, Sam. 2019. *Trauma-Informed Mindfulness With Teens: A Guide for Mental Health Professionals*. New York: WW Norton and Company.

Johnston, Emily R. 2014. Trauma Theory as Activist Pedagogy: Engaging Students as Reader-Witnesses of Colonial Trauma in Once Were Warriors. *Antipodes* 28(1): 5–17.

Ladson-Billings, Gloria. 1992. Culturally Relevant Teaching: The Key to Making Multicultural Education Work. In Carl Grant (ed.), *Research and Multicultural Education: From the Margins to the Mainstream* (pp. 106–121). New York: Routledge.

Lewis, Paul H. 2002. *Guerillas and Generals: The "Dirty War" in Argentina*. Westport, CT: Praeger.

Mattar, Sandra. 2011. Educating and Training the Next Generations of Traumatologists: Development of Cultural Competencies. *Psychological Trauma: Theory, Research, Practice, and Policy* 3(3): 213–214.

Mayo, Peter. 1999. *Gramsci, Freire, and Adult Education: Possibilities for Transformative Action*. London: Zed Books.

Morcillo, Santiago, and Cecilia Varela. 2017. Any Woman: Abolishing Prostitution in Argentina. *Sexuality, Health, and Society* 26: 213–235.

Newman, Elana. 2011. Teaching Clinical Psychology Graduate Students About Traumatic Stress Studies. *Psychological Trauma: Theory, Research, Practice, and Policy* 3(3): 235–242.

O'Donnell, Jennifer L. 2017. Seguimos Luchando: Women Educators' Trajectories in Social Movement Based Popular Education Projects in Buenos Aires, Argentina. Ph.D. Dissertation, University of Massachusetts, Amherst.

O'Donnell, Jennifer L. 2018. The Promise of Recognition and the Repercussions of Government Intervention: The Transpedagogical Vision of Popular Educators in Buenos Aires, Argentina. *Gender and Education* 30(8): 1078–1097.

O'Donnell, Jennifer L. 2020. I Let Not Just Their Knowledge, But Their Worlds Inform What I Teach: Difficult Knowledge in the Popular Education Classroom in Buenos Aires, Argentina. *Anthropology and Education Quarterly* 51(1): 66–89.

O'Donnell, Jennifer L. 2021. Anger and Disillusionment in Argentinian Feminism, 2011–2015: An Ethnography of Feminist Activism in Popular Education in Buenos Aires. *Gender and Education.* https://doi.org/10.1080/09540253.2020.1866171

Pantas, Susanna, Sean A. Miller, and Shanti J. Kulkarni. 2017. PS: I Survived: An Activism Project to Increase Student and Community Trauma Awareness. *Journal of Teaching in Social Work* 37(2): 185–198.

Pitt, Alice, and Deborah Britzman. 2003. Speculations on Qualities of Difficult Knowledge in Teaching and Learning: An Experiment in Psychoanalytic Research. *International Journal of Qualitative Studies in Education* 16(6): 755–776.

Schugurensky, Daniel. 2003. Two Decades of Neoliberalism in Latin America: Implications for Adult Education. In Stephen Ball, Gustavo Fischman, and Silvina Gvirtz (eds.), *Crisis and Hope: The Educational Hopscotch of Latin America* (pp. 43–64). New York: Routledge Falmer.

Sirvent, María Teresa, and Sandra Llosa. 1998. Jóvenes y Adultos en Situación de Riesgo Educativo: Análisis de la Demanda Potencial y Efectiva [Youth and Adults at Educational Risk: Analysis of the Actual and Potential Demand]. *Revista del Instituto de Investigaciones en Ciencias de la Educación, Facultad de Filosofía y Letras de la UBA,* 7: 77–92.

Toubes, A., and H. Santos. 2006. *Experiencias de Educadores de Jóvenes y Adultos en la Argentina. Análisis de Problemas y Dificultades: 1985–2000 [The Experiences of Youth and Adult Educators in Argentina. Analysis of Problems and Difficulties: 1985–2000].* Buenos Aires, Argentina: Cuadernos de Cátedra, OPFYL.

Ungar, Michael. 2014. Diagnosing Childhood Resilience: A Systemic Approach to the Diagnosis of Adaptation in Adverse Social and Physical Ecologies. *Journal of Child Psychology and Psychiatry* 56(1): 4–17.

Ungar, Michael. 2015. Social Ecological Complexity and Resilience Processes. *Behavioral and Brain Sciences* 38: 1–79.

Vanden, Harry. 2007. Social Movements, Hegemony, and New Forms of Resistance. *Latin American Perspectives* 34: 17–30.

Weber, Max. 1968. *Economy and Society.* New York: Bedminster Press.

Zembylas, Michalinos. 2014. Nostalgia, Postmemories, and the Lost Homeland: Exploring Different Modalities of Nostalgia in Teacher Narratives. *Review of Education, Pedagogy and Cultural Studies* 36(1): 7–21.

Zurbriggen, Eileen L. 2011. Preventing Secondary Traumatization in the Undergraduate Classroom: Lessons from Theory and Clinical Practice. *Psychological Trauma: Theory, Research, Practice, and Policy* 3(3): 223–228.

12 "Stones One Day, Flowers the Next"

The Struggle for Itinerant Schools in the Landless Workers Movement (MST), Brazil

Nisha Thapliyal

Introduction

The *Movimento dos Trabalhadores Rurais sem Terra* (MST, Landless Workers Movement Brazil) is a social movement of approximately 1.5 million poor, landless rural families. The struggle of the Brazilian landless has taken place in a countryside organized under colonial and capitalist logics of economic and social development. As in most Latin American societies, poverty in Brazil has historically been constructed as inferiority and poor people have been denied recognition as subjects and bearers of rights and dignity (Soares 2001; Dagnino 2010). Since independence from Portuguese colonialism two hundred years ago, the history of the Brazilian landless has been characterized by violent exploitation, material deprivation, cultural and political exclusion (see also Harnecker 2003).

Historically, Brazil has one of the most unequal distributions of cultivable land in the world. Even after land ownership laws were reformed in the sixties, vast swathes continue to be owned privately by a small elite group of *fazendeiros* (plantation owning families) and multinational corporations and used for environmentally destructive monocultural farming (e.g. eucalyptus and sugarcane) or simply left unproductive. While slavery officially ended in 1888 (making Brazil the last Western nation to ban slavery), feudal, exploitative working conditions remain a brutal reality for landless women, men, and children who remain trapped in an endless cycle of debt bondage and callous disposability. The term *sem terra*, which literally means landless, has long been used to disparage and dehumanize the rural working poor in Brazil. Resistance to oppression has been suppressed with targeted violence against indigenous people, *quilomberas*,[1] peasants, and agricultural laborers. These acts of violence have been carried out by private landowners and their private armies as well as Brazilian police, which have largely gone unpunished, most recently in the northeastern Amazonian region of Brazil. MST activists and their families have been repeated targets of violence including death threats, assault, torture, imprisonment, attempted murder, and murder since the movement was founded.[2]

DOI: 10.4324/9781003258223-15

The MST was officially established in 1984 and has worked to transform the historically dismissive and derogatory term *sem terra* into a powerful, collective identity *Sem Terra* (Landless). It is currently organized in 23 out of 26 Brazilian states. Movement philosophy and political practice are premised on a rejection of capitalist discourses of competition, economic efficiency, and entrepreneurship that normalize and reproduce conditions of precarity and disposability. The movement has inspired and draws inspiration from other collective sites of resistance to privatization and neoliberal restructuring in the Global South. The movement slogan – Occupy, Resist, Produce – speaks to the goals of organizing marginalized rural peoples to gain access to and participate in the political, economic, and social arrangements that embody the rights of citizenship. The movement has become synonymous with the politics of occupation[3] and successfully mobilized hundreds of thousands of landless families to claim land for those who work it from those who own it (Wolford 2005). If precarity means to be uncertain, insecure, and vulnerable, then the act of occupying public spaces represents a symbolic expression of resistance to precarity.

Beyond the struggle for land, the MST struggle encompasses all aspects of the lives of the landless, including the domain of public education. Over the last four decades, the MST has demonstrated how rural schools (and education more broadly) can become sites of collective struggle. These struggles exemplify how dominant social relations and imaginaries about development and democracy that legitimize and normalize structurally imposed conditions of precarity can be questioned, interrupted, and transformed. In this chapter, I analyze the MST struggle for itinerantItinerant schools (*Escolas ItinerantItinerantes*) to explore how the movement politicized and transformed precarious conditions in public education in the state of Rio Grande do Sul. Itinerant schools are mobile schools that respond to the itinerant nature of the existence of the rural landless and their struggle for land; in other words, these schools move with the children and families engaged in MST land occupations. The MST claimed not only access to schooling for the landless but also the right to self-determination, to envision and enact their own educational project. In doing so, they resisted and transformed dominant discourses of precarity, which have historically worked to stigmatize the landless as incapable and unworthy of being bearers of rights and dignity.

Conceptual Framework

Rubin (2004) states that social movements offer a "unique view of politics because they create new forms of organization and representation at the interaction of formal institutions and daily life" (p. 106). He also argues that the creation and resilience of movements can only be understood through attention to the interplay of culture, economics, and politics including the interconnectedness of state and social movements (Rubin 2004). From this perspective, movements do not only emerge as a response to a particular hardship or historical moment. Furthermore, movements are neither homogenous nor monolithic but instead constituted by complex moral economies (Wolford 2010). Accordingly, this analysis of the collective struggle to occupy rural public education emphasizes the significance of sociohistorical context as well as diverse activist subjectivities and identities.

The MST struggle for the right to education on their own terms emerged out of and is rooted in the marginal locations imposed on the landless by the capitalist labor market (Millar 2017). Thus, precarity is approached as an analytical category that "sheds light on the ways inequality is politicized in late capitalism . . . under conditions that make manifest in everyday life . . . the dialectic between the expanded reproduction of capitalism and dispossession" (Señorans 2020, p. 81).

Methodology

This research project begins with the premise that the ways in which activists make meaning about and represent their struggles are complex, contingent on and embedded with multiple dimensions of power (Polletta 1998, 2009). The analysis presented here draws on a larger qualitative research study undertaken between 2005 and 2010 that sought to document and analyze the movement's struggle to transform rural education policy and practice. It is empirically informed by in-depth interviews with a total of 20 MST educators and Education and Gender Sector leaders, which took place between November 2004 and January 2005 in the central state of Rio de Janeiro (Thapliyal 2006, 2013) and again in June 2010 in the southeastern states of Rio Grande do Sul (RGS) and Parana (Thapliyal 2019). During both periods of fieldwork, I also interviewed MST allies including academics, lawyers, and elected leaders and collected and analyzed a range of movement artifacts including MST print and digital publications, news articles, and research publications.

Two key informants figure prominently in this chapter: Marli Zimmerman de Moraes and Elisabete Witcel, who played a central role in the creation and expansion of the first Itinerant schools in Rio Grande do Sul (Zimmerman de Moraes & Witcel 2010). They gave their consent for their real names to be used in dissemination of research findings and are hereafter referred to as Marli and Beti; pseudonyms are used for the other MST activists quoted in this chapter. I lived with Marli and Beti and their families for a week in the winter of 2010 in Rio Grande do Sul. The title of this chapter comes from a dialogue with Beti during this time about her journey to becoming a teacher in the itinerantItinerant schools. Our conversation about their experiences with the itinerantItinerant schools continued in 2013–2014 in the form of a research collaboration, which also included leading MST scholar Dr. Rebecca Tarlau. The collaboration led to a panel presentation at the 2013 conference of the World Council of Comparative Education Societies

(WCCES) and an open-access journal special issue on learning activism (Zimmerman de Moraes & Witcel 2014; Thapliyal 2014; Witcel 2014).

Occupying Education in the Brazilian Countryside

Public education is one of the last remaining spheres of contestation in capitalist democracies. This is why the struggle for the MST itinerant schools (which were closed in 2011) was and remains significant not only to the movement but to debates about rural education and development as a whole. The MST struggle for the right to an education of the countryside (*Educação do Campo* in Portuguese) represents a comprehensive critique of capitalist education and development in Brazil. As with the struggle for land redistribution and agrarian reform, MST educational activism has exposed the historical role of the state in protecting and furthering the interests of elite ruling classes and private capital. Two hundred years of official rural education policy in Brazil have denied and diluted the constitutionally mandated right to education for the rural poor and other marginalized communities including the landless, the indigenous, and Afro-Brazilians (Plank 1996; Soares 2001; Thapliyal 2006). These policies have contributed to the legitimation and reproduction of an unequal social order (stratified by class, race, indigeneity, gender, the rural-urban divide, and so forth) and an unsustainable development project. However, the MST political project to occupy public education is predicated on a rejection of a worldview and public discourse where the suffering and dehumanization of the rural landless can be blamed on the landless themselves, and their rights have been reduced to needs (see also Señorans 2020). The MST has mobilized to not only demand access to existing rights and entitlements enjoyed by other Brazilians but also construct an alternative political discourse and imagination that exposes the fundamental limitations of capitalist, liberal democracy and development. In this alternative political project, the state is compelled to become a public space and construct public policies in collaboration with movements of historically marginalized groups instead of acting only to protect and promote the interests of private capital (Stédile 2003).

This is why the struggle to occupy education began almost as soon as the MST began to occupy land:

> When we began our struggle, we believed that land alone would be enough to get people out of poverty. We were wrong. We learned that the enemy was not just the large estates. We learned that there are other fences besides the ones that kept campesinos off of the land. We learned that the lack of capital is a fence. We learned that ignorance, a lack of knowledge, is a fence. The MST focuses on literacy because no matter how much land a *campesino* has, there is no chance of participation in society without literacy.
>
> (Stédile 2003, p. 22)

The MST has an alternative vision for rural education – called a "Pedagogy of the Land" – which recognizes and affirms the diverse knowledge traditions in rural Brazil (MST 1996). The first schools were established by parents and community members, predominantly women, who were determined that their children would experience a different kind of schooling that recognized and affirmed their cultures and lived experiences (Camini 2009). The interests, cultures, and lived experiences or realities of learners and educators were and remain a starting place for learning along with values for social justice; personal human connections; cooperation and interdependence; solidarity; and participatory, deliberative democracy (see also McCowan 2003). Learning is understood as a continuous and lifelong process, which should enable individual and social transformation (MST 1996). MST curricula and pedagogy are explicitly critical of capitalist education values such as the importance of mental over manual work, individualism, competition, and profit. Key influences include educational thinkers associated with socialist projects in Brazil, Cuba, and the Soviet Union such as Paulo Freire, Josué de Castro, Anton Makarenko, and Moisey M. Pistrak (see also Tarlau 2012).

The Education Sector is now one of the oldest sectors (or collectives) in the internal organizational structure of the movement (along with Political Education, Agricultural Production, Communications, International Relations and more recently Health, Gender, Environment, Human Rights and Youth). Its development and expansion has been led primarily by women who first pressured the movement for schools for their children and then continued to demand greater space for education, as well as gender equality on the movement agenda (see also Thapliyal 2019). Over the last four decades, the movement has educated thousands of infants, children, adolescents, and adults who have been stigmatized and abandoned by a capitalist education system. It has also prepared thousands of teachers from within the movement and cultivated a movement-wide culture of study (Harnecker 2003). Today, education in the MST encompasses the entire domain of public education including preschools, primary and secondary schools, literacy education, and the Florestan Fernandes National university. These educational spaces are recognized by the state apparatus, and often but not always supported with public resources (see also Thapliyal 2013; Tarlau 2019).

In the remainder of this chapter, I present a chronological account of the struggle for the Itinerant schools and highlight the specific ways in which the MST politicized and transformed the landless experience of precarity. The discussion highlights the role of MST children and educators in the struggle as well as the complex and situated ways in which activists understood the nature of the struggle for their right to education.

The Struggle for the Itinerant Schools in Rio Grando Sul (1995–2010)

The first "official" itinerantItinerant schools emerged in the mid-1990s during land occupations in the southern state of Rio Grande do Sul (RGS) during the administration of Governor Antônio Britto of the Brazilian Democratic Movement Party (PMDB). The MST was officially founded here by landless peasants descended from German, Italian, and Portuguese landless workers. Rio Grande do Sul is the fourth richest state in Brazil with the fifth highest population (Brazilian Institute of Geography and Statistics [IBGE] 2011). This was a time of change for the political culture of the region amidst high levels of protest and collective activism by workers, peasants, teachers, and others throughout the state including MST mobilizations to occupy lands as well as public schools.

Between 1996 and 2009, an estimated 7,000 landless people (children and adults) would participate in the itinerant schools that accompanied land occupations in Rio Grande do Sul. These families, consisting of both the rural landless and some urban homeless, were seeking to break an endless cycle of poverty and reclaim their dignity and autonomy. The process of land occupations can be long, uncertain, and dangerous.[4] As readers may know, families may participate in multiple marches and occupations until the official process of land redistribution occurs. In occupation camps, families live in tents made of bamboo and black plastic until the government officially resettles them, which usually takes months if not years (see also Harnecker 2003).

The Sem Terrinha and the Right to Education

MST activists sought to politicize these conditions of precarity by demanding the right to education for their children. Early experiences with mobilizing landless families for occupations had taught activists that families were more likely to participate if they were assured that their children's schooling would not be interrupted (Marli 2010 interview data). Rural landless families were also determined to provide their children with a different kind of education that affirmed rural identities, knowledge, and cultures instead of an urban-centric, industrialized worldview (Soares 2001). Marli (2010 interview data) described the disconnection and alienation that dominated the experiences of landless children in mainstream public schools as follows:

> The teacher is up there, and they have to copy and do whatever they say. They are discriminated against because they don't have shoes, because their clothes smell of the smoke from their camps, because they can't have regular baths without water in the camps.
>
> (Marli 2010 interview data)

In 1994, the MST Education Sector organized the first statewide Children and Youth Congress. It was attended by hundreds of students who participated in organized learning activities about the right to education and agrarian reform. They made signs, learned songs, and talked about the nature of public protest. The second Children and Youth Congress was held in 1995 where children, youths, and adults read and discussed the 1990 Brazilian Statute on the Rights of the Child (SRC). These two meetings led to the articulation of the demand for the access to schools for landless children while they participated in land occupations. For the MST, these meetings were also a key space in which to recognize and amplify the voices of working-class children[5] and an educational project premised on solidarity rather than self-interest (Caldart 2011).

MST activists then developed a formal proposal titled "A proposal for an alternative pedagogy" for the state government to recognize and fund schools that would accompany families engaged in the struggle for land. Like all MST negotiations, the proposal framed its demands in explicit relation to existing educational legislation, which affirmed the right to education for all Brazilian children including the 1971 Education Law and 1990 Statute for the Rights of Children and Adolescents (SRCA). In addition, the proposal incorporated the MST vision for an education that was responsive to the needs and lived realities of the children in the movement:

> We constructed a proposal to meet the needs of our children. The challenge for learning was how to become human, how to understand the other. Education is nothing else is it? You have to understand personally, and you also have to understand the person you are working with. You have to believe that transformation is possible. This is what the movement fights for – to arouse people with the will to live, to fight, to do something about your miserable situation.
>
> (Beti 2010 interview data)

They received help in writing this proposal from a former popular educator and Catholic nun called Sister Alda Moura appointed by the Britto administration to liaise with social movements. The movement then mobilized for the next year with support from a diverse group of allies including politicians and media until the proposal was finally considered by the State Education Advisory Board.

MST children played a prominent role in these mobilization actions, which received prominent media coverage. In late 1995, one hundred children marched to the state Department of Education (DOE) to present the proposal for the itinerant schools. The children sang songs, shouted protest chants, and read out the SRCA in front of the DOE building in Porto Allegre. A year later, with mounting public support, hundreds of *Sem Terrinha* marched again to the DOE, and the Secretary reluctantly agreed that the State Education Advisory Board (SEAB) would consider the proposal. The MST took advantage of this opening in characteristic fashion and ensured that the proposal was not given merely token consideration. The *Sem Terrinha* again played a critical role in the events of the day. Marli (2010 interview data) described the events as follows:

> We learned that our proposal for the schools was last on the agenda for the SEAB so what did we do? We filled two buses with children carrying placards and pamphlets. We arrived at the Council meeting and sang, played games, chanted. The Councilors arrived, saw the room full of children and didn't know what to do. The schools were placed first on the agenda and approved unanimously. Not a single Councilor had the courage to say no – that these children couldn't go to school – that they didn't have the right to study. They had no other option isn't it? This was a thoughtful and useful strategy.

The proposal was approved as a two-year experimental project where the movement had complete autonomy over the educational philosophy and processes of the school. With official recognition as public schools came resources for the construction of itinerant schools, wages for qualified teachers, and basic materials including chairs, chalkboards, and textbooks. Families contributed time and labor to build the schools and set up classrooms for the first four years of primary schooling. The schools were closely watched by education bureaucrats and funding was often delayed (Camini 2009). Nevertheless, official recognition and support for these schools was considered a major victory for the movement because it occurred during a period of intense repression by a hostile federal government. The itinerant schools also came to occupy a unique place within movement discourse because they foregrounded landless children as agents and political actors who were capable of understanding and claiming their rights.

The Movement Is a School

The itinerant schools expanded and flourished under the next regime of Governor Olívio Dutra. In 1998, the progressive Workers Party gained power with heavy support from the left-leaning social movements in the region. Dutra was personally committed to the idea of participatory governance (see also Gandin & Apple 2002) and significantly expanded support for the itinerant schools and land occupations. Dozens of schools were built in occupation camps and MST leaders were invited to join the Dutra administration, including the education department. In 2002 when he left office, there were 16 itinerant schools serving several thousand students in first through eighth grades (Camini 2009).

Activist memories of this period emphasized the challenges and possibilities of learning and teaching on the March and in the occupation camps:

> To construct schools within a movement is a great challenge. We have to construct another imagination for schooling that is connected to our

life experiences, to what we learn while living in the "black tents" (the MST encampments) and on the road from one occupation to the next. The goal of learning for the men and women in our schools and in the movement is to understand the meaning of the phrase "Hope for a life that is more just and human."

(Zimmerman de Moraes & Witcel 2010, p. 44)

Beti talked about constructing educational processes where "the rhythm of our studies matched the rhythm of the spaces in which we were studying." Carina described how teachers created lessons based in children's everyday lives including topics as diverse as vegetable gardens, popular music, football, and capoeira. Learning activities utilized the day-to-day activities of children such as agricultural work as well as arts and crafts and theater.

The experience of occupying land was a critical part of the curriculum:

Great marches were organized during that time. The families walked all day, all morning. When they stopped to rest and eat, we organized schools for the children. Tired as we were from walking, we studied the route of the march, the municipality, the distance we walked, what the children saw as they walked. All this was transformed into curriculum, into knowledge, based on the realities of life during the occupations. To be without food. To sleep in the cold. All this was discussed in the school and then the children learned in one way or another to write and document these experiences. We had a very big field of study with this kind of vision

(Marli 2010 interview data)

The diversity of socioeconomic backgrounds and lived experiences of the children also provided a challenge for educators. For many educators, this was their first encounter with families who had experienced urban poverty:

We received children who were from incredibly miserable situations. They have to find food to eat in the garbage. They have misery and violence in their homes. When they come to school, the educator has to first – before anything else – discover what stimulates these children to life – with affection, caring, dedication, attention. There are children who assault the teachers violently one day. And when you come back the next day, they bring the teacher flowers. To see the children light up when they write, when they make these discoveries and you know that you contributed. It is very satisfying when you can plant seeds – seeds of love, seeds of education, seeds of human values. There are no words to describe this feeling of satisfaction. This is what we learned in the classrooms. This is not in books.

(Beti 2010 interview data)

Teachers were expected to continuously learn and study in keeping with the movement's goal of constructing and maintaining a "culture of study" at all times. While they had been selected by their communities because they indicated that they liked working with children and valued family, most had little schooling themselves. The high degree of collaboration between state and social movement during this period enabled these novice educators to continue their own education and eventually gain official state teacher qualifications. Individuals like Marli and Beti experienced a journey of intense personal transformation from seeing themselves as uneducated to becoming educators who were capable of constructing an alternative rural educational project on their own terms.

In order to attain these qualifications, the teachers attended the independent high/secondary school established by the MST in 1995 called the Educational Institute of Josué de Castro (IEJC). Shaped by the MST vision for rural education and development, the IEJC allowed activists to complete their high school qualifications (Thapliyal 2013). The itinerant school teachers attended IEJC for part of the year and then returned to their camps to put their teaching into practice with continuing support from the state Education Sector. In the camps, these teachers were continuously supported through teacher networks and Education Sector Coordinators like Beti and Marli in designing curriculum, developing weekly lesson plans, and regular reflection consistent with a Pedagogy of the Land (Zimmerman de Moraes & Witcel 2010). The student teachers prepared research reports on this experience and – on completion of all requirements – were awarded a high school degree as well as a teaching certification "Teacher Training for the Land" (see also Diniz-Pereira 2005).

During the Dutra administration, MST education coordinators like Marli and Beti were paid to travel between camps to support the continuing development of teachers. The Dutra administration also funded regular regional and statewide seminars for continuous teacher training. Last but not least, in 2000 and 2002, the Dutra administration opened two civil service exams for state teachers that enabled successful candidates from the MST to enter the official public education system as teachers and administrators, in which many remain today. These exams represented a critical moment in the resilience of the MST education project because there would be no civil examinations for another decade. MST-trained educators who passed this examination became official state teachers with job security against political hirings and firings.

By the end of this unprecedented collaboration between state and social movement, the itinerant schools enjoyed widespread recognition and support and flourished throughout the state. Issues with state bureaucracy persisted, and salaries and funds for educational materials often arrived late and continued to be inadequate (Maria 2010 interview data). However, the movement's capacity to provide education in occupation camps continued to grow. In the next state elections, the PMDB returned to power under the leadership of Germano Rigotto (2002–2005). This administration stopped all support but allowed the schools to continue to function in occupation camps. In response, teachers and communities shared resources, and the schools continued to play an integral role in maintaining high morale in the occupation camps.

The Nature of the Struggle

In 2006, the deeply conservative Brazilian Social Democratic Party (PSDB) came to power in RGS under Yeda Crusuis. The PSDB has historically advocated for market-based economic policies and framed all left-wing politicians and movements, particularly the MST, as dangerous communists and a fundamental threat to the rule of law[6] (see also Carter 2015). The regime launched a full-scale violence attack on the MST using police to disband occupation camps and disrupt MST meetings. The political project to undermine the itinerant schools took much longer and required collaboration between two government agencies: the DOE and RGS Public Ministry (PM, a supposedly independent body similar to the state public prosecutor's office). In 2008, the PM launched an official inquiry into the itinerant schools in response to complaints from landowners about illegal activities in four MST occupation sites. The inquiry report concluded that the itinerant schools functioned completely outside the control of the government and that MST curriculum was replete with dangerous ideologies about class revolution. By the end of the year, the DOE and PM cosigned a document titled "Terms of Commitment to Adjust Conduct" (TAC), which mandated that the state government could close the itinerant schools.

Approximately 600 to 700 children were told to attend the nearest government school even though many were located over 50 kilometers away from the camps and there was no guarantee of spaces in those schools. This action was supported by the powerful conservative owned media, which misrepresented the movement as criminal and the schools as secretive and illegal. Activists highlighted the inherent contradictions in the highly mediatized discourse of child welfare that was deployed to justify the school closures:

> In discussions they told us "we only want the wellbeing of the children. We are here as mediators to ensure that the children have seats reserved in city schools and that the parents send them to these schools." But they evicted families in the middle of winter and assaulted our activists.
> (Maria 2010 interview data)

The ways in which MST activists analyzed the closure of the schools in RGS provides key insights into how they understand the nature of the struggle and why the closures represented an inevitable but temporary setback similar to their experience with land occupations.

We are in a class struggle, aren't we? We have learned that when you challenge the power structure, then you are attacked in many ways. You are criticized and massacred and labelled violent *baderneiros* (trouble-makers). We really made a difference to these families, you know. The schools gave them motivation to continue the struggle. We always say the government closed the schools because they contradicted the principles of capitalism. The schools rescued the people, their dignity.

(Beti 2010 interview data)

Education Sector Leaders like Marli, Beti, and Maria (2010 interview data) all emphasized the speed with which government agencies acted and collaborated to protect private property in stark contrast to the bureaucratic delays that dominated the relationship between the state and the movement in this period. They argued that closure of the schools allowed the state to take back sole control over education, and in doing so, demoralize and fragment the families involved in the land occupations. They also highlighted the larger project of education privatization of the Crusius administration, which closed down another 200 rural schools in order to construct more schools in urban areas and introduced market-oriented reforms including teacher merit pay and high-stakes testing despite resistance from teachers' unions.

Due to the sustained and organized resistance mobilized by the movement, it would take several years to shut the schools down completely. Teachers continued to teach without salaries and resources. Parents continued to send their children to school despite legal threats and police intimidation to send children to city schools. The MST and its allies organized marches and protests including prominent Brazilians such as Nita Freire, wife of Paulo Freire, and members of the judiciary, elected representatives, human rights organizations, and academics. The *Sem Terrinha* were prominent in these mobilizations; they marched in large numbers in 2009 and 2010 under the banner "Closing the Schools is a Crime!" The protests received national attention and sympathy including from congressional representatives.[7]

Conclusion

In this chapter, I have discussed how the MST claimed the right to education for landless children in RGS and in doing so politicized and transformed the precarious conditions that characterize their lives. The itinerant schools represent a site of struggle containing multiple and situated forms of dissent, resistance, and transformation – which emerge and are enacted in enduring conditions of precarity. For individual activists, *Sem Terrinha* and *Sem Terra*, the struggle was a site for personal transformation, overcoming cultural stigmas, and learning about the possibilities and contingencies of constructing collective or popular power. In and through the struggle, landless learners and educators were constructed not as inferior, needy, and uneducable but rights-bearers and creators of valuable and legitimate knowledge on their own terms. Thus, for the movement, the act of occupation can be seen to represent a control of territorial space that is necessary for the politicization of its members (Vergara-Camus 2009). For society as a whole, the occupation of education as public space, confronted and challenged the inequalities, exclusions, and sociocultural hierarchies that constitute capitalist conceptions of education and social relations in Brazil.[8]

In concluding, I will highlight particular aspects of the discourse of rights and citizenship that enabled the movement to challenge and resist an educational project designed to normalize and legitimize a national and global culture based on precarity. Zygmunt Bauman (2009) describes this as a global culture of liquid modernity based essentially on notions of superfluity manifest in the language of excess, redundancy, waste, and waste-disposal. For Bauman (2009), this is not a culture of continuous and relational learning and knowing but instead a culture of disengagement, discontinuity and forgetting. Human beings deemed insufficiently productive or vulnerable are relegated to inferior, needy, and disposable status who must eternally compete with each other in a race to the bottom while a tiny elite are positioned as rights-bearers deserving of a life with dignity and autonomy.

In this sociohistorical context, the struggle for the itinerant schools provides situated insights into how the movement goes about envisioning and expanding the meaning of rights, making these rights visible, and transforming power relations between citizens and the state in order to make them reality. As previously discussed, the necessity for the itinerant schools to exist exposed significant tensions, contradictions, and fractures in the capitalist development project. The MST demands that the Brazilian state meet its responsibilities to its landless citizens who have historically been positioned as clients by a paternalistic political culture of clientelism (Dagnino 2010) or simply dismissed as anonymous, disposable statistics.

More specifically, the demand for the itinerant schools was articulated in terms of the right to education for landless children to expose a fundamental tension in capitalist education and development that has historically excluded and stigmatized the rural poor. Along with the unequal distribution of land and the neglect of rural education, rural development policy as a whole has historically been configured to protect and promote the interests of private capital. In this context, the struggle for the itinerant schools compelled the Brazilian state to reimagine and enact a different kind of relationship with the landless: a relationship premised on dignity; the right to self-determination; and collective, deliberative decision-making and governance.

Like other Brazilian movements, the MST discourse of rights – to land, to education – is partly situated in rights recognized and affirmed in the existing legislation. These include the 1964 Land Law, the 1988 Constitution, the 1990 Statute for Children and Adolescents, and the 1996 Education Law (Thapliyal 2006; Soares 2001). However, movement rights discourse in the MST and some other Latin American movements goes far beyond existing institutional rights to claim the right to have rights on their own terms and within their particular historical, cultural, and political contexts (Alvarez, Dagnino, & Escobar 1998). In this context, the itinerant schools represented an alternative vision for education and society that is shaped by the lived realities of the working classes:

> The schools recognized that children in the struggle for land also need access to school . . . they represent the historical desire of the working classes to educate their children . . . they represent one more chapter in the struggle for denied rights to education
>
> (Zimmerman de Moraes & Witcel 2010, p. 12, translated by author)

Thus, the social imaginary and educational practice manifest in the spaces constituted by the schools is shaped by the relationship between the landless and the land, lived experiences of systematic and systemic dispossession, political marginalization, and cultural stigmatization as well as collective struggle.

These spaces also reflect a transformative conception of the state as a public space. Recognition and inclusion of the schools in the public education system represent the kinds of structural transformation that are possible when states are willing to work with movements. Reclaiming the state as a public space is central to movement imaginary and practice:

> We have learned that the State is losing power and control over what should be public. The public is becoming private. Social movements are a force that work with the established powers of the State in the struggle for rights and for social transformation. In this case, schools, for the Movement, are public, and therefore, of the people and for the people. Of the countryside and for the countryside.
>
> (MST 2004, p. 151)

As demonstrated by the struggle for the Itinerant schools, this political work of reclaiming the public is ongoing and continuous (contrary to linear, causal narratives about collective mobilizations and movements that dominate the scholarly literature as well as popular imaginations about what doing alternative democracy can look like). The MST is able to politicize and transform conditions of precarity through a politics constituted by processes of internal education, mass mobilization, continuous negotiation with state apparatus, and strategic political alliances. This political project has endured and thrived in an electoral democracy where a three-year electoral cycle ensures that the movement can never take any of its victories for granted.

Through this Gramscian war of position approach, the movement has repeatedly demonstrated that it is possible for popular power to coexist with state power in contingent ways in varying conditions of precarity (see also Harnecker 2003; Wolford 2010). That being said, it is important to acknowledge that the MST is not the only rural or urban social movement in Brazil that has contributed to the expansion of participatory and deliberative spaces of democracy. However, the project to occupy and transform rural public education through the itinerant schools exemplifies the ways in which the MST has effectively politicized and transformed precarity in rural Brazil. Through these and other education struggles, the landless have claimed the right to education and knowledge instead of being relegated to superfluous, exploitable, or disposable surplus.

Notes

1. Descendants of escaped African slaves who established free African strongholds called *quilombos* for more than 100 years during Portuguese colonialism.
2. See also a three-part video series in English of the history of the MST at www.mst-brazil.org/video/story-mst-part-i
3. It is important to emphasize here that the MST occupies land that is legally deemed eligible for redistribution under the existing law.
4. As recently as August 14, 2020, 65 families were violently evicted from the Quilombo Campo Grande encampment in the state of Minas Gerais. During the eviction, the police deliberately destroyed the Eduardo Galeano School. The school educated not only from the encampment but also from the surrounding area in topics such as agro-ecology and also had a vibrant adult literacy program.
5. MST publications regularly highlight the voices and educational experiences of the *Sem Terrinha* including the *Revista Sem Terrinha* and the *Jornada das Crianças Sem Ter-rinha e a Ciranda Infantil*. See https://mst.org.br/revista-sem-terrinha/
6. Other social movements including the women's peasant movement, teachers unions, rural workers, city workers, and street people were also labeled as lawless and criminal and subject to police brutality.
7. Three months after I completed my interviews in 2010, PT gubernatorial candidate Tarso Genro easily defeated Yeda Crusius on a platform to end the criminalization of social movements and bring back the itinerant schools. However, the sustained and violent repression by the previous regime had weakened the movement's position in the state. Land occupations declined significantly and there were no longer enough children in the occupation camps to justify restarting the schools. In addition, a number of leaders left the movement citing ideological and strategic differences.
8. The struggle in RGS sparked similar struggles and victories in other states including in Paraná (2003), Santa Catarina (2004), Goiás (2005), Alagoas (2005) e Piauí (2008) (Camini 2009). Currently, the schools only continue to function in Paraná.

References

Alvarez, Sonia, Evelina Dagnino, and Arturo Escobar (eds.). 1998. *Cultures of Politics, Politics of Cultures: Revisioning Latin American Social Movements*. Boulder, CO: Westview Press.

Bauman, Zygmunt. 2009. Education in the Liquid-modern Setting. *Power and Education* 1(2): 157–166.

Brazilian Institute of Geography and Statistics (IBGE). 2010. *Population Census*. https://www.ibge.gov.br/en/statistics/social/population/18391-2010-population-census.html?=&t=sobre

Caldart, Roseli, and the Movement of Landless Workers. 2011. Pedagogy of the Landless: Brazil. In Terry Wrigley, Pat Thomson and Robert Lingard (eds.), *Changing Schools: Alternative Ways to Make a World of Difference* (pp. 71–84). New York: Routledge.

Camini, Isabela. 2009. *Escola Itinerante: Na Fronteira de Uma Nova Escola* [Itinerant Schools: A New Kind of School]. São Paulo: Expressão Popular.

Carter, Miguel (ed.). 2015. *Challenging Social Inequality: The Landless Rural Workers Movement and Agrarian Reform in Brazil.* Charlotte, NC: Duke University Press.

Dagnino, Evelina. 2010. Citizenship: A Perverse Confluence. In Andrea Cornwall and Deborah Eade (eds.), *Deconstructing Development Discourse: Buzzwords and Fuzzwords* (pp. 101–111). Oxford, UK: Oxfam GB.

Diniz-Pereira, Julio Emilio. 2005. Teacher Education for Social Transformation and Its Links to Progressive Social Movements: The Case of the Landless Workers Movement in Brazil. *Journal of Critical Education Policy Studies* 11(2): 91–123. www.jceps.com/archives/505

Gandin, Luis Armando, and Michael W. Apple. 2002. Can Education Challenge Neo-Liberalism? The Citizen School and the Struggle for Democracy in Porto Alegre, Brazil. *Social Justice* 29(4): 26–40.

Harnecker, Marta. 2003. *Landless People: Building a Social Movement.* São Paulo: Expressão Popular.

McCowan, Tristan. 2003. Participation and Education in the Landless People's Movement of Brazil. *Journal for Critical Education Policy Studies* 1(1): 124–150. www.jceps.com/archives/402

Millar, Kathleen M. 2017. Toward a Critical Politics of Precarity. *Sociology Compass* 11(6): 1–11.

Movimento Sem Terra (MST). 2004. Educação no MST Balanço 20 anos. (20 Years of Education in the MST) *Boletim da Educação* 9. https://mst.org.br/download/mst-boletim-da-educacao-no-09-educacao-no-mst-balanco-20-anos/

Movimento Sem Terra (MST) 1996. Princípios da Educação no MST. (Principles of Education in the MST). *Caderno de Educação* 8.

Plank, David. 1996. *The Means of Our Salvation: Public Education in Brazil, 1930–1995.* Boulder, CO: Westview Press.

Polletta, Francesca. 1998. Contending Stories: Narrative in Social Movements. *Qualitative Sociology* 21(4): 419–446.

Polletta, Francesca. 2009. *It Was Like a Fever: Storytelling in Protest and Politics.* Chicago: University of Chicago Press.

Rubin, Jeffrey W. 2004. Meanings and Mobilizations: A Cultural Politics Approach to Social Movements and States. *Latin American Research Review* 39(3): 106–142.

Señorans, Dolores. 2020. "The Right to Live With Dignity": Politicising Experiences of Precarity through "Popular Economy" in Argentina. *Bulletin of Latin American Research* 39: 69–82. https://doi.org/10.1111/blar.12707

Soares, Edla de Araújo Lira. 2001. Diretrizes Operacionais para a Educação Basica nas Escolas do Campo – Resolução CNE/CEB No. 1 [Operational Directives for Basic Education in Rural Schools]. Ministry of Education (MEC), Brasilia, DF. http://pronacampo.mec.gov.br/images/pdf/mn_parecer_36_de_04_de_dezembro_de_2001.pdf

Stédile, João Pedro. 2003. Globalisation and Social Movements: A Brazilian Perspective. Colloquia Paper, Centre for Research on Latin America and the Caribbean (CER-LAC), York University, October 2. Presented in a public lecture at University of Toronto, Toronto, January 2004.

Tarlau, Rebecca. 2012. Soviets in the Countryside: The MST's Remaking of Socialist Educational Practices in Brazil. In Tom Griffiths and Zsuzsa Millei (eds.), *Logics of Socialist Education: Engaging With Crisis, Insecurity and Uncertainty* (pp. 53–72). Dordrecht: Springer.

Tarlau, Rebecca. 2019. *Occupying Schools, Occupying Land: How the Landless Workers Movement Transformed Brazilian Education.* London: Oxford University Press.

Thapliyal, Nisha. 2006. *Education, Civil Society and Social Change: A Case Study of a Brazilian Social Movement.* Doctoral Dissertation, University of Maryland, College Park.

Thapliyal, Nisha. 2013. Reframing the Public in Public Education: The Landless Workers Movement (MST) and Adult Education in Brazil. *Journal of Critical Education Policy Studies* 11(4): 106–113. www.jceps.com/archives/456

Thapliyal, Nisha. 2014. Learning, Knowledge and Activism: Introduction to the Special Issue. *Postcolonial Directions in Education* 3(1): 3–17. www.um.edu.mt/library/oar// handle/123456789/19651

Thapliyal, Nisha. 2019. "Legitimate But Not Legal": Learning Power in the Landless Workers Movement (MST), Brazil. *New Directions for Adult and Continuing Education* 164: 11–22. https://onlinelibrary.wiley.com/doi/abs/10.1002/ace.20352

Vergara-Camus, Leandro. 2009. The MST and the EZLN Struggle for Land: New Forms of Peasant Rebellions. *Journal of Agrarian Change* 9(3): 365–391.

Witcel, Elisabete. 2014. A Little Bit of My Story in the Landless Struggle. *Postcolonial Directions in Education* 3(1): 42–56.

Wolford, Wendy. 2005. Agrarian Moral Economies and Neoliberalism in Brazil: Competing Worldviews and the State in the Struggle for Land. *Environment and Planning* 37(2): 241–261.

Wolford, Wendy. 2010. *This Land Is Ours Now: Social Mobilization and the Meanings of Land in Brazil.* Durham, NC: Duke University Press.

Zimmerman de Moraes, Marli, and Elisabete Witcel. 2010. Escola Itinerante: Pontos e Contrapontos de uma Escola em Movimento [Itinerant Schools: Advances and Setbacks in a Movement School]. *Cadernos da Escola Itinerante* 3(5): 15–36.

Zimmerman de Moraes, Marli, and Elisabete Witcel. 2014. The "Responsibility" of Being Educators in a Social Movement School. *Postcolonial Directions in Education* 3(1): 42–56.

13 Radical Consciousness and Movements in Defense of Black Lives

The Lineage of Detroit's League of Revolutionary Black Workers and the Promise of Education for Liberation

Bianca Ayanna Suárez

Introduction

Since the founding of the U.S. nation state, control over the minds of the oppressed has served to perpetuate a fundamentally racist capitalist society (Du Bois 1968; Douglass 1845). Educational thinkers and scholars have examined the historical struggle for education to secure freedom in social, cultural, and economic terms (Watkins 2001; Anderson 1988). In particular, there is a bold history of social movement building and the promise of education for liberation (Rickford 2016; Biondi 2012; Muñoz 2007; Perlstein 2002. This chapter contributes to this history through examination of the relationship between a radical Black social movement and the development of radical consciousness in *and* beyond schools. Moreover, this exploration uncovers and highlights how Black social movements have played a decisive role in spearheading possibility for educational transformation. Additionally, this history provides a context to consider how social movements can discern precarious contradictions and offer an alternative vision of society (Kelley 2002). From here, we may then better understand the potential for transformation related to today's precarious conditions. Non-oppressive forms of educational practice are at the center of this newly curated social order.

Methodology and Analytical Framework

This chapter examines oral history interview data, archival research, biography/memoir, and secondary source material. Drawing on precepts of anti-colonial social thought, this chapter excavates how Detroit's League of Revolutionary Black Worker's (LRBW) quotidian and revolutionary analysis of race/racism informed the founding of the Black Student United Front (BSUF) and Parents for Community Control of Schools in Detroit. Drawing on precepts of decolonial methodologies, I employ a relational historical

DOI: 10.4324/9781003258223-16

ethnography approach (Tuck & McKenzie 2015; Smith 2012; Emerson, Fretz, & Shaw 2011). Data sources include oral history interviews approved by the Institutional Review Board of the University of California Berkeley, participation in Detroit grassroots activist spaces, and archival research conducted in 2015–2018. I draw on theoretical precepts from Fanonian (2004) theory of consciousness and Gramscian (2010) conception of organic intellectuals (and Lipsitz's [1995] extended concept of organic intellectuals) to excavate Detroit radical social thought and the role of educational consciousness as interstitial to a broader conception of freedom struggle. Together, Fanon and Gramsci provide an analytical framework through which to situate oral history and archival research data producing the following core themes which structure this chapter: Black workers as the vanguard of a revolutionary process, education as a tool of racial capitalism and social reproduction, and freedom struggle as a multi-front movement.

Secondarily, I draw on conceptual devices of the internal colonial model (Allen 2005; Muñoz, Barrera, & Ornelas 1972) to analyze the political economic context underlying the emergence of radical thought and activism in Detroit. These devices include the conceptual categories of a colonial social system and political powerlessness. Kwame Ture and Charles Hamilton (1992) argue "Black people in the United States have a colonial relationship to the larger society, a relationship characterized by institutional racism" (p. 6). Ture and Hamilton explain that a hegemonic white power structure defines the terms of incorporation into the democratic and capitalist social system, a differential process based on racial logic (Dill 2015; Schulze-Oechtering 2016). This assertion, referred to as the semicolony thesis, is described as distinct from the classic colonial relationship. The classic model is found, for example, in the overt and direct colonial rule and subjugation of African land and peoples by European nations, while the semicolony thesis accounts for the structural and ideological relation of domination present within contexts where the colony is not external to the colonizing structure. This semicolony relationship, also referred to as the internal colonial model, is characterized by subjugation and domination operating from within a national context. From this standpoint, the internal colonial model theorizes the terms of racial minorities' incorporation into the U.S. social polity, thereby illuminating the contours of racialized education oppression.

Findings

The findings presented in this section provide context and history related to the rise of the League of Revolutionary Black Workers and the alliances they foster in work toward social and educational change. This history lays a foundation for an analysis of the role that social movements play in transforming consciousness and a new social order.

Rise of the League of Revolutionary Black Workers and Building Counterhegemonic Consciousness

The formation of the League of Revolutionary Black Workers can be tied to what has been described as the Black radical tradition (Robinson 2021). Preceding from this historical collective consciousness of liberation struggle (Robinson 2021, p. 171), when Detroit erupted on July 23, 1967, in what became known as the Great Rebellion, several lessons were drawn that encouraged radical actors to focus on the plight of the Black worker. In Fall 1967, the *Inner City Voice* (ICV) newspaper was founded by a core group of radicals as a tool to build consciousness of the concrete conditions delimiting Black liberation. Analysis of U.S. imperialism and Third World revolutionary struggles were also featured themes in the newspaper. Such exchanges elevated the symbiotic relationship of the plight of colonized people in the Third World and the oppressed of the domestic United States (Young 2006).

General Gordon Baker Jr. was a key figure in this core group seeding Detroit movement radicalization. Baker was a seasoned activist and Dodge Main automotive plant worker who honed his politicization through a 1964 trip to Cuba to study Marxism and participation in the UHURU student organization at Wayne State University (Goldberg 2014). General Gordon Baker Jr. recruited other Black workers to visit ICV headquarters and Mike Hamlin, another ICV co-founder, began to write articles based on the experiences of these workers (Mike Hamlin, personal communication). Hamlin would conduct dialogue-based interviews of the workers. Through this dialogical process, the ICV served as a platform to engage ideas emanating from a deeply local perspective of conditions faced by Black workers. Subsequent ICV articles heightened the awareness of the preeminent contradictions of society, interpreting the objective conditions of the social complex (Gramsci 2010, p. 10). Engaging and communicating the plight of oppressed people from the standpoint of ordinary workers in the city proved to be a radical intervention.

The ICV efforts seeded the formation of the Dodge Revolutionary Union Movement (DRUM), stewarded through the coalitional efforts of General Gordon Baker Jr. and Dodge Main worker Ron March. DRUM was formed in 1968 at the Dodge Main plant in Hamtramck, an autonomous small municipality surrounded by the city of Detroit. Dodge Main was comprised of a majority of Black workers. However, the management positions were filled exclusively by white workers. Through the organizing efforts of Baker, March, and others, a wildcat strike was launched to openly contest forced speed-ups, without regard to worker safety, and racial segregation in job positions (Georgakas & Surkin 2012, pp. 32–41). The wildcat strike led to the formation of DRUM, which came to serve as a model for independent Black worker organizing. Other RUMs quickly formed across metro-Detroit manufacturing plants (Bird, Lichtman, & Gessner 1970).

The founding of additional RUMs created a good problem, a need to bring cohesion and a unifying vision to the Black worker struggle. Founded formally in 1969, the League of Revolutionary Black Workers was charged with doing just that. The League was comprised of a seven-member executive board representing a spectrum of Black, working-class, revolutionary and intellectual positions. The founding members include General Gordon Baker Jr., Mike Hamlin, Ken Cockrel, Chuck Wooten, Luke Tripp, John Watson, and John Williams. The League's analysis and direct actions can be understood as the outcome of increasing radicalism of the Black freedom struggle (Elbaum 2006).

The League believed Black workers were the vanguard of the revolutionary Black working class and operated along two predominant theoretical contexts, revolutionary nationalism and Marxism-Leninism. The guiding principle of its vision, outlined in the League's constitution, was the belief that Black workers occupied a strategic and historical position in anti-imperialist liberation struggles,

> We the super-exploited Black workers recognized the historic role that we must play and the grave responsibility that is ours in the struggle for the liberation of Black people in racist U.S.A. and people of color around the world from the yoke of oppression that holds all of us in the chains of slavery to this country's racist exploitative system.
>
> (Dan Georgakas Collection n.d.)

Rather than appeal to their established union, United Auto Workers (UAW), the League marked a shift toward engaging in open and direct action in the interest of Black workers (Hamlin 2013, p. 41). A 1970 film titled *Finally Got the News* provides a visual and interview-based portrait of the League's perspective. "Black workers have historically been the foundation stone upon which the American industrial empire has been built and sustained, it began with slavery over 400 years ago . . . and [Black people were] used to produce surplus value . . ." asserts League co-founder John Watson in the opening scene (Bird, Lichtman, & Gessner 1970). Through various member study groups, the League developed a systematic understanding of the role of the Black worker in the development of a modern world economy. In this way, the plight of the Black worker was connected to the plight of all oppressed people amid imperialism.

League members were involved in radicalism outside of formal League activity including participation in more traditionally established groups representing an array of social issues. In fact, the League developed a network of activism challenging multiple sites of oppression in the city (Georgakas & Surkin 2012, pp. 76–78). On a practical level, Detroit schools existed in an explicit and direct relationship to the interests of the League. The Detroit Public Schools had developed into a fundamentally racially segregated system. From this system, working-class Black students were being funneled into a segregated dual wage system. This relationship became a central site of the League's involvement and ideological influence (Gramsci 2010, p. 10).

The Formation of the Black Student United Front and Parents and Students for Community Control

In order to build the kind of movement that could transform society, the League insisted on developing and aligning with a network of organizations to support the Black worker struggle. On reflection of this crucial need, in "Finally Got the News," League co-founder Kenneth Cockrel explains efforts to help build the BSUF as rooted in a recognition of the necessity of having student support as well as the practical activist support students could provide. Cockrel adds, "The League relates concretely to the whole of [the] familiar category of problems that is stated when one relates to the so-called ghetto" (Bird, Lichtman, & Gessner 1970). In this way, the League conceptualized localized social problems as symptomatic of a broader condition of domination, a colonial social system (Allen 2005, p. 4). For the League, any distinction between the plight of the Black worker and the Black student struggle was artificial because of an overarching power relationship "and its structures of domination and subordination" (Allen 2005, 4). Moreover, the Detroit youth were already actively involved in open educational protest against the inferior education afforded them (Gregory 1967). As DRUM and the ICV gained visibility, many Detroit youths were drawn to the Black worker cause and vision.

Constitutive to Detroit's formation is the introduction of chattel slavery and land colonization, two practices of domination foundational to the construction of the U.S. nation-state (Miles 2017; Nakano Glenn 2015; King 2013). These formative interlocking capitalist structures, mediated by a racial logic, were reflected in the genesis and evolution of the city. The Detroit Public Schools (DPS) played a central and decisive role in mediating, expanding, and legitimizing this hegemonic structure. Since its inception in 1842, the DPS were a racially segregated system (Katzman 1973; Stephensen 1962). By the mid-1960s, the DPS were organized into 22 constellations comprised of several elementary schools, a few junior high schools, and a high school. Four of these constellations were almost completely Black and five were nearly completely white (Johnson 2008, p. 84). By 1966, Black students represented 57% of total DPS enrollment, though the white electorate exhibited enormous influence over school policy (Johnson 2008, p. 84). As the voting populace remained predominantly white, buttressed by a broader colonial social system, Black Detroit was resigned to a state of educational political powerlessness (Muñoz, Barrera, & Ornelas 1972).

The politics of race and class that had shaped district hiring practices, attendance zone policies, and historical practices of Black student containment, allowed the development of a dual school system: one for white students and one for Black students. The 1960s represented an era of increased radicalization in opposition to this historical reality. It is in this context that the BSUF was formed. The BSUF, an umbrella organization for local Black student organizations operating in several Detroit junior high schools and senior high schools, formed an integral arm of the League of Revolutionary Black Workers' structure. In fact, many BSUF members held dual membership in the League (Hicks 2009, p. 27). At its height, the BSUF was active in 22 of the district's high schools. From 1968 to 1971, the BSUF organized and/or supported seven student-led strikes and developed two Freedom Schools alongside these protest efforts. Although the BSUF was not the only militant educational protest group in the city, their embrace of League ideology and political strategy informed their distinctive perspective on the predominant educational issue of this period: racial segregation, its origins and deleterious effects.

Founding BSUF member Gregory Hicks explains that the BSUF initially began as a way to politicize students who, like their parents before, were tracked into a substandard education that aimed to produce a docile workforce (Hicks 2009, p. 30). The BSUF developed the *Black Student Voice* (BSV) newsletter as a tool to bring cohesion to the varied militant Black student groups comprising the BSUF and to build consciousness. The BSV was imagined as a mechanism to "train strong political student organization, in unity with the League for the decisive battle against racism and oppression" (General Gordon Baker Jr. & Darryl Mitchell Personal Papers). Affiliated groups printed their own edition of the BSV covering conditions specific to their school/community, while the city-wide BSV edition reflected district issues and provided direct guidance to affiliates. The BSV newsletters were printed in the same facilities as the ICV and the DRUM newsletters (Darryl Mitchell, personal communication). Editions of the BSV reveal how Black students experienced inferior education and their efforts to demand an education that would achieve liberation in social, cultural, and political economic terms.

The revolutionary nationalist and Marxist-Leninist orientation of the League was demonstrated in BSUF condemnation of a dual inferior school system and emphasis on the revolutionary role of Black students. In an October 1970 edition of the city-wide *Black Student Voice*, Volume 1 Number 1, a notation cites the edition as intended to provide organizational context for local affiliates. The leading article titled "Black Youth the World is Yours, Take it!" explains,

> The Black Student Front was created as a result of the ever worsening conditions in the schools in an effort to build a black student movement to end the misery and suffering that we endure during the years that we spend in racist schools. We are aware that the real issue that black people have to address themselves to is not integration, but racism. The racism that brought about a situation of inequality in the schools in the inner-city where we live with the schools located in the fringe areas of the city where the whites live.
>
> (General Gordon Baker Jr. & Darryl Mitchell Personal Papers)

BSV articles emphasize the revolutionary potential of collective student activism. A popularized BSUF slogan printed in the varied BSV editions reflects the ideological orientation of the League. In the Volume 2 Number 10 edition of the *Black Student Voice*, an advertisement to student readers posits the revolutionary potential of students, much as the League espoused the revolutionary capacity of a mass movement of Black workers: "Our heroes are not Huey P. Newton's nor are they Stokely Carmichael, Our heroes are you! The masses of Black students involved in struggle" (General Gordon Baker Jr. & Darryl Mitchell Personal Papers).

As BSUF affiliates continued to challenge individual school grievances, political education afforded access to a conceptual language to more fully discern how the education system participated in a global project of racial and economic oppression. BSUF members participated in political education classes, similar to those offered to League members (Mike Hamlin, personal communication). Participation in political education classes exposed students to classical Marxist theory as well as anticolonial social thought such as that of Frantz Fanon and Amilcar Cabral (Hicks 2009, pp. 38–39). The influence of this shifting consciousness was represented in the BSV articles. In the Osborn High School BSV Volume 1, Number 1 edition, one article titled "American is the Black Man's Battle Ground" was directed toward discouraging Black students from joining Osborn High School's ROTC Training Corp. BSUF activists write,

> Can Black youth go along with the suppression and killing of courageous freedom fighting peoples throughout the world (i.e. the non-white Vietnamese and Laotians, struggling in Asia, the Black Revolutionary forces of Guinea-Bissau, Mozambique, and Rhodesia in Africa, the Liberation minded people of Brazil, Peru, Uruguay, Mexico, and Paraguay in Latin America) under the logic of stopping the so-called threat of "communism." . . . Our fight for freedom and justice are within the shores of this United States of American, not in some far off foreign country.
>
> (General Gordon Baker Jr. & Darryl Mitchell Personal Papers)

Another League co-founder, John Watson, approached the notion of educational struggle akin to his general view on the Black worker struggle. Watson emphasized to student activists that regarding the burgeoning community control of schools, the goal remained the same, seize power (Gregory Hicks, personal communication). By the end of the 1960s, the BSUF routinely attended Board of Education meetings, engaged in student walkouts, developed Freedom Schools, and were demanding community control of schools. In 1969, the Detroit Board of Education (BOE) was forced by state legislation to put forth plans for decentralization, a policy mandate to address racial segregation. Decentralization legislation mandated the creation of new feeder school patterns and the establishment of regional boards of education. The League and BSUF perceived the decentralization mandate as an opportunity to seize power.

The League's success in recruiting members and galvanizing community was partially the result of their active involvement in out-of-plant organizing. Watson himself completed a stint at Wayne State University, a bastion of militant student radicalism in the 1960s (Boyd 2017, p. 190) and transitioned to the directorship of a highly regarded community agency, the West Central Organization (WCO). The WCO built its reputation through housing justice efforts in the city. Watson assumed leadership of the WCO while continuing his work with the League. When the BOE announced it would consider plans for how best to establish the boundaries of a decentralization plan, Watson mobilized the WCO to support the development of what would become known as Parents and Students for Community Control (PASCC), also known as Black Parents and Students for Community Control (BPSCC) (Gregory Hicks, personal communication).

To achieve decentralization, the Detroit Board of Education was mandated in a bill approved by Governor Milliken on August 11, 1969, to create a new district plan containing 7 to 11 regional contiguous school districts with a range of 25,000–50,000 students in each regional district. The WCO organized a conference to support community efforts to develop a united approach to the legislation and propose their own plan. As reported in the January 5, 1970 article "People's Conference" in the Cooley High School *Black Student Voice*, the People's Decentralization Conference was hosted December 27–31, 1969, on the campus of the University of Detroit, attended by some 300 student and community members representing at least 70 organizations (General Gordon Baker Jr. & Darryl Mitchell Personal Papers). In advance of the conference, the WCO partnered with the Detroit Geographic Expedition and Institute (DGEI), a youth-led initiative, which conducted research to create a decentralization plan that would produce majority Black student regions (Warren & Katz 2012). This strategy envisioned to culminate in the election of predominantly Black regional boards.

The BSV article reports on the final day of the conference, which featured speak-outs and teach-ins, participants ratified several resolutions alongside city-wide Black student demands. These student demands included a demand of removal of all police/guards from schools, amnesty for student activists, institutionalization of Black Studies, and community control of Black schools (General Gordon Baker Jr. & Darryl Mitchell Personal Papers). The DGEI unveiled their proposed decentralization plan, known as the Black Plan, which was ratified at the conference. The conference led to the formation of the PASCC, which formed the organizational body backing the Black Plan. Like the League and BSUF, the PASCC "came to see itself as the beginning of a permanent citywide network of communications and action. Hundreds of rallies and meetings took place, and PASCC representatives made regular appearances on radio, on television, and in schools" (Georgakas & Surkin 2012, p. 76).

The newly formed PASCC adopted an ideological orientation akin to that espoused by the LRBW and BSUF, influenced by both revolutionary nationalism and Marxist-Leninism. A flyer circulated states, "Although we understand the true nature of the Decentralization Bill, Public Act No. 244, which gives No real power, we must struggle to capture that control" (General Gordon Baker Jr. & Darryl Mitchell Personal Papers). The Black Plan sought to put the Black youth under control of people who cared about them. The Plan would ensure Black control in six out of eight newly formed regions (Dan Georgakas Collection n.d.). The PASCC outlook represented a different and divergent approach to racial segregation in the schools.

Instead of endorsing the busing of Black inner-city students to white schools, in an outline of their approach to the question of integration, the PASCC raised the question of, "Why not fight for quality education for Black schools in the inner city" (General Gordon Baker Jr. & Darryl Mitchell Personal Papers). In this way, community control was conceptualized as a tool to challenge the notion that quality education for Black students could be achieved through integration alone. In contrast, the PASCC believed that nothing short of complete control over school budgets, curriculum, and administration could affect real change. Ultimately, the Black Plan was opposed by an alliance of the BOE as backed by UAW leadership (Geschwender 2009, p. 50). Nevertheless, the LRBW-BSUF-PASCC alliance excavates the depth and breadth of the vision offered by the League of Revolutionary Black Workers.

Discussion

As a case study, this historical portrait excavates educational protest that centers analysis of racial and class oppression simultaneously, rather than treating either form of oppression as epiphenomenal. The LRBW-BSUF-PASCC alliance situated educational protest within a broader historical analysis of racial capitalism. The League's revolutionary analysis informed a vision of education that rejected reformist approaches, such as a call for racial integration of the city schools or settling for inclusion of culturally relevant curriculum. As a result, the BSUF and PASCC called for nothing less than the complete community control of Black schools. Even in this demand, the BSUF and PASCC demonstrate an understanding of education in service of liberation as interstitial to the Black worker global struggle. Put another way, the demand for community control of schools was not an end to itself, but a strategy in service of a broader freedom struggle waged by the revolutionary vanguard of the Black working class. Through the development of consciousness of the historic role of the Black worker struggle, the BSUF and PASCC root their conception of community control within a historical Black radical tradition.

Such history deepens examination of the function of schooling in the contemporary moment. Urban education systems have in particular been cited as bastions of educational inequity, particularly along race and class cleavages. Critical education researchers argue that educational administrative practices and achievement outcomes of such systems are relational to the social context in which school systems are situated (Lipman 2011; Rury & Mirel 1997). The history of the LRBW-BSUF-PASCC alliance suggests a broader historical analysis of social context as interstitial to trajectories of urban school systems, and education more broadly. Moreover, how social movements discern social contradictions that underlie social problems, such as education inequity, and contribute to transforming consciousness fostering social change, are central lessons gleaned from this history.

Conclusion: Movements in Defense of Black Lives and Social Consciousness

This chapter is not a complete history of any of the formations explored. Instead, this chapter has sought to excavate why we might consider the contributions of social movements to the promise of education for liberation. Anti-colonial thought surmised the maintenance and reproduction of an enduring colonial condition as interstitial to, though not singularly contingent on, the continuous dehumanization of colonized people (Fanon 2004, pp. 6–7). Key herein is the ideological and physical processes by which the colonizer inculcates within the colonized a debased conception of self. Critical educational stakeholders, thinkers, and activists have argued that transformative education can disrupt this process and (re)humanize colonized peoples (Biondi 2012; Muñoz 2007; Perlstein 2002; Freire 2003). Rejection of debased conceptions of self and community, a social learning process, can seed new futures. However, often elided are the grassroots movements that have identified the very societal structures that must be transformed and reimagined in order to fulfill the promise of education for liberation.

In recent years, there have been efforts to build small independent schools and education-centered movements. Yet, we might do well to consider education researcher and activist Jean Anyon's assertion that such schools (and movements) are frankly unable to transform societal level political economic oppression (Anyon 2005, p. 5). Anyon suggests that educators must pursue the promise of education while cognizant of the broader political economic dynamics. We must deem any distinction between the call for education justice and broader freedom struggle as artificial, just as the League of Revolutionary Black Workers did. This battle cry is perhaps more pressing than ever as we consider how to seed an educational vision in the wake of the continued assault on Black lives and the COVID-19 global pandemic. As Anyon (2005) urges, we must pursue educational justice as a collective across axes of struggle. It is from this purview that we should consider how the varied alliances and formations associated with the movement(s) in defense of Black lives contribute to our understanding of the interlocking systems of oppression that use schools to perpetuate the dominant social order.

The origins of the hashtag that birthed a movement is well documented. On February 26, 2012, African American teenager Trayvon Martin was murdered as he walked back home from a convenience store in Sanford, Florida. In the hours after the acquittal of Trayvon Martin's murderer on July 13, 2013, Alicia Garza wrote what she termed a love letter to Black people on Facebook (Garza 2014). Soon after, Patrisse Khan-Cullors re-shared Garza's message adding the Twitter hashtag, #BlackLivesMatter. This hashtag catalyzed what has been observed as the formation of a multi-front abolitionist global social movement, Black Lives Matter (BLM). In 2013, Alicia Garza, Patrisse Khan-Cullors, and Opal Tometi together stewarded the development of a nascent social movement that grew to become a global network (Garza 2014). This global network galvanized the spirits, minds, and bodies of a new iteration of social protest and led to the founding of Black Lives Matter chapters around the world. Alicia Garza (2014) has described BLM as affirmation of Black life and as "a tactic to (re)build the Black liberation movement." Affirmation of Black lives is a repudiation of anti-Black racism, a global and historical construct imbricated within the development of the modern world.

At the time of writing, BLM has evolved through various waves of development and organization. The original founders have pursued new allied interests and there are multiple books and coverage of the BLM evolution (Garza 2020; Khan-Cullors & bandele 2018; Ransby 2018). Over the years, BLM as a campaign, platform, and various associated organizations has engaged countless in local direct actions, social policy work, and intimate conversations with the aim of challenging the distinctive assault on Black life, while nourishing the development of an alternative vision of society. Historian Barbara Ransby traces the antecedents of the Black Lives Matter movement situating its genesis within a broader history of radical Black and feminist movements against state violence (2018). As an inclusive movement approach that does not sacrifice the particularity of lived reality (Khan-Cullors & bandele 2018), we might interpret BLM-informed movements, direct actions, and organizations as educative processes that reflect a continuous study of life at the margins, creating platforms for work in defense of forgotten places and people. Critical geographies scholar and prison abolitionist Ruth Wilson Gilmore (2018) charges, "Forgotten places, then, are both symptomatic of and intimately shaped by crisis" (32). I argue that the organizing work of BLM movements, this continuous study at the site(s) of the grassroots crisis, has provided distinct conceptions of contemporary precarious conditions. This process and analysis seed the development of counter-hegemonic consciousness empowering a critical understanding of our objective conditions and the capacity to think and act beyond them (Freire 2003).

In the documentary *Stay Woke: The Black Lives Matter Movement*, African American studies scholar Keeanga-Yamahtta Taylor describes how the synergies of early BLM history, represented in the 2014 Ferguson uprisings in response to the extrajudicial murder of Michael Brown, demonstrate the ability of BLM to affect mass consciousness (Grant 2016). Through the use of social media technologies and network building, the BLM movement has transformed sensemaking of localized struggles and effectively provides scaffolding to link the local to the global. Live streaming and first-person accounts of street-level protests have allowed the masses to learn about the social context of state violence against Black communities across cities that range from Ferguson to London, UK (McNair 2019). Moreover, the growth of BLM from hashtag to global network has produced counter-hegemonic ideas challenging dominant notions of democracy, equality, and the pursuit of freedom. For example, on August 1, 2016, the Movement for Black Lives (MB4L), a coalition of 50 Black-led organizations, issued a policy agenda known as the "Vision for Black Lives: Policy Demands for Black Power, Freedom and Justice." Situating BLM within a historical continuum of the Black radical tradition, historian Robin Kelley describes this Vision "as a plan to transform the entire nation, save the planet, and ultimately end racial capitalism" (Robinson 2021, p. xiii).

Each phase of BLM development, from the hyper-local to the global, is reflective of a shared consciousness developing organically in relation to the quotidian struggles of each locale (Lipsitz 1995, p. 236). In 2020, while the world grappled with the COVID-19 global pandemic, countless took to the streets to protest the continued assault against Black people. In the wake of the extrajudicial murder of George Floyd on May 25, 2020, social protest and direct actions across the world emerged in mass. In Detroit, social protest developed into the BLM-influenced entity Detroit Will Breathe (DWB). Writing in *Left Voice*, DWB organizers, William Lewis and Tristan Taylor (2020), detail, "It is a movement sitting atop hundreds of years of racist terror and capitalism, and exploding within the context of the ongoing triple crises of the Covid-19 pandemic, the economic slump, and police brutality" (para. 2). Moreover, Lewis and Taylor explain, "The current movement against racism and police violence has sustained itself for weeks because in each city it has taken on a life of its own" (para. 2). This social analysis exemplifies how lived experience and social struggle contribute to the discernment of present conditions in flux (Khan-Cullors & bandele 2018). This is only knowable because of an insistence on continuous study at the grassroots level, and the leadership of the grassroots themselves.

In this dialogical learning process, we are offered a portrait of an educational process that centers eradication of anti-Black racism in the curation of a new social world. This is important for the field of education, and more broadly for all concerned social actors who have a desire to work toward the development of non-oppressive forms of educational practice. In order to understand how race and class are interactive, and indeed co-constituted systems of oppression, I argue for the need to examine and engage with social movement formations that center analysis of racial capitalism regimes.

Contemporary educational movements such as the Journey to Justice movement, the Detroit Independent Freedom Schools, and grassroots education resistance to neoliberalism in Oakland, New Orleans, New York, and beyond have provided inroads to unpacking the tethered relationship between racial capitalism and educational oppression. Understanding how such formations are engaging in serious study and engagement with grassroots conditions and social movements may illuminate how traditional forms of schooling can realize their contribution to the promise of education for liberation more fully.

References

Allen, Robert L. 2005. Reassessing the Internal (Neo) Colonialism Theory. *The Black Scholar* 35(1): 2–11.

Anderson, James. 1988. *The Education of Blacks in the South 1860–1935*. Chapel Hill, NC: University of North Carolina Press.

Anyon, Jean. 2005. *Radical Possibilities: Public Policy: Urban Education and a New Social Movement*. New York: Routledge.

Biondi, Martha. 2012. *The Black Revolution on Campus*. Berkeley and Los Angeles: University of California Press.

Bird, Stewart, Rene Lichtman, and Peter Gessner, in Association with the League of Revolutionary Black Workers. 1970. *Finally Got the News*. Black Star Productions.

Boyd, Herb. 2017. *Black Detroit: A People's History of Self-Determination*. New York: Amistad.

Dan Georgakas Collection. n.d. Walter P. Reuther Library, Archives of Labor and Urban Affairs, Wayne State University, Detroit, Michigan.

Dill, LeConté. 2015. Poetic Justice: Engaging in Participatory Narrative Analysis to Find Solace in the "Killer Corridor". *American Journal of Community Psychology* 55(1–2): 128–135.

Douglass, Frederick. 1845. *Narrative of the Life of Frederick Douglass, an American Slave, Written by Himself*. Boston: Published at the Anti-Slavery Office. Accessed February 20, 2021. http://utc.iath.virginia.edu/abolitn/dougnarrhp.html

Du Bois, W. E. B. 1968. *Black Reconstruction: An Essay Toward a History of the Part Which Black Folk Played in the Attempt to Reconstruct Democracy in America, 1860–1880*. Cleveland, OH: Third World Publishing Company.

Elbaum, Max. 2006. *Revolution in the Air: Sixties Radicals Turn to Lenin, Mao, and Che*. New York: Verso.

Emerson, Robert M., Rachel I. Fretz, and Linda L. Shaw. 2011. *Writing Ethnographic Fieldnotes*. Chicago: University of Chicago Press.

Fanon, Frantz. 2004 [1961]. *The Wretched of the Earth* (Richard Philcox, Trans.). New York: Grove Press.

Freire, Paulo. 2003. *Pedagogy of the Oppressed*, 30th Anniversary edition. New York: The Continuum International Publishing Group.

Garza, Alicia. 2014. A Herstory of the #BlackLivesMatter Movement. *the feminist wire*, October 7. https://thefeministwire.com/2014/10/blacklivesmatter-2/

Garza, Alicia. 2020. *The Purpose of Power: How We Come Together When We Fall Apart*. Random House Audio: Audible.

General Gordon Baker Jr. and Darryl Mitchell Personal Papers.

Georgakas, Dan, and Marvin Surkin. 2012. *Detroit: I Do Mind Dying*, 3rd edition. Chicago: Haymarket Books.

Geschwender, James A. 2009. *Class, Race and Worker Insurgency: The League of Revolutionary Black Workers*. New York: Cambridge University Press.

Gilmore, Ruth Wilson. 2018. Forgotten Places and the Seeds of Grassroots Planning. In Charles R. Hale (ed.), *Engaging Contradictions: Theory, Politics, and Methods of Activist Scholarship* (pp. 31–61). Berkeley: University of California Press.

Goldberg, David. 2014. Detroit's Radical. *Jacobin Magazine* online, May 27. www. jacobinmag.com/2014/05/detroit-s-radical-general-baker/

Gramsci, Antonio. 2010. *Selections From the Prison Notebooks of Antonio Gramsci*. New York: International Publishers.

Grant, Laurens, directors. 2016. *Stay Woke: The Black Lives Matter Movement*, May 26. Black Entertainment Television (BET).

Gregory, Karl. 1967. The Walkout: Symptom of Dying Inner City Schools. *New University Thought* 5: 29–54.

Hamlin, Mike, and Michelle Gibbs. 2013. *A Black Revolutionary's Life in Labor: Black Worker's in Detroit*. Detroit: Against the Tide Books.

Hicks, Gregory. 2009. The League of Revolutionary Black Workers and Detroit's Black Student United Front: Social Exchange and Leadership Development Select Interviews With Members of the Black Student United Front. Master's Thesis, Wayne State University.

Johnson, Arthur. 2008. *Race and Remembrance: A Memoir*. Detroit: Wayne State University Press.

Katzman, David M. 1973. *Before the Ghetto: Black Detroit in the Nineteenth Century*. Urbana, IL: University of Illinois Press.

Kelley, Robin D. G. 2002. *Freedom Dreams: The Black Radical Imagination*. Boston: Beacon Press.

Khan-Cullors, Patrisse, and asha bandele. 2018. *When They Call You a Terrorist: A Black Lives Matter Memoir*. Macmillan Audio: Audible.

King, Tiffany Jeannette. 2013. In the Clearing: Black Female Bodies, Space and Settler Colonial Landscapes. Ph.D. Dissertation, University of Maryland.

Lewis, William, and Tristan Taylor. 2020. Marches, Assemblies, and a Public Tribunal: How Detroit Activists Are Building Power. *Left Voice* online, June 25. www.leftvoice. org/marches-assemblies-and-a-public-tribunal-how-detroit-activists-are-building-power

Lipman, Pauline. 2011. *The New Political Economy of Urban Education: Neoliberalism, Race, and the Right to the City*. New York: Routledge.

Lipsitz, George. 1995. *A Life in the Struggle: Ivory Perry and the Culture of Opposition*. Philadelphia: Temple University Press.

McNair, Kimberly. 2019. Beyond Hashtags: Black Twitter and Building Solidarity across Borders. In Abigail De Kosnik and Keith P. Feldman (eds.), *#Identity: Hashtagging Race, Gender, Sexuality, and Nation* (pp. 283–298). Ann Arbor: University of Michigan Press.

Miles, Alicia Tiya. 2017. *The Dawn of Detroit: A Chronicle of Slavery and Freedom in the City of the Straits*. New York: The New Press.

Muñoz Jr., Carlos. 2007. *Youth, Power, Identity: The Chicano Movement*, 2nd edition. New York: Verso Press.

Muñoz Jr., Carlos, Mario Barrera, and Carlos Ornelas. 1972. The Barrio as Internal Colony. In Harlan Hahn (ed.), *People and Politics Urban Society* (pp. 463–498). Beverly Hills: Sage Publications.

Nakano Glenn, Evelyn. 2015. Settler Colonialism as Structure: A Framework for Comparative Studies of U.S. Race and Gender Formation. *Sociology of Race and Ethnicity* 1(1): 52–72.

Perlstein, Daniel H. 2002. Minds Stayed on Freedom: Politics and Pedagogy in the African-American Freedom Struggle. *American Education Research Journal* 39(2): 249–277.

Ransby, Barbara. 2018. *Making All Black Lives Matter: Reimagining Freedom in the Twenty-First Century*. Oakland, CA: University of California Press.

Rickford, Russell. 2016. *We Are an African People: Independent Education, Black Power, and the Radical Imagination*. New York: Oxford University Press.

Robinson, Cedric. 2021. *Black Marxism: The Making of the Black Radical Tradition*, 3rd edition. Chapel Hill: The University of North Carolina Press.

Rury, John L., and Jeffrey Mirel. 1997. The Political Economy of Urban Education. *Review of Research in Education* 22: 49–110.

Schulze-Oechtering, Michael. 2016. The Alaska Cannery Workers Association and the Ebbs and Flows of Struggle: Manong Knowledge, Blues Epistemology, and Racial Cross Fertilization. *Amerasia Journal* 42(2): 23–48.

Smith, Linda Tuhiwai. 2012. *Decolonizing Methodologies: Research and Indigenous Peoples*, 2nd edition. London and New York: Zed Books.

Stephensen, William. 1962. For a True System of Free Schools Should Afford Equal Opportunities for All: Integration of Detroit Public School System During the Period: 1839–1869. *Negro History Bulletin* 26(1): 23–28.

Tuck, Eve, and Marcia McKenzie. 2015. Relational Validity and the "Where" of Inquiry: Place and Land in Qualitative Research. *Qualitative Inquiry* 1(6): 1–6.

Ture, Kwame, and Charles Hamilton. 1992. *Black Power: The Politics of Liberation*. New York: Vintage.

Warren, Gwendolyn, and Cindi Katz. 2012. In Conversation at The CUNY Graduate Center, Center for the Humanities. Accessed February 20, 2021. https://vimeo.com/111159306

Watkins, William H. 2001. *The White Architects of Black Education: Ideology and Power in America, 1865–1954*. New York: Teachers College Press.

Young, Cynthia A. 2006. *Soul Power: Culture, Radicalism, and the Making of a U.S. Third World Left*. Durham, NC: Duke University Press.

Conclusion

14 Precarity in Educational Spaces

Reflecting Back and Moving Forward

Amira Proweller, Ann Frkovich &
Karen Monkman

Introduction

Educational spaces are increasingly precarious throughout the world in these times. Educational endeavors – formal schooling, nonformal education, and incidental learning – are more complex and messy, with an increasing range of pressures and pace of change, along with compounding challenges layered one on top of another. Precarious forces outside of education (Butler 2009; Fine, Greene, & Sanchez 2016; Ahmed 2020; Perry, Aronson, & Pescosolido 2021) have made their way into educational spaces as well. While these challenges can be overwhelming, becoming more cognizant of them creates a gateway for a new understanding of and commitment to equity, and a vision for human care and responsibility toward others.

Precarious Educational Spaces

What is precarious about educational spaces? The most evident manifestations in these times relate to the global pandemic (UN 2020; USDOE 2021). All educators have had to change their approaches to teaching, pivoting to online instruction with no warning or guidance. This latest example of precarity impacting education is layered on top of the existing but also rapidly changing influences of neoliberalism, specifically policies that undermine teacher autonomy, narrow curriculum, and take educational responsibility out of the hands of schools and educators (Brewer & Lubienski 2019). Global politics, violence, and natural disasters that impact mobility, especially for refugees and immigrants are also layered upon other forms of precarity (Ertorer 2021). Related are the changing notions of tolerance for diversity that situate people lacking social power to be more affected by these changes, destabilizing their lives (Sherhan 2020; Rogers et al. 2017). All of these instances (and others) of increasing precarity within education originate from the outside. Educators are then pressed to react quickly. Reactions that are not informed by a full analysis of the forces can be limited in their effects, or even detrimental to positive outcomes.

DOI: 10.4324/9781003258223-18

What makes these times of precarity different from earlier times, which also involved difficult challenges, is the layering, rapidity, and destabilizing nature of the forces at play (Standing 2016). Time for critical reflection is then limited. We are called to question our own assumptions; become aware of how we are socially conditioned to think and act in particular ways; and step back to recognize the scope of global, national, and local forces that originate outside of educational spaces. Even though these phenomena often come from outside, they impact our daily lives, also shaping our identities.

In this volume, the chapters in *Part I – Precarious Entanglements: Situating the Self* – examine how identity is shaped at the nexus of individual agency and forces from the outside. Forces acting on identity are seen in Chapter 2, where Zuniga Fuentes discusses "dangerous" conditions, manifested as tension points between pressures to assimilate and desires to embody an authentic ethnic identity, all of which change over time as social norms about diversity shift. Language is one such example: being bilingual or monolingual affects identity differently, relative to the social pressures to assimilate or identify ethnically. This can affect Latinx, Arab American, Asian American, and other populations in culturally diverse societies. These identity shifts are also seen by Jaber (Chapter 3) in the ways that racial, ethnic, religious, and gender-based violence impact identity for Arab American women and girls in predominantly white educational spaces. The demonization of this particular group within society (the United States in this case) creates a tremendous insecurity and impacts the ways their lives are perceived by others. This dynamic is notably evident in educational spaces in the post-9/11 United States, in particular, how white-dominant school cultures and communities function as "gatekeepers to inclusion." In Jaber's chapter, we come to better understand how Muslim women and girls experience precariousness as intersectional.

In Chapter 4, Wang and Goldstein reveal the many spaces Chinese Americans inhabit – home, school, and university life in the United States, and travel to their ancestral homelands in China. We see how easily identity can become destabilized as different spaces reify distinct social messages about identity priorities, enabling a more hybrid identity as they negotiate "Chinese" and "American" values. Reflecting on their identities as white Jewish women, Catlett and Proweller (Chapter 5) critically interrogate how systemic oppression across race, class, and gender have shaped their lives and informed social justice work with Jewish-American teen girls focused on addressing gender-based oppression within their community and beyond. Anti-Semitism and gender-based violence are interwoven with white privilege, situating the authors and the teens in a youth PAR project in a unique space to recognize and push back against precarity – their own and others'.

The self is under assault in precarious times and spaces. Situating the self becomes, for participants and authors in all of the studies in this section, a complex shifting and layered effort, impacted by various precarious social forces at once. It is through reflective processes of identity construction and how we are differently and similarly situated that enables an emerging and dynamic sense of self, along with a deeper understanding of the spaces, conditions, and social forces that are salient. Reflection is a fundamental and necessary educational practice (Zeichner & Liston 2013).

In *Part II – Educational Practice in Precarious Spaces* – the authors highlight how educational practice reacts to and engages with precarious conditions. It is not enough to consider educational practice as teaching methods alone. In addition to pedagogy, curriculum matters and context matters.

In Chapter 6, Derrah, Clark, and Ballou examine how university educators and their students in Japan reacted to the global pandemic. The authors used Bourdieu's (1990) concept of *habitus* to highlight how students came to engage in an education that was now online. Traditional ways of being socialized into their desired work settings beyond the classroom became unavailable due to the pandemic, which forced students to redefine how they used their time, discovering a value in being with family and developing hobbies. They also lamented the impacts on their futures without the traditional means of networking in preparation for their careers.

Educational practice has also become increasingly precarious as the hate rhetoric of right-wing politics has created instability and divisiveness in schools serving minoritized students, and makes teaching that much more difficult, as shown by Waly (Chapter 7). Teachers come to understand the necessity of cultivating pedagogical practices that account for ever-changing sociopolitical conditions while also promoting learning, inclusion, belonging, and empowerment. In many situations, teachers work against the undercurrents of political agendas and educational policy that prioritize teaching to the test and narrowing of the curriculum (e.g., to sidestep political agendas or avoid talk about race). These forces undermine teachers' abilities to teach young people in ways that enable purposeful learning toward a meaningful life.

As neoliberal dynamics have markedly redefined and reshaped the norms of education itself, educators are increasingly seeing themselves situated at the crossroads of their obligations toward their students and inability to work in the best interest of students, as Frkovich and Carter-Richardson describe in Chapter 8. Instead, educators must navigate various power relationships, political and policy agendas, and social terrain related to social class, race and gender that are often overt, but go unrecognized or willfully ignored. Often, having to navigate this terrain ends up being a necessity of the job of education itself.

Educational practice also faces precarious conditions when populations are rendered stateless due to violence and fear of death, among them, refugees and asylum seekers. Children, sometimes with their families, are displaced, often for years, as shown by Aljaffery (Chapter 9). Schooling is interrupted and often of low quality for refugees. Along the way, they feel most supported by teachers who have an understanding of the precarious conditions they experience, or who are actively open to learning about them. Positive influences served to support the students to find a sense of home at school, and later in life.

Across these chapters, we see that educators and students are often expected to do the impossible: to teach and to learn. In contexts such as these where change is unpredictable, multifaceted, and destabilizing, educators cannot rely on a conventional toolkit for teaching, or to assume that learners are able to learn in the conditions that prevail within precarious spaces. It is important for educators to develop an intersectional mindset that accounts for sociopolitical and environmental dynamics and histories. Experiences of precarity change how we need to foreground curricular decision-making and pedagogical choices that reconcile the tension points across what educators understand is best for the learners, what is expected of them, and what is possible.

In the last section, *Part III – Pushing Back Against Precarity* – the authors examine the importance of radical pedagogies, activism, and social movements, all of which are designed to challenge and alter the underlying structures of social inequities and oppression, along with the conditions of precarity (Almeida 2019). The four chapters in this section engage very different histories, locations, and dynamics, although they share a key point about collective solidarity as the basis for working toward robust and sustainable social change.

González and Snyder (Chapter 10) reveal the difficulties of teaching about social conditions and feminist pedagogical processes in what was planned as a study abroad program until the COVID-19 pandemic prohibited travel. Despite these challenges, the authors created new possibilities for connecting across borders virtually and building transnational collaborations among students, activists, and educators. They found that online teaching and activism can still challenge the status quo through transnational dialogue, when in-person engagement is not possible. The authors explain how this virtual – "spectral" – engagement forces changes in how to connect with people and issues, how to teach and learn, and how to be an activist. They point to the ways that neoliberal policy undermines educators' ways of engaging students in virtual spaces, by preventing many of the supportive structures that were otherwise available in on-site educational contexts.

Activism around gender-based violence is the focus of O'Donnell, John, and Valdivia's Chapter 11. They show how neoliberal policies have undermined the public education system and increased the fragility of life for the poor, particularly for women and girls. In response to this, popular educators have supported learners through collective opportunities to publicly grieve their pain as they work to transform their lives. The "difficult knowledge" (Britzman 2000) of gender-based violence is engaged through trauma-informed pedagogy, building community, and empowering women and girls as change agents as they heal together.

Thapliyal (Chapter 12) shows us how the Landless Workers Movement activists in Brazil evolved through their struggle for itinerant schools, as they fought for a right to education. The activist narratives of landless women educators reveal a life-changing learning process as they came to see themselves as activists, pressuring the government to provide schooling for their families. Although they made gains, the schools were later closed by the government. In facing the continuing challenges of being landless along with inadequate schooling for their children, their identities were changed forever, due to their newly developed commitment to activism. While activism and social movements can advance positive change, paths through precarious conditions can be uneven and the outcomes are often unpredictable.

In Chapter 13, Suárez confronts the deep history of racism in the United States through a historical examination of the alliances between the Black labor movement and the Black student movement, highlighting the potential of collective activism against racial and class oppression in the interests of transformative change. Race and class intersect in this work within alliances across different sectors and generations. The value of "unpacking the tethered relationship between racial capitalism and educational oppression" becomes clear when analyzing social activism and grassroots resistance to neoliberalism. This approach also provides historical context for understanding the emergence of social movements today, like Black Lives Matter (BLM) and others.

Examining activism and social movements can provide a new way of understanding educational endeavors. This enables a deeper analysis of the relationship of sociopolitical and economic contextual dynamics with what goes on within educational spaces. It surfaces a clearer vision of the forces that create and perpetuate inequities and the layering of precarity that is experienced by many. While the chapters in this section focus on activism and social movements, one can see elements of reflection and educational practice that are embedded in these activist processes. The intertwining of reflection, educational practice, and activism provide a foundation for the next generation to live and act differently in this world.

Engaging Precarity Through Reflection, Pedagogy, and Activism

Across these chapters, authors have given us insight into how precarity is experienced.

Precarity is multilayered, unpredictable, and complex, and thus it is felt more intensely than discrete forms of oppression. As such, engaging with precarity requires a more nuanced educational approach. This is why this book is organized around reflection, pedagogy, and activism, not as separate processes, but as integrated and fundamental to realizing purposeful teaching, meaningful learning, and social change in the contemporary moment.

We see in the contributions to this volume how precarity upends the work of educators and learners in various ways, but also how it compels shifts in thinking in response to newly emerging problematics. Critical forms of reflection facilitate nuanced insights related to one's own situatedness, histories, and experiences, along with a deeper understanding of the lived realities of others, including students, adult learners, colleagues, and community members. Pedagogies built on knowledge and insights gained from reflective processes lay the terrain for envisioning a future built through activism. Activism extends learning beyond the limits of formal academic spaces to what is meaningful for life in the interest of changing inequitable social dynamics. Education, in or out of schools, should not be just about learning a predetermined curriculum. Rather, it is also about learning to engage in life so that it is made better for oneself and others (Greene 1977). Through new ways of thinking, we can gain a clearer understanding of precarious spaces, how to adjust or shift our educational practice, and how to push back as part of the project to eliminate inequality and oppression (Zembylas 2019).

In addition to the negative dimensions of precarity, it can also be recognized as a catalyst for engaging in educational and social change processes. Fine, Greene, and Sanchez (2016) argue that precarity can be a site of forming "radically new solidarities" (p. 511) as learning takes place. Similarly, Casas-Cortés (2021) argues that precarity can make a space for a more politicized awareness; as that awareness emerges, identities change, and ways of engaging in social movements and processes expand. This politicized awareness becomes an impetus for change, leading to new political possibilities. She explains: "Besides trouble, precarity movements flip vulnerability upside down in such a way that experiences of insecurity and dispossession [can] lead to initiatives of collective agency and organized resistance" (pp. 511–512). The chapters in this book understand and engage precarity in a variety of ways, revealing both the negative impacts it has on lives and educational experience and also the potential as a springboard for positive change.

Concluding Remarks

Educators are invited to look more deeply at precarity as played out in varied spaces and communities, to understand more fully the nuanced conditions in which we currently find ourselves. We invite readers to put aside unexamined assumptions and unsubstantiated public discourses, so as to open space for a richer, nuanced, and grounded understanding of today's challenges. Moreover, thinking about precarity in these ways creates an opportunity to envision a world different than what we are now facing.

We conclude this book as the third variant of COVID-19 emerges, and over five million people globally have died from the virus (Diaz 2021). Populist movements with exclusionary and divisive rhetoric continue to grow around the world (Sherhan 2020), and the expansion of neoliberal policies in and beyond education continues (Schneider & Berkshire 2020; Kumashiro 2020). Climate change remains an increasing threat to the globe, while the countries most responsible for global warming hesitate to take full responsibility (New York Times 2021), and poverty and violence have been exacerbated by these events. Teaching and learning are increasingly challenging due to varying forms of precarity in the world today. In reflecting on our own experiences of precarity, and those evoked in the chapters herein, we cannot ignore that the continuing challenges in these times are characterized by fragility and disruption, unpredictability and complexities. While we do not have a clear road map forward, we leave readers to ponder these challenging experiences as opportunities to think differently about how we are situated in particular and layered contexts, and to seek out a more nuanced understanding of the experiences of others, starting with those we are engaged with in educational and community settings. Readers are invited to consider ways of educating that engage with broader social processes, evoking activism and participation in social movements with a view toward changing our collective future for the better.

References

Ahmed, Nabeela. 2020. Everyday and Everywhere Bordering and Precarity Under COVID-19. *SPERI Blog*, May 13. Sheffield Political Economy Research Institute (SPERI). http://speri.dept.shef.ac.uk/2020/05/13/everyday-and-everywhere-bordering-and-precarity-under-covid-19/

Almeida, Paul. 2019. *Social Movements: The Structure of Collective Mobilization*. Berkeley: University of California Press.

Bourdieu, Pierre. 1990. *The Logic of Practice*. Cambridge: Polity Press.

Brewer, T. Jameson, and Christopher A. Lubienski. 2019. Introduction: Teaching as a Profession in an Age of Privatization: Issues, Advocacy, and Approaches. In Christopher A. Lubienski and T. Jameson Brewer (eds.), *Learning to Teach in an Era of Privatization: Global Trends in Teacher Preparation* (pp. 1–14). New York: Teachers College Press.

Britzman, Deborah P. 2000. If the Story Cannot End: Deferred Action, Ambivalence, and Difficult Knowledge. In Sharon Rosenberg, Roger I. Simon, and Claudia Eppert (eds.), *Between Hope and Despair: The Pedagogical Encounter of Historical Remembrance* (pp. 27–57). Lanham, MD: Rowman and Littlefield.

Butler, Judith. 2009. *Frames of War: When Is Life Grievable?* London: Verso.

Casas-Cortés, Maribel. 2021. Precarious Writings Reckoning the Absences and Reclaiming the Legacies in the Current Poetics/Politics of Precarity. *Current Anthropology* 62(5): 510–538. DOI: 10.1086/716721

Diaz, Jaclyn. 2021. The COVID-19 Pandemic Has Now Killed 5 Million People Around the World. *National Public Radio*, November 1. www.npr.org/2021/11/01/1051020063/the-covid-19-pandemic-has-killed-5-million-people-globally#

Ertorer, Secil E. 2021. Asylum Regimes and Refugee Experiences of Precarity: The Case of Syrian Refugees in Turkey. *Journal of Refugee Studies* 34(3): 2568–2592. https://doi.org/10.1093/jrs/feaa089

Fine, Michelle, Cory Greene, and Sonia Sanchez. 2016. Neoliberal Blues and Prec(ar)ious Knowledge. *The Urban Review* 48(4): 499–519. DOI: 10.1007/s11256-016-0365-x

Greene, Maxine. 1977. Toward Wide-Awakeness: An Argument for the Arts and Humanities in Education. *Teachers College Record* 79(1): 119–125.

Kumashiro, Kevin. 2020. *Surrendered: Why Progressives Are Losing the Biggest Battles in Education*. New York: Teachers College Press.

New York Times. 2021. 6 Takeaways From the U.N. Climate Conference. *New York Times*, November 13. www.nytimes.com/2021/11/13/climate/cop26-climate-summit-takeaways.html

Perry, Brea L., Brian Aronson, and Bernice A. Pescosolido. 2021. Pandemic Precarity: COVID-19 Is Exposing and Exacerbating Inequalities in the American Heartland. *Proceedings of the National Academy of Sciences of the United States of America (PNAS)* 118(8): e2020685118. https://doi.org/10.1073/pnas.2020685118

Rogers, John, Megan Franke, Jung-Eun Ellie Yun, Michael Ishimoto, Claudia Diera, Rebecca Cooper Geller, Anthony Berryman, and Tizoc Brenes. 2017. *Teaching and Learning in the Age of Trump: Increasing Stress and Hostility in America's High Schools.* Los Angeles, CA: UCLA's Institute for Democracy, Education, and Access.

Schneider, Jack, and Jennifer Berkshire 2020. *A Wolf at the Schoolhouse Door: The Dismantling of Public Education and the Future of School.* New York: The New Press.

Sherhan, Yasmeen. 2020. Populism Is Morphing in Insidious Ways: The Political Movement Defined Democracies Around the Globe in the 2010s: It's Not Going Anywhere. *The Atlantic*, January 5. www.theatlantic.com/international/archive/2020/01/future-populism-2020s/604393/

Standing, Guy. 2016. *The Precariat: The New Dangerous Class.* London: Bloomsbury Academic.

United Nations (UN). 2020. *Policy Brief: Education during COVID-19 and Beyond.* www.un.org/development/desa/dspd/wp-content/uploads/sites/22/2020/08/sg_policy_brief_covid-19_and_education_august_2020.pdf

United States Department of Education (USDOE), Office of Civil Rights. 2021. *Education in a Pandemic: The Disparate Impacts of COVID-19 on America's Students.* US Department of Education. www2.ed.gov/about/offices/list/ocr/docs/20210608-impacts-of-covid19.pdf

Zeichner, Kenneth M., and Daniel P. Liston. 2013. *Reflective Teaching: An Introduction,* 2nd ed. New York: Routledge.

Zembylas, Michalinos. 2019. The Ethics and Politics of Precarity: Risks and Productive Possibilities of a Critical Pedagogy for Precarity. *Studies in Philosophy and Education* 38: 95–111. https://doi.org/10.1007/s11217-018-9625-4

Index